The Insoluble Problems of Crime

The Insoluble Problems of Crime

ROBERT P. RHODES
Edinboro State College

JOHN WILEY & SONS
New York Santa Barbara London
Sydney Toronto

Library of Congress Cataloging in Publication Data:

Rhodes, Robert P
The insoluble problems of crime.

Includes index.
1. Criminal justice, Administration of—United States.
2. Crime prevention—United States. 3. Law enforcement—United States. I. Title.
HV8138.R5   364'.973   76-46275
ISBN 0-471-71796-7
ISBN 0-471-71799-1 pbk.

Preface

There are two levels of defense against serious crimes such as murder, assault with injury, forcible rape, large-scale larceny, and armed robbery. The first level provides the kind of political and social structure in which violence, extortion, theft, and greed are minimized. The second level provides an effective criminal justice system to prevent or, failing that, to contain criminal behavior when it does occur while protecting the rights of the innocent.

This is a book about crime policy. It is designed for the second level of defense. By necessity, it is also an analysis of the political process and structure that shapes and limits crime policy, including the behavior of actors in and around the criminal justice system. I do not ignore the relationship between the social structure and crime, but I am principally concerned with the possibilities for generating policy that presently can be realistically implemented to reduce street crime and victim suffering. The scholarship to which I am indebted and freely draw on is thoroughly interdiciplinary—law, sociology, political science, economics, history—but the focus remains crime policy analysis.

A frustrated state executive in a planning agency once described the criminal justice system as an "octopus." Its tentacles reach out in different directions; its purposes are often at odds with one another. Yet the organism is one. No less confusing are the varying perspectives on the "crime problem" of scholars and intellectuals: the sociologist looks for causes of crime and behaviors determined by class and social institutions; the political scientist is interested in decision-making elites, particularly in the courts; the lawyer insists that understanding procedure is crucial to solving the crime problem; the economist refuses to look at anything that cannot be reduced to a mathematical construct (I hasten to add that exacting measurement is often what we *do* need in policy analysis); the historian is resigned to generalizing about past behavior in criminal justice while suppressing his frustration at the lack of data.

I have brought together relevant empirical literature from a number of disciplines on a series of crime policy issues. All the issues treated here—drugs, hand gun control, delinquency, deterrence, corrections, court delay, and bail bond—are contentious. All have their own partisans arguing one side or the other. The criminal justice system's objectives are, of course, to protect the innocent, keep the peace and maintain order, provide due process for the accused, maintain a humane and hopefully rehabilitative correctional system, and foster political liberty. But its comprehensive objective is to protect the often forgotten component of criminal justice—the victim.

I would like to acknowledge the assistance of some of the many people without whose thoughtful help this book would not have been completed. John Gardiner read the manuscript twice and made many insightful suggestions. James F. Short, Jr., Peter K. Manning, and Michael Mulkey made helpful suggestions at the earlier stages of the manuscript, and Charles R. Tittle, Abraham S. Blumberg, and Elizabeth M. Suval provided detailed, scholarly comment on the later revisions. I also benefited from many conversations with my brother, William Rhodes (one of the economist-criminologists whom I earlier slighted). My colleagues in the Criminal Justice Program at Edinboro State College, Samuel Kushner and Ernest Wood, read much of the manuscript and offered useful criticism and needed encouragement. The Research Council of Edinboro State provided funding for much of the typing and some released time from the classroom, while my students provoked my mind to think through the material here. Joan Kindred typed and edited the manuscript and thereby improved my prose. Finally, Jacky Lachmann and Dick Baker at Wiley provided skillful assistance and friendly encouragement at every step.

My greatest debt—to my family—is acknowledged elsewhere. Of course, responsibility for the final product is mine alone.

ROBERT P. RHODES

Contents

TO CAROLINE,
ANNE, AND RUTH

1

CRIMINAL JUSTICE— A POLICY LORELEI

Democracy is an approximate solution to insoluble problems.
Reinhold Niebuhr

The title of this volume may strike current reformers in the field as excessively pessimistic. Nevertheless, I feel that the problems of crime are, as presently understood, susceptible to approximate solutions of very limited potency. This conclusion rests on the premise that both conflicts of interest in American society and lack of awareness of the multidimensional nature of criminal justice problems prevent public discussion of realistic, feasible policy alternatives to reduce property and violent crime that are consistent with current standards of due process and a humanistic correctional system. It is trite to repeat that as a body politic, we cannot agree on effective solutions for crime. It is more meaningful to say that we cannot even agree on the nature of the problems.

Incremental improvement in the criminal justice system has been made in recent years, and the potential for effective, concerted anticrime policy exists. We do not have to be fated to a problem-solving treadmill that produces more of the same temporizing solutions. But we need to ask the right questions regarding what goals we wish to adopt for what is vaguely referred to as criminal justice. This is the heart of the political dilemma. Raising the proper questions is difficult, since various groups in the political community disagree over the goals of justice and are very reluctant to challenge previous value commitments. Moreover, reluctance to reassess goals is likely to persist as long as questions of "law and order" continue to be discussed with partisan stridency.

Yet the political prognosis of this volume provides limited encouragement that the criminal justice system can solve our crime problems. Much of our crime results from social and historical forces that cannot be altered by police and courts. As is true with most policy efforts, we will probably "muddle through" our problems of criminal justice without coherently defining the nature of problems or devising realistic policy to deal with those problems. We will "muddle through" partially because of inherent conflicts of interest—and, therefore, of problem and goal definition—within our political life and culture, and partially because we were not sure what to do about crime, irrespective of conflicts of interest. The politics of crime is replete with value conflict and chiliastic crusaders from both the right and the left. Moreover, patience is a virtue somewhat rare in the character of Americans who, as a people, are noteworthy for their crusading optimism and immediate expectations. We are a problem-solving people, with enormous faith in human progress and in technology. Americans have always been characterized by limitless energies for reforming human behavior—both its serious inhumanities and its many peccadillos. We do not like to be told that there are limits to what can be expected by public policy.

Nor will this book be reassuring for those who vigorously advocate "reform" with sacerdotal assurance that the advantage of the reform is self-evident to the initiated who understand the "real" situation. Many reformers have their favorite devils—unenlightened police, a punitive and parsimonious public, the capitalist system on the one hand, or tender hearted liberals who shackle the police on the other. The politics of crime abounds in such uplifting cliches and scapegoats. Many reforms have been confidently urged by very distinguished scholars through prestigious bodies such as the 1967 President's Commission on Law Enforcement and the Administration of Justice and the recently convened 1973 National Commission on Standards and Goals in Criminal Justice. However, as a member of the 1967 Commission indicated recently,[1] many of the recommendations represent the personal and political opinions of the members, not scholarly conclusions based on data. Also, many recommendations are contradictory in their purpose.

For example, there is little evidence that the size of probationary caseloads has much effect on recidivism,[2] in spite of frequent recommendations to reduce probation and parole caseloads. There is considerable evidence that departments of correction, like most government bureaus or agencies, will support measures that expand their personnel, provide promotional opportunities, and enhance their status. It is also clear that local or state politicians will oppose such expansion if it is not supported by taxpayers. Without data, the scholar is no more than an articulate advocate of one side or the other, promoting a personal political

[1]James Q. Wilson, "Crime and the Criminologists," *Commentary* (1974), 58:52.

[2]J. Robinson, et al., *The San Francisco Project,* Report to NIMH, 1969; see Department of HEW, *Correctional Treatment in Community Settings* (Washington, D.C.: U.S. Government Printing Office, 1972), p. 18.

program. Scholarship becomes nonpartisan expertise when data supports a policy consistent with achieving objectives for which there is no disagreement.

Such a convergence of data and political consensus on objectives would be a rare occurrence. For example, it is as difficult to find a consensus on the functional objectives of probation as it would be to find a consensus on most other functions of the criminal justice system. Probation is regarded by judges as a lesser punishment, as well as a correctional device. They are not the same objectives at all: one is jurisprudential, involving guilt and punishment and general deterrence for the community; the other is treatment for an individual. Probation can also be considered as a humanistic alternative to prison, apart from its impact on jurisprudential meaning or its merits for corrections.

Without quarreling with the need for federal aid to assist law enforcement,[3] one can caution against oversimplifying criminal justice problem definitions and levels of success that breed frustration, impatience and, finally, recriminations against the courts, the police, the intellectuals, or other scapegoats when unrealistically high expectations exceed practical possibility. Considering the degree of value conflict that presently envelops the criminal justice system, solutions leading to reduction of criminal behavior, or of any other conceptualizations of "reform," will be of their nature incremental. We will not "solve" the problem of excessive drug use or burglary, although we may reduce its incidence. At worst, crusading actions that purport to produce an immediate solution may have dysfunctional consequences. Certainly, one has to balance publicly advertised drug suppression campaigns with the heightened prospect of unwarranted searches and wiretaps, the moral ambiguities of the informer system, and increases in police corruption that seem epidemic in vice and narcotics squads. And the uncritical rhetoric of penal reformers that "corrections are not correcting" (as if they were designed to) and that "treatment" should substitute for "punishment" (as if they were logically opposites) often bears ironic consequences not considered by the rhetorician. Many behavior modification treatment programs[4] have been far more brutal and dehumanizing than treatment by a traditional prison administration that neglects the inmates' psychic-social status,[5] in favor of leaving them alone and allowing them to finish their terms.

[3]Bordua and Haurek argue that police budgets actually decreased between 1902 and 1960. David Bordua and Edward W. Haurek, "The Police Budget's Lot," *American Behavioral Scientist* (1970), 13:669-670.

[4]Once hailed as a humane and scientific alternative to "punitive" prison sentences, behavior modification has fallen out of favor in federal prisons recently. The U.S. Department of Justice announced in the spring of 1974 it would no longer fund the behavior modification programs of the Federal Bureau of Prisons where inmates were subjected to forced administration of drugs and electric shock treatments for not conforming to the programmed behavior established by the therapist.

[5]The historical irony of correctional reform for juveniles is aptly reviewed by Anthony Platt. Platt's study modifies the traditional image of penal reformers as disinterested social engineers and humanis-

Many of our problems of criminal justice reflect inherent conflicts of long standing. Oliver Wendell Holmes once wrote that "law, in the main, is the rationalization of the dominant group." Certainly, criminal law is no exception to what is true of legislation in general. But the rationalizations of the dominant group—or groups, as the pluralists would prefer—are much more subtle and complex than the statement suggests. If we define politics as the study of who gets what, when and how—that is, what values are allocated to whom—criminal justice involves two kinds of justice. As Aristotle thought, it involves retributive justice, in the sense of *lex talionis,* or making a punishment proportionate to an individual crime; it also involves distributive justice—the allocation of special privileges and benefits for those whose political social contribution is proportionately greater when judged by those who enjoy power—in the distribution of resources and rewards to conduct policy.

For example, there are obvious distinctions in retributive and distributive justice for "functional" theft. Cheating on income tax payments or providing large sums of money from corporation coffers for political campaigns or for the personal use of prominent politicians are not punished as severely as larcenies involving small sums for the personal use of the lower-class thief. The resources to deter, to apprehend, and to convict are also not equal when one compares the relative legal assistance for the corporation or the wealthy with that of the common thief. Recently, the President of Gulf Oil Corporation was fined $1000 and his company fined $5000 for an illegal $100,000 contribution to the Committee to Re-elect the President, under the apparent assumption that special favors would be rendered to the company by the federal government. Considering the structure of our economy and society, locking up the Gulf Oil Corporation is out of the question, legally and practically, since its role in an interdependent economy is too vital. The same cannot be said of the common thief. This is not to say that the sanction for illegal contributions cannot be increased or altered in such a manner that would permit enforcement consistent with modern organization. But the nominal statutory sanction that was provided by law reflected the interests of the dominant group.

Dominant group interests are also reflected in organizational life and process and in job and role security within formal and informal groups. Perhaps the most important variable affecting organizational behavior in the criminal justice system has been the low priority accorded its departments and agencies when budgets are constructed. Meager budgets mean untrained, harried, or overworked police, part-time prosecutors and public defenders, and overcrowded lockups and pris-

tic experts "rescuing" without consulting the rescued. Anthony Platt, "The Child Savers: The Emergence of the Juvenile Court in Chicago" (unpublished Ph.D. dissertation, University of Chicago, 1968), p. 4. This dissertation subsequently has been published as a book, entitled *The Child Savers: The Invention of Delinquency* (Chicago: University of Chicago Press, 1969).

ons with brutal conditions. Coupled with heavy law enforcement responsibilities and crowded dockets, the lack of resources requires roles adapted to evading, or avoiding altogether, the rules of procedure or professional conduct in order to maximize limited resources for getting the job done.

FROM GROUP POLITICS TO PERCEPTION POLITICS

The most important impediment to consensus on the problems of crime goes beyond conflicts of interest and of organizational behavior, although it is closely related to both. The major difficulties are the distinctly separate perceptions of how to evaluate the seriousness of the crime problem and the impact of public policy on these problems. Organizational and cultural vantage points for policemen, academics, consultants, judges, probation officers, correctional officials, and turnkeys—all of these positions, their roles and their interests—create particular "mind-sets." Problems are defined in sharply different ways; evaluation models, goals, and indicators of success are quite distinct, and word-symbols of success in reform have sharply divergent meanings. All this makes it quite likely that the debate on criminal justice reform will continue to be rhetorical, contentious, and political (political in the sense of clashing purposes and values).

The most immediate and subtle barriers to reform in criminal justice, then, are perceptual variations in problem definitions. These problem definitions flow from ideological positions of police officers, attorneys, correctional officials, intellectuals, and others—all of whom see the problem from their own institutional vantage point with little consciousness of their theoretical differences. Criminal justice decision making is replete with perennial questions of value that have been unresolved since at least the time of Socrates. Ideology continues to exert a powerful influence on the policies and procedures of those who conduct criminal justice, although the degree and kinds of influence it exerts are largely unrecognized. As Walter B. Miller has written, "Ideology is the permanent hidden agenda of criminal justice."[6]

CRIMINOLOGY AND THE LIMITS OF CRIME POLICY

The influence of ideology and perspective is particularly subtle and unrecognized in research and teaching. Scholars who have specialized in criminology and criminal justice present a special problem of perspective, if for no other reason than that the claim of objectivity through modeling, statistical analysis, and esoteric language is ably defended. Police officers tend to be more straightforward with their biases.

[6] Walter B. Miller, "Ideology and Criminal Justice Policy," *Journal of Criminal Law and Criminology* (1973), 64:189.

Criminology for many years has been dominated by the perspective of the social-psychological setting for criminal behavior; it has rejected "rational" theories of crime associated with the legal philosopher John Austin and his teacher, the utilitarian Jeremy Bentham. Austin and Bentham still represent the foundation of a traditional jurisprudence against which there has been a reaction from both legal scholars of the legal realism school (Pound, Llewellen, Holmes, and others) and from social scientists. Bentham's underlying psychological assumption regarding crime and punishment was that individuals calculate the pains and pleasures of crime and pursue illegal behavior if the latter exceeds the former. The structure of the law, according to Austin, was hierarchical in order to make clear who was giving command under the law. Individuals who violated legal proscriptions were either ignorant of its proscriptions or were calculating that no serious sanction would follow if the sanction were not applied.

Certainly this is a simplistic application of the complexities of psychology to legal behavior. According to Sutherland and Cressey, two distinguished and respected modern criminologists, the psychology of Bentham's utilitarianism, found in the classical works of Beccaria, were too "individualist, intellectualistic and voluntaristic."[7] The classical school, characterized by Sutherland and Cressey, assumed "freedom of the will in a manner which gives little or no possibility of further investigation of the causes of crime or of efforts to prevent crime."[8] Criminal behavior, they argued, is not the result of rational calculation, of weighing advantages and disadvantages according to the delicate balance of a jeweler's scale.

Faulting the utilitarian explanation of crime and a number of other explanations (biological, Marxist, feeble-mindedness) Sutherland, while he was alive, outlined what has become the dominant theory or "principle," as his associate Cressey now prefers to call it, of differential association. Oversimplified in our description, since the theory is complex and recognizes multiple causation of crime, differential association "is a principle of normative conflict which proposes that high crime rates occur in societies and groups characterized by conditions that lead to the development of extensive criminalistic sub-cultures."[9] Such subcultures, Cressey and Sutherland add, are themselves the product of broken homes, emotionally insecure environments, and poverty, although these are not causes of crime but are only associated with criminal behavior.

The theory of differential association seems plausible and convincing as an explanation of the basic social setting for a great deal of violent criminal behavior. However, we are not as certain that Cressey and Sutherland's theory, or contem-

[7]Edwin H. Sutherland and Donald R. Cressey, *Criminology* (Indianapolis: Lippencott, 1970), pp. 50-51.

[8]Ibid., p. 51.

[9]Ibid., p. 89; see pp. 75-91.

porary criminological theory in general, is necessarily more advantageous for public policy than the seemingly discredited utilitarian approach. The reason is that sociological explanation, typical of criminological thought in the modern age, concerns itself almost entirely with the root causes of crime; at the same time, it has little to say, based on research and data, about what public agencies can realistically do to reduce criminal conduct short of wholesale transformations of the social structure to alter the "root causes." The police and courts cannot be an effective agent for increasing affection in the home or eliminating poverty and unemployment in the ghetto. A realistic, feasible crime policy must have objectives that are limited to the capacities of the criminal justice system. A social policy whose objective is strengthening the family unit, providing more opportunity for the disadvantaged, and improving nutrition may indirectly deal with root causes of crime, perhaps, through programs such as income redistribution, public service jobs, or community health service. Clearly, poverty, poor housing, unemployment, and family structure are closely associated with street crime. But it does not follow that criminal justice agencies are equipped (or can be equipped) to deal with these problems, even if the root causes of crime are clear.

Positivist criminology, such as that represented by Sutherland, has been taken to task by many other criminologists, most especially by those who emphasize the interactive qualities of social reality and definitions of deviancy. Generally referred to as the "labeling" theorists,[10] they criticize the root cause approach of the positivist school and emphasize that criminal behavior, like all deviant behavior, is defined by the social structure as well as by the so-called deviant. Thus, applying a "criminal label" such as juvenile delinquency to juvenile destruction of property on Halloween can transform with maturity youthful excesses that are deplorable but correctable into products of a criminal mind. At this point a tautological, social definition of the individual deviant occurs. The "criminal act" is initially labeled pathological or abnormal. Then, the youngster's act is considered "caused" by a pathology and the youngster is classified as an official "deviant."

The interactionist criticism of "official" or conventional labels for criminal offenders has properly cautioned against drawing rigid distinctions between criminal behavior and respectable behavior. But, with few exceptions, criminologists, including those of the interactionist school, have been singularly unwilling to explore crime policy with one exception—they have consistently argued persuasively in favor of decriminalization of much of the criminal law. However, they have taken little notice of what to do in the immediate future about serious

[10] Leading scholars of this persuasion are David Matza, *Delinquency and Drift* (New York: Wiley, 1964); Howard S. Becker, *Outsiders* (New York: The Free Press, 1963); Erving Goffman, *Asylums* (New York: Doubleday, 1961); Richard Quinney, *The Social Reality of Crime* (New York: Little, Brown, 1970).

crime (homicide, armed robbery, forcible rape); their theoretical framework implies that all crime is the product of the neutral social science construct, "socially defined realities."

Although the utilitarian approach is very limited in terms of a model to explain or deal with the root causes of crime I believe it may be very useful in analyzing the effect of police practices, the speed of adjudication, and the administration of justice or deterring crime, consistent with other social aims as well. The economist Gordon Tulloch, a typical advocate of the utilitarian approach[11] through the vehicle of welfare economics, demonstrates the relevance of deprivation and reward systems in motor vehicle violations, tax evasion, and other areas of the criminal law. Parking ticket policy is a good illustration. Normally, we think the policy objective of issuing parking tickets is simply to prevent illegal parking. That is not necessarily so; the function of the fine, assuming honest and efficient law enforcement, is determined largely by the size of the fine. If income revenue from the fines were the object, the optimal fine for revenue purposes would be large enough to cover the cost of policing illegal parking, but small enough not to discourage unduly illegal parking by those who find illegal parking convenient. If the fine for all-day illegal parking is merely $2, while parking in a nearby garage legitimately is $1, it may be that busy and affluent individuals would gladly pay the fine for the convenience of parking, albeit illegally, near their destination. In this case the function of the fine is to discourage illegal parking for those of lesser means and more time while permitting, even assisting by reducing demand, illegal parking of affluent individuals who have tight schedules. One could safely assume, however, that illegal parking would diminish quickly if the fines were increased to $10 or if illegally parked cars were towed away after a short time.

The above utility model has nothing to do with root causes of crime; it is concerned only with the utility curve of progressively increased sanctions on illegal parking behavior. The model assumes reasonableness and calculation on the part of the drivers who are its components, a fact that makes the utilitarian approach unsuited to many problems of impassioned criminal behavior, as Sutherland and Cressey rightly point out when criticizing Bentham and Beccaria. However, policy-oriented approaches that may be realistically followed by criminal justice agencies have been unduly ignored by criminological theory, while causation or general analyses of social structure have continued to dominate the area. Surely the study of crime causation is important to inform our future

[11]Gordon Tulloch, *The Logic of the Law* (New York: Basic Books, 1971), p. vi. See Chapters 8 to 13. There is a growing literature in economics that is similar in orientation. For examples, see Gary S. Becker, "Crime and Punishment: An Economic Approach" *Journal of Political Economy* (1968), 78:526-536; Llad Phillips, "Crime Control: The Case for Deterrence," from *The Economics of Crime and Punishment,* ed. Simon Rottenberg (Washington, D.C.: American Enterprise Institute for Public Policy Research, 1973), pp. 65-84.

directions, but policy analysis to assist those who must contain criminal behavior *today* has its own validity.

This is a book about crime policy and the political and organizational environment that shapes the manner in which we state our crime problems and solutions. Second, it is an attempt to come to grips with a whole range of problems and suggests what criminal justice agencies can realistically do about them.

Part One

THE POLITICS OF CRIME

Chapter 1 introduces the broad dimension of the politics of crime in a democratic society. The theme specifically focuses on the chasm between public perception of crime and its episodic and ephemeral interest in what is actually done. It provides little comfort for democratic theorists since, as far as crime policy and legislation are concerned, public opinion and attitudes are generally irrelevant. The same is not true, however, of specifically interested criminal justice publics, particularly in the politics of criminal legislation. Criminal legislation and crime policy are forged in a political environment not unlike any other public problem, with their own elites, interest groups, and allocation of values. The perception of crime problems reflects the broader dimensions of political culture, however. Answers to the question "Is there a crisis of law and order and what should we do about it?" inevitably affect the historical bias of our own generation's higher expectations of how others should behave.

Within the political culture, particularly in agencies and departments, the actors in the criminal justice system are influenced by the structure of their organizational setting. Their role, or expected behavior as they relate to others, will be influenced by that setting. Their occupational and organizational roles generate unique perspectives regarding what the problems and solutions are in criminal justice and affect their choices as they go about their everyday tasks.

Chapters 2 to 7 explore the structure of criminal justice, its social-political organization, and how its institutions affect the role and perception of its actors. Each chapter also devotes attention to the policy implications of the environment for police, prosecutors, and defense counsel, judges, and correctional officials. Chapter 3 introduces the reader to the criminal justice system. Chapters 4 and 5 examine the influence of the organizational and working environment of the police officer and the dilemma that environment poses for police reform. Chapters 6 and 7 do the same for the attorneys who fill the offices of prosecutor, defense counsel, and judge.

2

THE PUBLIC PERCEPTION OF CRIME

There ought to be a law.
American maxim

Whenever people read the newspapers or tuned in on local newscasts in the late 1960s or early 1970s, they were apt to be reminded of the "crisis of law and order" that most Americans assumed to exist, particularly in our nation's cities. Certainly the Federal Bureau of Investigation's criminal statistics gave credence to that view. From 1963 to 1975, the national rate of reported violent crime against persons increased at an annual rate of 10 percent.[1] Persons arrested under the age of 25 years accounted for at least 63 percent of all crime.[2] With the exception of 1971, according to the FBI's Uniform Crime Report, person-to-person crime shows little sign of slowing its alarming increase. Why?

One popular assumption has been that the increase of violent crime in the United States during those years reflected the evolution of American society from a relatively stable, pastoral, agrarian order to our present metropolitan society and its crisis of law and order. Conservatives are apt to see our present moral decline as resulting from the loss of the family's traditional authority, from the secularization of American society and loss of morality, from the erection of Constitutional barriers against effective police action, and from flaccid judges who refuse to make the punishment of sufficient severity to fit the crime. Liberals point to the social conditions that, they are likely to argue, breed criminogenic circumstances: poor housing, lack of opportunity, racial discrimination, overcrowding,

[1]FBI *Uniform Crime Report* (Washington, D.C.: U.S. Government Printing Office, 1972), p. 61.
[2]Ibid., p. 34.

and inadequate education.[3] Many distinguished criminologists during the same period spent considerable effort in challenging the existence of a significant increase in crime at all!

Have we experienced a decade of "crisis" in law and order? Or is the very measurement of crime subject to the vicissitudes of politics, reflecting—as some charge—the political interests of law enforcement agencies for favorable consideration from appropriation committees during budget hearing time? Doubtless, the FBI has utilized, wherever possible, crime data to justify budgetary expansion. Yet the difficulty of measuring crime goes far deeper than interagency politics or justification for budgets.

The question, "Is there a crisis of law and order?" has many levels of understanding. The question may not be resolved unless three additional questions are raised: (1) What role does political culture play in determining crime problem definitions? (2) How do social phenomena such as organizational role, class, and regional setting influence the conceptualization of criminal behavior? (3) What are the universes, uses, and limitations of contemporary criminal statistics?

The role of political culture is important, since public perception and attitudes, the functions of values and experiences within the political culture, help to shape definitions from which crime statistics are drawn. The widely shared beliefs, attitudes, and sentiments of a political culture define public issues and how they will be raised, public policy goals and what their accepted scope and limits are, and legitimate decision makers and how they may exercise power to achieve public goals. The crime problem is partly defined by its public perception and the extent to which public attitudes, beliefs, and sentiments about crime are linked to the actions of decision makers.[4] Obviously, many of the discretionary activities of criminal justice actors do not represent formal decision making, nor can they be linked to public perceptions of what the problem is. Police behavior in particular is reflexive and is guided by the rules and boundaries of street culture and police culture. The concept of political culture is singularly useful in explaining police and prosecutor behavior and, to a lesser extent, in explaining other practitioners' behavior in the criminal justice system, because of the latitude of discretion permitted without serious review within the organizational life of those who perform these roles. But the public also defines the bounds of propriety for the practitioner and, therefore, public perception is an important ingredient. The question of political culture's relationship to public perceptions is discussed next.

[3] The best-known liberal critic of our criminal justice system is Ramsey Clark, *Crime in America* (New York: Simon and Schuster, 1970), p. 54.

[4] *International Encyclopedia of the Social Sciences* (1968), s.v. "Political Culture," by Lucian W. Pye.

PUBLIC PERCEPTIONS AND ATTITUDES

If security from violence and coercion is as much a state of mind as it is physical protection, then images and attitudes toward crime become as important as the actual number of incidents itself. For example, during the 1968 Presidential campaign, a reporter for the *New York Times* polled the citizens of Webster City, Iowa, which calls itself "Mainstreet, U.S.A." He found the overriding issue that year in Webster City to be "crime in the streets," with particular concern about riots and unruly demonstrations. When the interviewer inquired about crime in Webster City, however, the actual complaints were of youngsters drinking beer, driving too fast, and breaking an occasional window. Pressed for further details, the city fathers complained that trucks hauling turkey feathers through town were unlawfully failing to cover their cargoes to keep from littering Main Street. In another Midwestern town, Garnett, Kansas, another reporter during the same campaign found the town up in arms over crime. His investigations revealed that there had not been a rape in Garnett for 10 years, nor a murder for 21 years; the only person in jail was a 17-year-old-hot-rodder.[5]

There is considerable evidence that public tolerance levels for street crime are differentiated from community to community. Survey research reveals that public perception and concern about crime are not systematically related to crime rates. Thus, responding to the question, "Do you like living in this neighborhood?" 63 to 77 percent of the residents of four very high crime districts, two with predominantly white residents and two with largely black residents, responded affirmatively.[6] When asked what it is that they especially like about living where they do, 58 percent responded that it is "a nice place to live." Indeed, more than one fourth of the residents emphasized the "safety, quietness, and respectability of their neighborhood!"[7]

What reasons can explain these anomalies of perception for residents of high crime rate districts? Perhaps violence and crime are taken as matters of course by those who live approximate to, although most are not part of, areas containing violent subcultures.[8] Or perhaps those who had a lower tolerance for crime and slum conditions that exist in each area had already fled the area.[9] Certainly

[5]Fred P. Graham, "A Contemporary History of American Crime," in *The History of Violence in America: A Report to the National Commission on the Causes and Prevention of Violence,* ed. Hugh Davis Graham and Ted Robert Gurr (New York: Bantam Books, 1970).

[6]Albert J. Reiss, Jr., *Field Surveys III: Studies in Crime and Law Enforcement in Major Metropolitan Areas,* Vol. 1, Sec. II, Public Perceptions and Recollections about crime, Law Enforcement, and Criminal Justice, University of Michigan, Grant 006, Office of Law Enforcement Assistance, U.S. Department of Justice (probably 1966), U.S. Government Printing Office, table on p. 24.

[7]Ibid., p. 25, table on p. 26.

[8]Staff Report to the National Commission on the Causes and Prevention of Violence, *Crimes of Violence,* Vol. 12 (Washington, D.C.: U.S. Government Printing Office, December 1969), pp. 470-471.

[9]*Field Surveys III,* Vol. 1, Sec. II, p. 35.

residents' information levels about crime rates within their own district compared with other areas of the city were low. Most residents believed that their respective cities were experiencing higher crime rates (an incorrect assumption in 1965 at the time of the survey; crime rates had stabilized in both cities), but that their own neighborhoods were about average or even safer than other areas in their cities (an incorrect assumption, since their crime rates were among the highest in the city).[10]

National public opinion research tends to support the lack of relationship between street crime and public perception of increasing crime rates. Although crime has always been a favorite morality play dramatized profitably by local newspapers throughout our history, crime began emerging as a major concern in public opinion polls in the mid-1960s, particularly in 1968 when crime was a major issue in the presidential campaign. But the nature of public perceptions of crime (and therefore public opinions concerning its seriousness) appears to be influenced by events of general unrest and political protest. For example, the Harris Survey has repeatedly asked the question, "In the past year, do you feel the crime rate in your neighborhood has been increasing, decreasing, or has it remained the same as it was before?" Responses seem to vacillate with extraneous events. After the assassination of President Kennedy, 73 percent thought the crime rate was rising in their neighborhood (UCR reports indicated just the opposite for 1962 to 1963). By 1969, responses to the same question had dropped to 35 percent, perhaps a response to racial violence subsiding after the long, hot summer of 1967. But UCR reporting indicates a sharp increase in the crime rate for 1969! Again, when political antiwar protest in 1970 was in the headlines, 62 percent of those polled by the Harris organization responded that crime was increasing in their neighborhood. By October 1973, that response had dropped to 48 percent, strongly suggesting the influence of war protest quiescence resulting from the Paris Peace Agreement on Vietnam.[11]

Yet fear for safety on the streets has risen steadily since 1965 in all sectors of the population, particularly among women, the aged, and suburban and urban dwellers. Although a perception of increases of crime does not correspond to increases in criminal activity, fear of crime among a population is closely related to the actual level of victim suffering. Many individuals are afraid of being victimized without perceiving crime rates to be inordinately high in their neighborhoods. There is tragedy in this division between perception and loss of security, because the poor, the least educated, and the blacks are consistently most frightened of the streets in their neighborhoods. And these are the very

[10] Ibid., p. 36.

[11] This review relies heavily on an analysis of five polling agencies' efforts. Hazel Erskin, "The Polls: Fear of Violence and Crime," *Public Opinion Quarterly* (1974) 38:131-145, especially p. 131. See also Hazel Erskine, "The Polls: Politics and Law and Order," *Public Opinion Quarterly* (1975), 38:623-634.

categories of people who are *least* apt to vote or participate in the electoral process and political decision making that might respond to the crime problem. On the other hand, perception of rising crime rates appears to have no consistent relationship to socio-economic status. Perception of crime and insecurity because of crime are separate phenomena, and they separate the politically participatory from the politically impotent.[12]

Seriousness of crime is not adequately measured in statistical compilations of offenses, but must include in any equation public perspectives and attitudes that affect police activities and offical definitions of the crime problem found in their reporting and apprehension of crime. What is tolerable behavior for one social grouping or geographical area may be serious crime for another. If public support for enforcing prostitution or gambling laws is indifferent, police are free to establish enforcement policy independent of public attitudes. If important members of criminal justice decision making are opposed to rigorous enforcement, such as a mayor or chief of police who receive political contributions or bribes, obviously there will be no enforcement at all. Moreover, such corruption can exist even in the face of public opinions and attitudes regarding full enforcement. Public opinion and attitude alone are not sufficient to promote rigorous police enforcement for particular crimes. That there is no automatic linkage between attitudes and opinions on the one hand and between behaviors or policy on the other is a well-known maxim in social science. The public must not only support full enforcement in their opinions and attitudes; they must also know what the government is, in fact, doing about gambling, narcotics, prostitution, and other crimes. But the evidence is fairly strong that the general public has little knowledge of local policy. Its major sources or information are "episodic" newspaper accounts, and the public tends to discount newspaper exposés of local corruption that are not reinforced by the authority of outside institutions such as federal or state grand juries.[13]

Moreover, American democracy is characterized not by one public, but by many different "publics," each with its own interests and concerns. There are some concerned about lack of enforcement of vice laws. Others, who profit from vice, may engage in politics, legally or illegally, to continue nonenforcement. But abstract criminal justice issues, as opposed to a daring robbery or a brutal murder, do not command the attention of very many. Moreover, decision-making elites in criminal justice—mayors and chiefs of police, judges, and prosecutors—are characterized by a fragmentation of authority, a fact that will concern us in later chapters. A mayor cannot control the courts; a judge cannot reform the police.

[12] Erskine, "The Polls: Fear of Violence and crime," p. 132.

[13] For a superb review of the dynamics between public perspectives and official corruption in one urban setting, see John A. Gardiner, *The Politics of Corruption: Organized Crime in an American City* (New York: Russell Sage Foundation, 1970), especially Chapters 4 and 5.

Just as any constituency for criminal justice reform is small and scattered so, too, are the elites.[14]

POLICING IN THE PAST

Until very recently, law enforcement did not reach into particular geographic areas, including many rural areas and racial and ethnic ghettos within the city. For example, interviews by the author with senior police officials in Syracuse, New York, revealed that prior to 1960 police did not concern themselves with a great deal of "criminal" activity in the black ghetto, except in the case of homicide, destruction of property, or cases brought to their attention by the leadership of the neighborhood. Interestingly, now that police officers are enforcing the law with greater vigor where energetic law enforcement was absent in the past, it may be that more ghetto residents are reporting crimes as well. The consequence would be a geometric increase in the rate of reported crime.

The absence of vigilant law enforcement was the rule rather than the exception in the first half of the nineteenth century. Crimes such as public drunkenness and assault, while usually prohibited by statute, were virtually ignored during that period. Most major cities did not have a full-time police force until the 1830 to 1850 period, when the country sustained some of the most violent rioting in our history. At that time, rioting, burning and looting were periodic occurrences extinguished by vigilantes who were deputized for the occasion. Boston, in 1837 the paradigm of American civilization, was gutted by fire and rioting three times before the city fathers would pay for part-time police protection. Prior to that time, the customary practice was to permit the riot to burn itself out; law enforcement was limited to containing the conflagration within the boundaries of the inner city. Not until the Civil War would the citizens of Boston permit police officers to wear uniforms or to carry firearms.[15]

The American public historically has been suspicious of police forces. Even today there is a deep-seated distrust of centralized police activities, especially persistent when the subject turns to a discussion of a national police force or even national police academies. Earlier in our history this suspicion was even more pronounced. The early nineteenth century was an individualistic, uncomplicated age, where minor disputes were settled by informal means, often by fistfights. Given the agrarian socio-economic structure of the country, there was little need for the urgency in settling disputes that is present in a delicately balanced, technologically oriented, interdependent society. No doubt the thought of organized and armed police forces to the nineteenth-century American mind renewed

[14] Ibid., pp. 7-19, 101-102.

[15] Roger Lane, "Urbanization and Criminal Violence in the Nineteenth Century: Massachusetts as a Test Case," in *The History of Violence in America,* pp. 475-479.

memories of uniformed English troops, standing armies, and excessive prerogatives of power in the executive branch, be it mayor or governor.

Even after American police forces were well established, their function was almost exclusively social control, not law enforcement. New men were recruited for the force who had street sense and fighting skills; they were typically put out on the street with gun and badge, but with no training. Their function as peace officers required the very broadest levels of tolerance toward what today constitutes illegal activities that were not seriously threatening decorum and public order. That was especially true of vice.

In 1880 in Syracuse, New York, a city founded much earlier by the followers of Methodist John Wesley, a rookie officer was given this advice on his first day by his new captain: "Take it easy, O'Brien. You'll soon get the hang of it. Keep your mouth shut and remember you've got the police force behind you. Don't let anyone bluff you, but don't hunt for trouble, because if you do, you'll find it."[16]

Bluffing, in 1880, meant threatening a police officer with a beating. The successful officer called everyone's bluff and established a reputation for fistfighting. But maintaining public order did not mean interfering with the social order. According to the rookie, O'Brien:

> *The city in those days was what would now be called "wide open." I mean there were a lot of saloons, disorderly houses and gambling places in operation, not actually running by permission of anybody, but which could have been closed if public sentiment had demanded it. So long as nobody was robbed or murdered or cheated in too raw a way, the people were satisfied to let well enough alone. Occasionally, a reform wave would come along, but it never lasted long.*[17]

There would be a time soon after 1880 when Syracuse, New York would close the brothels and casinos that lined the Erie Canal, its subsidiary waterways, and the back streets of the city. The reform would be the result of higher standards of civility insisted on by the citizenry who had established roots and status in the community. The crime rate for gamblers, prostitutes, and young toughs would, of course, increase as the meaning of crime in the eyes of newly charged police officers changed in definition.

But in 1880 the political culture tolerated minor violence, commercial sex, and gambling. Fighting vice in a turbulent city of poor immigrants and discordant values and styles of life is a government expense that was neither desired by local businessmen nor affordable. One in four citizens between 1880 and 1890 in the Salt City, as Syracuse was known because of its commercially valuable salt

[16] William O'Brien, *Forty Years on the Force* (Syracuse: Syracuse Herald, 1926), p. 10.

[17] Ibid., p. 11.

deposits, was foreign-born,[18] and the population of the city took a quantum leap during that same period, jumping from 51,792 to 88,143, an increase of 51 percent.

Vice and violence were an accepted way of life in most American cities throughout the nineteenth century, particularly during the years of heavy immigration. The Quaker city of Philadelphia tolerated 517 brothels in 1880.[19] Physical beatings of children were normal and were frequently administered during that period in the tenements of Chicago, according to Jane Adams; and the problem of alcoholism was probably of more serious dimensions than it is today. As early as 1810, Albany, New York, with a population of 20,000, was consuming 200,000 gallons of liquor a year. That averages 1 gallon every 18 days for every man, woman, and child. New York City had over 1600 saloons and grog-selling grocery stores, while Chicago had a saloon for every 28 people in some wards.[20]

The instability of social norms and the existence of conflict in an uprooted population, to use Oscar Handlin's expression, produced a variety of police behavior that James Q. Wilson has called the "watchman style." Indeed, during the first quarter of the nineteenth century, and much later in some cities, there was no police force; it was generally assumed that such a force of armed men would represent a serious threat to liberty. Public order was nominally maintained by watch-and-ward societies or patronage appointees, often of advanced age. Criminal investigations or pursuit of offenders frequently depended either on the size of the reward, in the case of theft, or on the energies of the victim. Even after the establishment of police forces, as we have previously commented, law enforcement was limited to maintaining public order, and arrests were made only for more serious crimes. Reform in enforcement practices and public support for cracking down on vice and petty crime had to wait until there was a change in the political culture, affecting the perceptions of citizens and criminal justice practitioners alike.[21]

History represents a relativistic variable. Behaviors that are legal, illegal, or unenforced in one historical period are considered differently in a subsequent period. Infuriating as it is to many, there is considerable support in social history for Edward Banfield's provocative thesis in *The Unheavenly City Revisited.* Banfield argues that modern American cities are not experiencing a crisis, but that the definition of civility has reached a higher level corresponding to the growth of the middle and upper-middle classes in American society. These groups,

[18] Roscoe Martin et al., *Decisions in Syracuse* (Garden City, N.Y.: Anchor Books, 1965), pp. 24-25.
[19] Edward C. Banfield, *The Unheavenly City Revisited* (Boston: Little, Brown, 1974), pp. 74-75.
[20] Alice Felt Taylor, *Freedom's Ferment* (New York: Harper and Brothers, 1962), pp. 316-317.
[21] James F. Richardson, *The New York Police: Colonial Times to 1901* (New York: Oxford University Press, 1970), Chapters 1-3.

through their political and cultural activities, have redefined situations in the cities, such as housing, education, health, and social services, in a manner that transforms historically bad, but tolerated, conditons into "crises."[22]

The same phenomena of rising standards of acceptability regarding police procedures, vice and violence, and due process have tended to produce a crisis mentality over problems of criminal justice. One has only to recall that for most of our history public intoxication, use of cocaine, morphine, and marihuana, and assault all were more or less tolerated behaviors either because they were not illegal or because there was little public demand to enforce what criminal prohibitions did exist.[23]

CRIMINAL LEGISLATION

Max Lerner has pointed to the paradox of Americans' insisting on rigid law enforcement at the same time that they multiply laws or legal rules beyond the point of enforcement, and then violate the same laws. Lerner finds that the pragmatic temper of Americans provides a balance to the attitude that "there ought to be a law" for every social ill. Formal codes or procedures "go largely unheeded because it is believed by those administering their provisions that enforcement would cripple the practical needs of social life and violate the insistent impulses of man's nature." It becomes a question of organizational needs, such as manpower, efficiency, appropriations, and the need for public support, juxtaposed with the fullest possible enforcement of the rule of law.

> *The Americans have sought to solve the problem [of crime] by alternations of neglect and enforcement, as shown by their traffic regulations, their disastrous Prohibition experiment, their gambling and betting laws, their vice and narcotics laws. They have moved between the twin beats of Puritanism, silence and crackdown. There will be long periods of "patterned evasion" of the legal norms through corruption and the "Big Fix." Then there will be a crackdown on racketeers, "vice kings," fee-splitters, "ambulance-chasers," narcotic peddlers and addicts, gamblers, bookies, prostitutes, gang warriors, traffic violators, or just vagrants and bums. In this crackdown the police, prosecutors, judges, press, clergy, and politicians tumble over one another in an hysteria of legal enforcement, feeling at once virtuous and inwardly silly. Then a vast apathy will blanket the community, and the silence will be as before.*[24]

The attitudes and perceptions that accompany political culture shape the cli-

[22] Banfield, *The Unheavenly City Revisited,* Chapter 3.
[23] Lane, "Urbanization and Criminal Violence in the Nineteenth Century," in *The History of Violence in America,* pp. 468-483.
[24] Max Lerner, *America as a Civilization* (New York: Simon and Schuster, 1964), Vol. I, pp. 438-439.

mate for criminal legislation. As long as we consider criminal behavior apart from the political process, we are bound to have difficulty conceptualizing, and consequently measuring, behavior that is labeled criminal. Criminal behavior is not universally understood or agreed on. It is the product, like other legislation, of interest group activity and constitutent pressures influencing the judgment of the legislature. Yet American jurisprudence has regarded the convicted criminal as a member of an immoral social set, ignoring the interplay of group values that led to defining criminal behaviors. This is not surprising, given the central role that morals and community judgment play in criminal law and procedure. Even more interesting was the ease with which criminological and juridical theorists transformed criminal and moral categories into pseudo-scientific nosologies of deviance, mental illness, and delinquency. Social and behavioral science became the new priesthood, a development that continues today, as sin is replaced by the sciences of abnormality.

Until recently, most criminologists and reformers assumed that criminal behavior was both universal (a criminal in New York is the same as a criminal in Moscow or Cairo or Hong Kong) and a form of deviance, mental illness, or sociopathology. Traditional criminologists and reformers looked for causes of crime in the individual's personality or environment. They ignored or minimized the fact that "crimes" are defined by statute and statutes are products of a particular political culture. For example, in the early 1960s a young man in Moscow noted that the demand for female cosmetics far exceeded the supply permitted by Soviet planners, who were far more interested in the development of heavy industry than in the appurtenances of feminine life. Light consumer goods were low priority, and cosmetics had no priority at all. To fill the void in female demand, the enterprising individual manufactured lipstick in his cellar, marketed the product, and made an unsocialist profit. He was subsequently arrested by Soviet police and given life imprisonment for the kind of initiative and enterprise that would have earned him at least a Junior Chamber of Commerce award as Man of the Year if his operations had been in the United States.

Enforcement of the law and prosecution also reflect community standards. It has been noted that laws prohibiting petty crime were not vigorously enforced in racial or ethnic ghettos prior to World War II as they are today. It is also clear that illegal gambling may not be prosecuted as vigorously in some localities (Atlanta, for example, where it complements tourism) as it is in others (Maine, for example, where the tourists are campers and fishermen). What can be said of the penal law and statutory criminal procedures can be said of legislation in general. The history of criminal sanctions against drugs, gambling, and consensual, aberrant sexual practices has reflected the influence of strongly held belief systems of politically dominant groups much more than any rational assessment of the effectiveness of criminal sanctions in reducing these behaviors. Resolution of problems such as our high homicide rate, drug use (including alcohol), petty graft and organized crime, vice crime, and abortion cannot be anticipated until value conflicts in the political arena are reconciled with rational means for crime control.

We must look at criminal statutes themselves if we are to understand crime, and we must see the criminal statutes as products of the politics of legislation and the administration of justice, not merely as definitions of "deviancy" or "universally unacceptable behavior." To be sure, many kinds of human behavior—murder, larceny, and aggravated assault against members of the community—are proscribed in all societies. But, for the most part, criminal law, like all law, reflects the thoughts of Oliver Wendell Holmes that "law is in the main the rationalization of the dominant group." This is not to say that the dominant majority's notion of what is permissible is spurious or not well considered. Indeed, it is only to suggest that crime is a definition of behavior that is conferred on some people by other more influential people. Agents of the law (legislators, police, prosecutors, judges, and correctional personnel) represent segments of the body politic and are responsible for maintaining criminal law and enforcing it.

Crime, then, is a partially political phenomenon. For example, prior to 1914, gambling, narcotics use,[25] and prostitution in most parts of the United States were legal, or at least laws against such behavior were not vigorously enforced. Exploitation of child labor,[26] yellow-dog contracts,[27] and racial segregation[28] were not only legal several generations ago; they were practices protected, even required, by statutory and constitutional law. Child labor, yellow-dog contracts, and state-mandated racial segregation are now illegal, and such practices may result in criminal sanctions, while the production and sale of alcoholic beverages, once illegal, are now flourishing and respectable.

It is surprising that no systematic study of the politics of criminal legislation has been done, considering the intense interests of political scientists in the legislative process. A few topical studies have been completed on particular criminal laws, especially the Volstead Act, which ushered in prohibition,[29] short works emphasizing the historical-political evolution of specific criminal laws for

[25]The term narcotic is used in its popular sense, not according to its pharmaceutical properties, to embrace illegal stimulants, depressants, anaesthetics, and hallucinogenics. Obviously, many powerful and often equally dangerous drugs, such as nicotine, caffeine, and alcohol, are not considered narcotics in a popular sense because they are normally legitimized by the political culture. Howard S. Becker, *Outsiders* (New York: Macmillan, 1963), p. 138; Rufus King, "The American System: Legal Sanctions to Repress Drug Abuse," in *Drugs and the Criminal Justice System,* ed. James A. Inciardi and Carl D. Chambers (Beverly Hills, Calif.: Sage Publications, 1974), pp. 17-34.

[26]*Hammer* v *Dagenhart* 247 U.S. 251 (1918).

[27]*Civil Rights Cases* 109 U.S. 3 (1883).

[28]*Adair* v *United States* 208 U.S. 161 (1908); *Coppage* v *Kansas* 236 U.S. 1 (1915).

[29]For example, Peter Odegard, *Pressure Politics: The Story of the Anti-Saloon League* (New York: Octagon Books, 1966); Joseph R. Gusfield, *Symbolic Crusade: Status Politics and the American Temperance Movement* (Urbana, Ill.: Ill. University of Illinois Press, 1963).

sexual psychopaths,[30] and laws proscribing the use of marihuana[31] and narcotics use in general.[32] There are also a number of law journal articles that emphasize structural and technical changes, but not political behavior, in systematic fashion.

This discussion of the politics of criminal legislation will not fill this research gap, but it will provide a general overview[33] of the process and point out three important factors about that process. However, empirical evidence for these generalizations is somewhat shallow, and the conclusions are partially impressionistic.

1. The first is that interest groups lobby for criminal justice legislation just as they do for other legislation. Moreover, as is true with most legislative efforts, there is an absence of public information and interest in criminal legislation, thus maximizing the influence of those who are among the informed and interested.
2. There are important limits in the political culture beyond that legislators dare not trespass for fear of activating retaliation from individuals or groups that will defend the moral and political order.
3. There is an elite closely associated with the drafting of criminal law, with characteristics that benefit some social groupings but not others.

CRIMINAL LAW LOBBIES

The range of organizations, agencies, businesses, and groups that testify or otherwise participate in drawing up a criminal code and related legislation is enormous. In the 1973 Revisions of the criminal code of Pennsylvania, the Motion Picture Association, the Pennsylvania Library Association, and even representatives of the Book of the Month Club testified on obscenity proposals,[34] traditional associations, such as the Public Defenders Association, the District Attorney's Association, and the American Civil Liberties Union played a major role in the earlier draft. Interest groups concerned with criminal law can be usefully distinguished as either *ad hoc* groups, such as the Motion Picture Association, or more *permanent* groups, whose interest in the criminal law is more than transient. In

[30] Arthur Sutherland, "The Diffusion of Sexual Psychopath Laws," *American Journal of Sociology* (1950), 56:142.

[31] Becker, *Outsiders,* pp. 135-146.

[32] King, "The American System", pp. 17-34; Alfred Lindesmith, *The Addict and the Law.* (Bloomington: Indiana University Press, 1960)

[33] The discussion that follows relies heavily on two sources: my unpublished research in New York State and the Commonwealth of Pennsylvania, including interviews with key participants in the 1967 Revised Criminal Code in New York State, and research still in progress on the 1973 Revised Criminal Code of Pennsylvania. A second source from which I have borrowed extensively is John P. Heinz, Robert W. Gettleman, and Morris A. Seeskin, "Legislative Politics and the Criminal Law," *Northwestern University Law Review* (1966), 64:277-357.

[34] Pennsylvania House Committee on Law and Justice, *Hearing Report,* Harrisburg, Pa. October 11, 1973, pp. 2-3.

the latter category, in most states, would be state and large-city bar associations, chiefs of police associations (with particular reference to large, urban departments), state trial lawyer's associations, public defender associations, and government agencies such as corrections and state planning for Federal Safe Streets funds, the latter a newcomer. Probably the most influential force of all in drafting criminal codes is the consultation and testimony of prosecutors from the large urban centers of a state, centers such as Philadelphia, Chicago, and New York. Just how much influence these groups have and what role patterns each group and its elite play remains unclear. Probably the political influence and role formations will differ from state to state. Each group mentioned, however, has a continuing interest in the criminal statutes.

Most selective interest characterizes the *ad hoc* groups: pinball manufacturers who fear prohibition of their machines; the National Rifle Association whose militancy against gun regulation is well known; local telephone companies concerned that court-approved wiretaps will provide adverse publicity for their commercial interests; church organizations activated by code changes relative to abortion or sex crimes; and banking interests hoping to increase criminal penalties for illicit use of credit cards.[35] Such groups rarely are interested in criminal law, per se, except for specialized areas that directly affect the goals of their organizations, and their influence probably is proportionate to the degree of general public outrage that might be provoked if and when the bounds of propriety in political culture are trespassed.

Such a consequence was a distinct possibility at one stage in the drafting of Illinois' revised criminal code section on abortion provisions in 1961. While the original law permitted abortions only when "necessary for the preservation of the mother's life," the revised draft reviewed by the legislature would have allowed a physician to perform an abortion if "medically advisable because continuance of the pregnancy would endanger the life or gravely impair the health of the pregnant woman." The revised code also permitted abortion where the fetus was defective or where rape or incest resulted in pregnancy. The role of one interest group was described by Heinz just before a joint committee of the Illinois legislature was to vote on the revised code.

> *Predictably, the chief opposition to these provisions came from the Roman Catholic Church. The Church also opposed the repeal of the "crime against nature," which had covered both homosexual acts and bestiality. Bowman*[36] *recognized immediately, of course, that the Catholic Church was a formidable*

[35] Heinz, Gettleman, and Seeskin, "Legislative Politics," pp. 283, 308-317, 297, 305.

[36] Charles H. Bowman of the University of Illinois School of Law was the principal draftsman of the 1961 Revised Code.

opponent—even more formidable than the National Rifle Association. In 1960, the state's population was approximately 35 per cent Catholic, and over half of the population of the city of Chicago was Catholic. Had the Church waged an all out campaign, including denunciations from the pulpit, it could easily have influenced enough constituents to persuade many legislators that it was unwise to vote for the code. Thus, even if Bowman could have preserved the abortion provisions intact in the committee's recommendations, a code including those provisions might well have failed on the floor. Accordingly, he arranged a meeting with the Church's lobbyist, Claire Driscoll, a Chicago lawyer. Bowman and Driscoll proceeded to strike a bargain which was reasonably acceptable both to the Church and to the proponents of the code. Bowman agreed to drop the liberalized abortion provisions in return for the Church's agreement to cease its opposition to the other sex crime proposals, specifically the lack of any coverage of consensual homosexual acts . . . Both sides kept their agreement.[37]

Of course, the above narrative simplifies the relationship of political process with political culture. The Catholic Church was and continues to be a major opponent of liberalized abortion, but by no means exhausts the list of factors behind public opposition to such measures. The year 1961 predated the sexual revolution, the feminist movement was inchoate, and abortion reform was not a viable option in Illinois, or in other states, for that matter. By 1968 public opinion had probably changed on abortion, since culture had changed.[38]

Normally, legislatures prefer to delegate primary responsibility to expert drafting committees drawn from the ranks of attorneys who have political or prosecutorial experience and from the university law schools. Little opposition to the recommendations of code-drafting commissions will occur in the legislature as long as the code's measures remain within a value structure for which there is concensus in the political culture. Most measures pass with overwhelming votes on the floor.[39]

Obviously, whether a code draftsman is a law professor or a former prosecutor —two traditional possibilities—he must be sensitive to what the legislature, in fact, will approve. And what the legislature will approve cannot be determined simply by analysis of interest group formation around the legislative process; political culture and the values and symbols that government must defend, at least tacitly, play a subtle and powerful role. Thurman Arnold once wrote that many "criminal laws survive in order to satisfy moral objections to established modes of conduct," but they are unenforceable "because we want to continue our

[37] Heinz, Gettleman, and Seeskin, "Legislative Politics," pp. 323-324.
[38] R. A. Hudson Rosen et al., "Health Professionals" Attitudes Toward Abortion," *Public Opinion Quarterly* (1974), 38:159-173.
[39] Heinz, Gettleman, and Seeskin, "Legislative Politics," pp. 325-334.

conduct, and unrepealed because we want to preserve our morals."[40] Issues such as abortion, adultery, gun registration, homosexuality, and the privacy of hearth and home against telephone taps or warrantless search go far beyond churches, sportsmen's organizations, or associations of civil libertarians. "Legalized murder," "the right to control one's body," "a man's house is his castle," and "if citizens are disarmed, only criminals will have guns" are fervid slogans emerging from powerful values in the depths of culture. They represent neither the rhetoric of a special interest group nor the interests of an elite.[41] Yet it is this type of issue that is most likely to generate debate in a legislature.[42]

ELITES IN CRIMINAL LAW LEGISLATION

If an analysis of interest group formations may be insufficient to explain the source of criminal legislation, perhaps an analysis of elite decision making may fill the void. Again, research is virtually nonexistent in the area, other than generalized claims deduced from abstract political theory.[43] Certainly, lawyers are heavily represented in the legislature, in testimony, in drafting commissions, and as retained lobbyists. Moreover, in all of these capacities, the elites frequently interact professionally and know each other on a personal basis and are likely to represent, as we have said, prosecutorial concerns;[44] these concerns include plea bargaining, which requires various degrees of seriousness in a charge, and flexibility as to charge, which permits the prosecutor to throw a broad net with generalized language such as broad definitions of conspiracy. It is also correct that, until recently, few women and black representatives have served on codification commissions or otherwise participated in criminal law legislation, a fact that might reflect past stratification in the legal profession more than overt discrimination.

Most political theorists recognize the major role of political elites[45]—those

[40] Thurman W. Arnold, *Symbols of Government* (New Haven, Conn.: Yale University Press, 1935), p. 160.

[41] There is an enormous literature on the relationship between culture, custom, and law, the traditionally accepted view being that law is an institution in complex societies that grows out of, but is distinct from, custom. For a brief review see Lon Fuller, *Anatomy of the Law* (New York: New American Library, 1968), pp. 67-91. For a set of assumptions sharply at variance with ours, see Richard Quinney, ed., *Criminal Justice in America* (Boston: Little, Brown, 1974), pp. 26-29.

[42] New York and Pennsylvania both debated, at various stages, eliminating adultery, although few prosecutions for this popular crime have been recorded in decades. See also Heinz, Gettleman, and Seeskin, "Legislative Politics," pp. 320-323.

[43] For example, see Quinney, *Criminal Justice in America,* pp. 16-21. Quinney's Marxist position is that a ruling class in the United States has been created by the capitalist mode of production and that the state and its accompanying legal system reflect and serve the needs of the ruling class.

[44] Heinz, Gettleman, and Seeskin, "Legislative Politics," pp. 337-341.

[45] There is, however, a lively debate on the representativeness and competitiveness and on the cumulative nature of the elite's power. For representative authors see Peter Bachrach, *The Theory of Democratic Elitism: A Critique* (Boston: Little, Brown, 1967); Robert A. Dahl, *Pluralist Democracy*

with political skills of negotiation and mediation, with sufficient leisure and income to participate in politics or in official positions where they are privy to information that is not available outside of bureaucracy and to personal contacts that facilitate communication in their own interests. There are, however, heated debates concerning the socio-economic character of elites, and there is disagreement particularly on the degree of responsiveness of elites to nonelites. Moreover, the relationship between "elite status" and "power" remains murky.

There is little question, however, that the legal profession dominates the legislative process, and that dominance remains whether the elite influentials are noncontroversial, technical codifiers or moral entrepreneurs from the left or right. Both reforms and measures to maintain the status quo are carried out by elites in the legislative process for the criminal law.[46] A major reason for this dominance has to do with the technical complexities of law itself. For example, in the 1961 Illinois code, a major issue arose from the code's "Unlawful Use of Weapons" section. That section made it a crime to possess knowingly a firearm concealed in one's vehicle or on one's person, and then created an exemption or "affirmative defense" for certain kinds of persons under certain circumstances, including "licensed hunters or fisherman while engaged in hunting or fishing." The National Rifle Association was opposed to virtually any weapons control provision and, once given a forum to achieve this end, focused their opposition especially on this provision. The NRA and some field-and-game sportswriters, through attorney lobbyists, argued that the law as drafted was unconstitutional, since it would place on a defendant the burden of proving his innocence. The political issues involved related to sportsman opposition to gun control; the lawyerlike issue debated and resolved (in favor of the original draft) was the constitutionality of an affirmative defense as outlined.[47]

Given the esoteric character of technical questions of criminal law, it is understandable that the process generates little public interest so long as cultural symbols are not threatened. Gun control does threaten a minority group's values in a serious way, as do abortion, pornography, and gambling. Primarily, however, legal issues are not very exciting outside of a law school forum—questions of burden of proof, degrees of crime, and affirmative defenses are dull to the layman. Under these circumstances, legislators have little fear that they will be called to account for their vote. Consequently, customarily being lawyers themselves, they liberally delegate their authority to codifying commissions and routinely accept what appear to be noncontroversial changes proposed by expert members of their

in the United States: Conflict and consensus (Chicago: Rand McNally, 1967). For a superb review of past and contemporary elitist theory see David M. Ricci, *Community, Power and Democratic Theory: The Logic of Political Analysis* (New York: Random House, 1971).

[46] Heinz, Gettleman, and Seeskin, "Legislative Politics," pp. 352-355.

[47] Ibid., p. 322.

legal fraternity. That the appearance of noncontroversy can cloak striking reform —indeed that quiet change may be a major characteristic of reform in a pluralist polity—is one of the fascinating characteristics of American politics. For example, the drama and debate of the highly visible U.S. Supreme Court has overshadowed the potentially more comprehensive reach of statutory and code revisions, which are customarily adopted with little fanfare or public discussion.[48] Yet the latter would appear to have a greater impact on criminal justice than an appellate court.

REFORM AND THE MIDDLE-CLASS ETHIC

The very success of the American dream, the "middle classifying" of 80 percent or so of the population, has raised an additional barrier to more than incremental improvement of criminal justice, at least relative to the perceptions of public opinion. Concomitant with the growth of the middle class in American society and the multiplication of its politically active elites has been the growth of higher and higher levels of expectations regarding law enforcement and legal procedure.

Political research has long established a relationship between social class and voting participation.[49] Important characteristics of middle-class membership are the inner feelings of obligation toward "good citizenship" and relatively high expectations that individual participation in voting and other political activity does make a difference. Being a "good citizen" is synonymous with exercising one's duty to vote. Conversely, nonparticipation in voting is related to relatively lower levels of expectation as to the efficacy of citizen participation, such as is found among members of the lower class. For these reasons (and many others) members of the middle and upper classes exercise their franchise and generally participate in public affairs in disproportionately large numbers.

Edward Banfield has extended this relationship between status and a sense of public obligation. Banfield's conception of middle and upper class is that members from both its sectors are oriented toward the future and toward moral and material progress for the individual and for the society as a whole. The typical upper-class political active feels a strong obligation to try to improve not only himself but everything else: his community, his society, the whole world.[50] It is characteristically American to believe that, with sufficient efforts, all difficulties can be overcome and all problems solved.

The middle-class ethic has potential for high irony in its effects on serious attempts to conceptualize and generate policy to resolve the problems of crime,

[48] Arthur H. Sherry, "The Politics of Criminal Law Reform," *American Journal of Comparative Law* (1973), 21:201.

[49] Seymour Martin Lipset, *Political Man* (Garden City, N.Y.: Doubleday, 1963), p. 208.

[50] Banfield, *The Unheavenly City Revisited,* pp. 57-60.

particularly when the middle class identifies contending goals as crucial to reform. The reformer must confront the fact that the criminal justice system has multiple and often contradictory goals of equal validity. As an illustration, the criminal justice system has, as one of its objectives, the protection of due process for the criminally accused. The right to cross examine witnesses, protection against forced self-incrimination, and the right to counsel are among a myriad of constitutional and statutory protections for the defendant. But the system also has as an objective the apprehension and conviction of those who are culpable. At many junctures maximizing both due process and convictions for guilty offenders is not possible. Providing use immunity,[51] for instance, to obtain information on criminal colleagues in organized crime or government corruption does not fully protect the defendant (who is forced to testify) from public exposure or even from conviction if evidence for the defendant is evidence obtained independent of his testimony for which he has been granted immunity.

Plea bargaining provides a similar, if more complicated, example. As is now widely known, plea bargaining refers to negotiations between prosecutors and defense attorneys that, if successful, lead to a plea of guilty or *nolo contendere.* In return, the prosecutor agrees either to drop some charges, to recommend leniency in the sentence, or both. Estimates of the extent of plea bargaining in some cities run as high as 90 percent of all cases resulting in a conviction, although the average rate is closer to between 30 and 40 percent.[52] There is little question that the practice of permitting a reduction in charge in exchange for a guilty plea preserves the resources of the district attorney's office. Negotiating a guilty plea may involve minutes; preparing for trial and prosecuting at trial may involve days, or even weeks. Encouraging a defendant to plead, on the other hand, permits the district attorney to spend more time on difficult cases and minimizes the risk of losing at trial.

Plea bargaining affects offenders in discriminatory fashion, depending on the nature of the offense charged. The negotiation strength of the defense is stronger

[51] Until recently, immunity statutes were of two types, the most common being "transactional immunity." This standard provides for complete immunity from prosecution after a witness is compelled by the government to testify in exchange for a grant of transactional immunity. Spurred by antiorganized crime efforts of the federal government, some states have adopted "use immunity" standards. Under a grant of use immunity, only the testimony of the witness is immunized. The government may subsequently prosecute a witness with use immunity, but it is prohibited from introducing as evidence prior testimony of the witness. The federal government's "use immunity" statute from the 1970 Organized Crime Act goes further to protect the witness. Under a "use plus fruits" immunity, the U. S. government may not use the testimony of the witness while he was granted immunity or any of the "fruits" or leads from such testimony. "The Scope of Testimonial Immunity under the Fifth Amendment," *Northwestern Law Review* (1972), 67:107-108.

[52] National Advisory Commission on Criminal Justice Standards and Goals, *A National Strategy to Reduce Crime,* U. S. Department of Justice (Washington, D.C.: U.S. Government Printing Office, 1973), p. 146.

in a serious narcotics, rape, or tax evasion case where evidentiary motions, such as motions to suppress, are frequent; standards of admissibility of evidence are complex; police procedures are very refined; and the reliability and availability of government witnesses are open to question. Such cases tax a prosecutor's human and material resources in terms of time and personnel, and they raise the possibility of losing his case and reputation at trial after months of cooperation with detectives, drawing up search warrants, and preparing for trial. A typical burglary case or an assault or larceny defendant does not normally involve anywhere near the same expenditure of resources. Research in Pennsylvania revealed that prosecutors spent on the average no more than 30 minutes for dealing with such cases prior to trial preparation.[53] Consequently, defense counsel negotiating leverage will be relatively greater for a narcotics case than for a burglary.

The merits of plea bargaining have been vigorously debated at all levels of justice, from the U.S. Supreme Court to two presidential commissions and district attorney offices throughout the country. The Supreme Court has normally upheld negotiated pleas unless it has been shown that defense counsel was incompetent when advising a plea, the plea was not intelligently given, or the plea was coerced and involuntary. On this latter point, the Supreme Court's concept of coercion does not include calculation by a defendant that a plea would be advantageous because the weight of evidence is against him and conviction after trial may result in a more serious punishment than that administered after a plea. Nor can a guilty plea be rejected even if it may have been motivated, in part, by a coerced confession. The probability that the confession would or would not be rejected by an appellate court after trial was simply regarded by the Supreme Court as part of the acceptable calculation as to the advantages and disadvantages of going to trial.[54] Unconstitutional coercion is present in plea bargaining only when judges' or prosecutors' promised reductions in charge or sentence do not materialize after a plea of guilty is entered. Also unacceptable are legislated inducements to pleas whereby trial may result in capital punishment and a plea will not.[55]

In 1967 The President's Commission on Law Enforcement and the Administration of Justice recommended restructuring discretionary decision making in the negotiated plea by means of a memorandum outlining and explaining the

[53] These data are based on unpublished research conducted in 1973 for the Pennsylvania Governor's Justice Commission. Except for narcotics, our findings are supported by other available data. See Jacqueline Cohen et al., "Implementation of the Jussim Model in a Criminal Justice Agency," *Journal of Research in Crime and Delinquency* (1973) 10: Table 4 on p. 124; Table 2 on p. 122. For a breakdown of costs to the criminal justice system per index crime see The President's Commission on Law Enforcement and Administration of Justice, *Task Force Report: Science and Technology* (Washington, D.C.: U.S. Government Printing Office, 1967), Table 12 on p. 63.

[54] *McMann* v *Richardson* 397 U.S. 759 (1970); *Tollett* v *Henderson* 411 U.S. 258 (1973).

[55] *United States* v *Jackson* 390 U.S. 570 (1968).

negotiated disposition prior to sentencing. The Commission also recommended other procedures designed to provide fairness by increasing the visibility of the negotiation and making the procedure clearer to the defendant as well as to criminal justice personnel.[56] However, a more recent blue-ribbon commission, The National Advisory Commission on Criminal Justice Standards and Goals, has recommended the abolition of the negotiated plea by 1978. Even its recommendation for the interim period prior to 1978 goes beyond the American Bar Association's recommendation as well. Standards and Goals suggests a full statement in open court of the terms of every negotiated agreement and the judge's reasons for accepting or rejecting the plea.[57]

The debate over plea bargaining is likely to continue without a resolution of the issue, since the practice has, like many public practices, multiple goals. Defenders of the rights of the accused point to the discrimination and lack of vigorous advocacy by the defense counsel inherent in this practice. They argue, with considerable justification, that defense counsel is often the major influence on the defendant's decision to plead guilty, even when the defendant does not want to do so.[58] There is frequently economic incentive for a defense attorney, or for a part-time prosecutor for that matter, to dispense quickly with a pending criminal case, where remuneration will be small compared with a more lucrative civil law case. However, the preponderance of the evidence thus far disputes this motivation, at least in the case of public defenders, where the motivation to encourage a guilty plea is more likely based on a desire to expedite cases in which the evidence is overwhelmingly against the client and the defense counsel wishes to maintain a cooperative relationship with the district attorney, and vice versa.[59] Additionally, the statistic of 30 to 40 percent representing plea bargaining pleas nationwide is somewhat misleading. Prosecutors are often interested in justice as much as defense attorneys, and they will reduce the charge in cases where the legislature has mandated unreasonable sentences or where they believe the sentence is too severe for the particular situation. In making such a judgment, the district attorney and defense counsel refer to offenses in terms of the actual events surrounding the case, instead of a legal definition.[60] On the other hand, conserva-

[56]The President's Commission on Law Enforcement and the Administration of Justice, *Task Force Report: The Courts* (Washington, D.C.: U.S. Government Printing Office, 1967), pp. 9-13.

[57]National Advisory Commission, *A National Strategy to Reduce Crime,* pp. 46-49.

[58]Abraham S. Blumberg, "The Practice of Law as a Confidence Game," *Law and Society Review* (1967), 1:28, 33-34. There is general confirmation of this fact in the literature. See Lynn M. Mather, "Some Determinants of the Method of Case Disposition: Decision Making by Public Defenders in Los Angeles," *Law and Society Review* (1974), 8:200.

[59]Mather, "Some Determinants of the Method of Case Disposition," p. 209. Also see Jerome Skolnick, "Social Control in the Adversary System," *Journal of Conflict Resolution* (1967), 11:52-70.

[60]Mather, "Some Determinants of the Method of Case Disposition." Private attorneys, public defenders, and district attorneys readily confirm this to be the case in private conversations with me.

tives such as Arlen Specter, former district attorney for Philadelphia County, have argued that "the bargained plea is really no bargain. We should not settle for a system which simultaneously deprives the innocent defendant of the forum where the prosecutor is compelled to prove his case, and the public is victimized by excessive leniency for hard-core criminal repeaters."[61]

Plea bargaining could be ended theoretically by prohibiting the prosecutor from negotiating a plea for consideration. Yet, if the practice is ended, at the same time providing additional judges, prosecutors, detectives, and defense counsel in large metropolitan courts, at least, it is probable that the number of acquittals and dismissals would increase rapidly. There would be no other way for the prosecutor to devote his limited time to very serious cases than to limit the flow of cases through one of these two options. Of course, the proportion of cases going to trial would increase, well above the current 11 percent estimate of all felony cases disposed of by trial today. Punishments for those cases prosecuted to the full letter of the law would probably by greater, while other culpable offenders would go unpunished. On the other hand, many minor cases might never get beyond the station house and, to some defense-oriented attorneys, that is considered a compliment to the fairness of our system of justice.

But a vital instrument would be lost to the prosecutor to obtain information and testimony from recalcitrant defendants in return for a reduction of charge. The Special Prosecutor's office investigating Watergate has made abundantly clear what was not clear to a large portion of the public before, that plea bargaining through promise of immunity and reductions in charge is a principal law enforcement technique to elicit testimony and other evidence. Additionally, without this capacity, district attorneys would be powerless to expedite the court calendar by avoiding trials for which the certainty of conviction is in doubt by accepting a plea to a lesser charge. It is a standard principle among defense attorneys that as the mandated punishment is increased, which would be the case if no charges were reduced, the likelihood of such a case going to trial is increased.[62]

The point of this discussion, of course, is not to rationalize the inequities of the plea bargaining system, but to point out the contending goals inherent in criminal justice. Reform from the right or the left, without providing additional resources for the system, is apt to maximize one objective of the system at the expense of other, perhaps equally valid, objectives. Of course, views differ as to what relative weights of value are to be associated with due process, contrasted with criminal investigation and prosecutor effectiveness. But the problem becomes particularly sticky when one considers that eliminating plea bargaining may maximize one

[61] National Advisory Commission, *A National Strategy to Reduce Crime,* p. 147.

[62] This is particularly true of narcotics cases. See Alfred R. Lindesmith, *The Addict and the Law* pp. 80-81, footnote on p. 306.

due process goal at the expense of still another due process goal. Eliminating plea negotiation may, indeed, assure equal procedural attention to those cases the prosecutor does not prosecute. Administrative and procedural complexities that are not related to the offender's guilt (such as the time-consuming nature of a narcotics case) would become irrelevant after the decision to dismiss. But surely equitable punishment for similar offenses is also a goal of due process. Sentences are likely to increase in proportion to increases in the number of trials, if past dispositional patterns are an accurate barometer. People convicted after a jury trial are likely to be "hammered" in their sentence to make up for others who were dismissed for want of prosecutorial resources. Value conflict is the crucible for a politics of crime and can only be modified to maximize contending goal fulfillment. It cannot be eliminated.

There is still another source of irony in the middle-class ethic. Reformers may insist on higher and higher levels where new efforts to fulfill more expansive goals reach the point of marginal utility. The more lofty the expectations, the greater the chance for disappointment, frustration, and recrimination. The attitude may develop that the criminal justice system is failing to do its job when in fact, the standards of success have changed. Citizen and practitioner expectations have risen, resulting in a newly perceived gap between what is and what ought to be. We have seen previously how public and professional perceptions regarding the level of criminal activity were related to political culture in history, to social class, and to region. A similar case could certainly be made about civil liberty protections and effectiveness of prosecution; historical evidence is overwhelming that civil liberty protections for the criminally accused in the past were minimal compared to contemporary standards, and the prosecution of criminal offenses, at best, depended on the perfunctory police work of an earlier age. Thus, the problems of crime today are partially a product of the perception of a newly emerging middle and upper-middle class.

3

THE CRIMINAL JUSTICE SYSTEM

This chapter describes and explains the interrelated yet hydralike criminal justice system (Figure 3.1) as a heuristic aid for those unfamiliar with its arrangements. Obviously formal organizational diagrams and flow charts cannot convey to the reader the rich complexity of criminal justice. This is particularly so since the tasks and role definitions of the actors in each of the subsystems—police, courts, and corrections—are not agreed on, and often are contradictory. Moreover, hierarchical charts of police departments or courts give a false impression of clear lines of authority and seem to support the famous, if untenable, legal myth of the nineteenth-century father of jurisprudence, John Austin that "law is command."

Hierarchies of command and supervision do delineate responsibilities of special offices. The functional components and lines of authority for formal organization are not irrelevant variables. Customarily, assistant prosecutors do not publicy flaunt their disdain for the chief prosecutor's policies, and patrolmen do not disobey their chief's "orders of the day." When they do flagrantly disobey their superiors, either the organization must operate with no cohesive leadership and responsibility, or someone must be dismissed. However, the day-to-day social transactions of police, prosecutors, judges, probation officers, and the impact that police screening practices (to arrest or not arrest) have on prosecution caseloads, trial levels, and probation-parole caseloads (i.e., affect decision making by judges and prosecutors) cannot be understood by traditional organization charts or chains of command. Arrest practices, levels of criminal activity, particularly violent crime in a community, the structure of criminal law and procedure, resources available both to the criminal justice system and to social service agencies—all of these factors must be understood to have systemwide (systemic) influence. Such factors will influence the type and number of offenders that enter the system after commission of a reported crime (input), what decisions are made regarding the flow of cases at varying stages within the system (conversion), what dispositions and treatment are accorded each offender (output), and what influence such dispositions have on actors in the criminal justice system and on the degree of support provided by the broader political system (feedback).[1] Finally, the criminal justice system's impact on the problems of crime is a vital part of the system: Has crime policy in the system reduced criminal activity and victim suffering?

System approaches to evaluating public policy are frequently subject to serious criticism. Notable among such criticism is the tendency of the systems analysts to accept too readily official labels, such as crimes known to or reported by the police, without exploring the broader social dimensions that help define the differential applications of the label. Systems approaches also tend to assume homeostasis, as an implicit virtue, in spite of its nonnormative, empirical posture. Homeostasis is the organic balance in the operating machinery of the system, its component parts, its levels of support, and its capacity to react and adjust. Such an emphasis by the analyst influences a conservative outlook, one that emphasizes "tinkering" with the system to preserve its essential integrity indead of criticizing its fundamental assumptions. Such normative and nonnormative assumptions are that marihuana smoking is evil, treatment in correctional institutions really is effective, efficiency in processing cases is an unmitigated blessing, and criminal cases, not potential victims, are the essential focus, since certain arrest and punishment, among other things will reduce victimization. Nevertheless, understanding criminal justice as a system is very useful to the student who needs to organize his thoughts about a very complex set of interactions. With proper caution and theoretical consciousness regarding its limitations as an analytical tool, an approach to criminal justice as a subsystem in the larger political system is particularly useful for policy analysis.

The system operates as an organic, interrelated set of administrative gears (although there is no shortage of criticism about the *way* in which it operates). The system has a flow of cases whose sheer numbers represent an important variable that, coupled with time limitations and the seriousness of the charge, places varying pressures on police, prosecutor, and judicial decision making. In many but not all ways, as we shall see later, the flow is analogous to traffic. For example, a sudden surge of arrests for public intoxication will result in heavier demands on magistrates to arraign, plead and, perhaps, try inner-city alcoholics, many of whom appear before the bench on a regular basis. The inebriate "traffic" not only jams up the courts, but taxes police resources. In Erie, Pennsylvania, for

[1]The terminology follows David Easton's *The Political System.* For an application of the Eastonian system to the federal courts see Sheldon Goldman and Thomas P. Jahnige, *The Federal Courts as a Political System* (New York: Harper and Row, 1971).

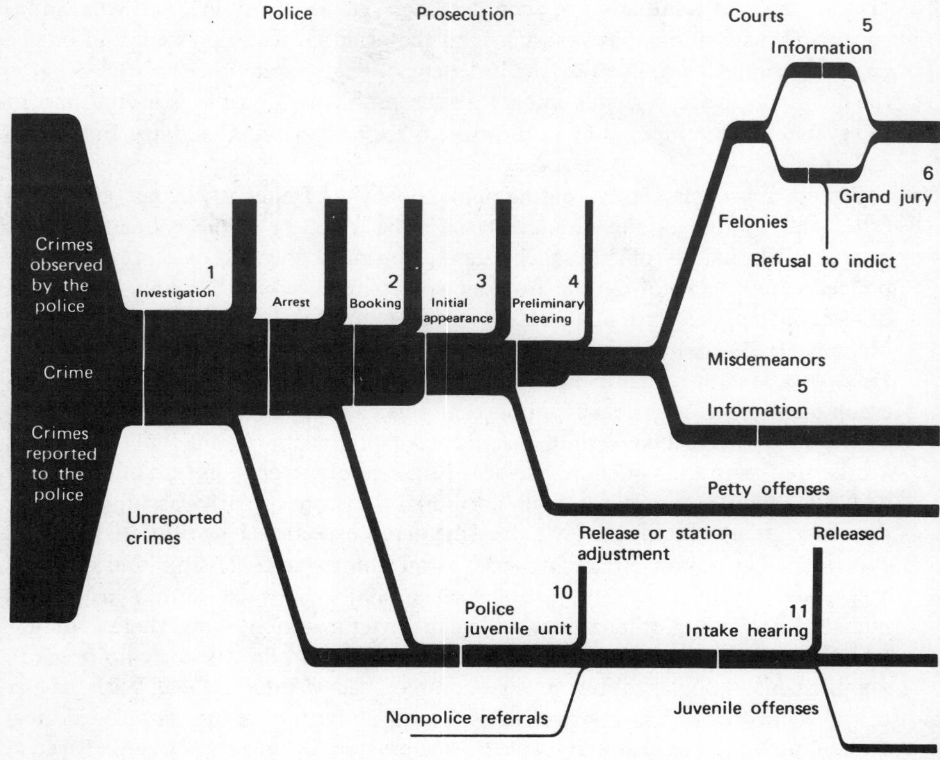

1 May continue until trial.
2 Administrative record of arrest. First step at which temporary release on bail may be available.
3 Before magistrate, commissioner, or justice of peace. Formal notice of charge, advice of rights. Ball set. Summary trials for petty offenses usually conducted here without further processing
4 Preliminary testing of evidence against defendant. Charge may be reduced. No separate preliminary hearing for misdemeanors in some systems.
5 Charge filed by prosecutor on basis of information submitted by police or citizens. Alternative to grand jury. Indictment; often used in felonies, almost always in misdemeanors.
6 Reviews whether Government evidence sufficient to justify trial. Some States have no grand jury system; others seldom use it.
7 Appearance for plea; defendant elects trial by judge or jury (if available); counsel for indigent usually appointed here in felonies. Often not at all in other cases.

Figure 3.1 A general view of the criminal justice system. This chart seeks to present a simple yet comprehensive view of the movement of cases through the criminal justice system. Procedures in individual jurisdictions may vary from the pattern shown here. The differing weights of line indicate the relative volumes of cases disposed of at various points in the system, but this is only suggestive, since only limited data of this sort exists.

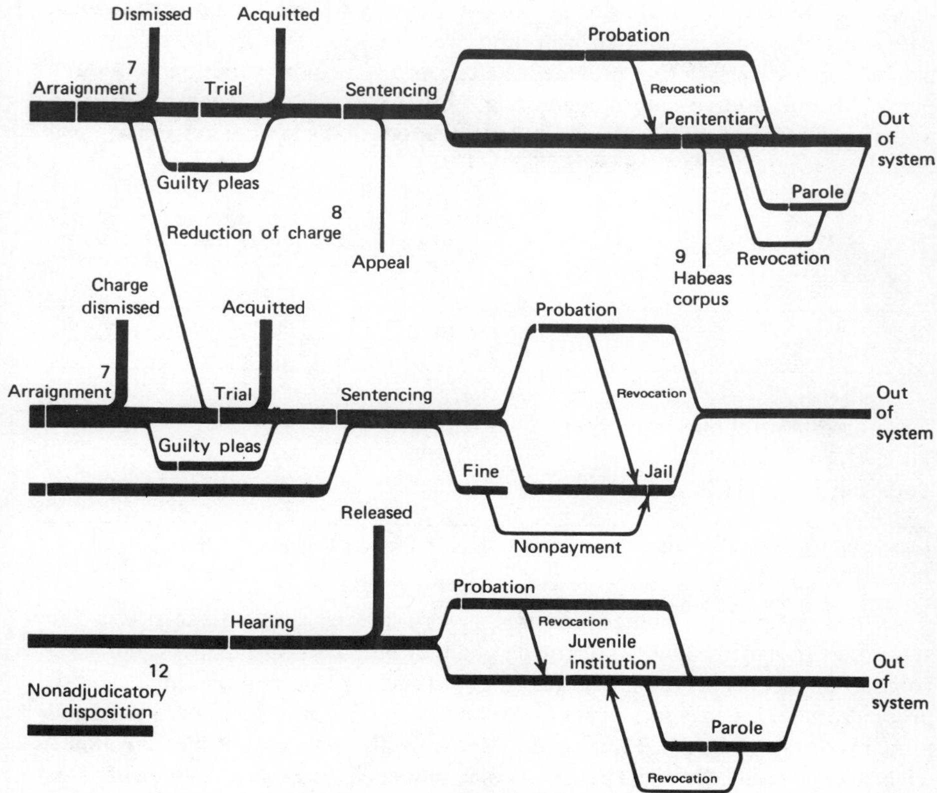

8 Charge may be reduced at any time prior to trial in return for plea of guilty or for other reasons.
9 Challenge on constitutional grounds to legality of detention. May be sought at any point in process.
10 Police often hold informal hearings, dismiss or adjust many cases without further processing.
11 Probation officer decides desirability of further court action.
12 Welfare agency, social services, counselling, medical care, etc., for cases where adjudicatory handling not needed.

example, each arrest consumes an average of three police hours[2] for transportation, booking, providing medical treatment, and incarcerating a public inebriate, often under demeaning circumstances. Moreover, the hapless inebriate still must be charged, plead, or be tried and sentenced in a police court.[3] In 1971 a

[2] Data collected from the Pennsylvania Governor's Justice Commission for the City of Erie, Pennsylvania, Northwest Regional Office, 1973.

[3] Northwest Regional Office, Pennsylvania Governor's Justice Commission, Cross Roads Police Pick-up Program, unpublished evaluation report, p. 7.

crossroads pick-up program was initiated in this city whereby public intoxicants, who had otherwise committed no crime, were referred by a police officer to a civilian pick-up service that provided shelter, meals, medical attention for a short period of time, and voluntary counseling.[4] By 1972 when the program was fully operational, the magnitude of systemwide changes that such a diversionary program can produce can be seen in Table 3.1

Table 3.1 Impact of criminal justice resources of public intoxicant diversionary program

	1970	**1971**	**1972**
Total arrests of public intoxicant	2075	1570	261
Total court cases	800	756	43
Total days sentenced and served	2035	1515	180

Source. Pennsylvania Governor's Justice Commission, Northwest Regional Office.

As the volume of imputed criminal cases increases and interacts with the system, a myriad of other systemwide changes may be projected. As increased volumes of cases enter the prosecutor's office (whose resources remain constant), prosecutors and judges may work harder or may work at an unaltered pace and prepare sloppy cases. *Nolle prosequis* and dismissals may go up, time-consuming trials may go down. Or court calendars may influence the relative volume of cases and, hence, prosecutorial decision making. *Nolle prosequis* may increase and guilty pleas may decrease. Or, while the plea rate remains constant, the final bargains struck between the prosecutor and defense attorney may not be as successful from a prosecutor's point of view. Excessive delay, usually pleasing to the defense but not to the prosecution, may result from an overtaxed and unprepared prosecutor's office. But delay is also the consequence of the kind of offenses with which an accused is charged (Table 3.2), as well as other variables, such as whether or not there is a plea, or trial by jury, or trial before a judge (Table 3.3), or whether the defense counsel is privately retained, a public defender, or court appointed.

[4]For the concept of diversionary programs for public inebriates see Charles W. Weiss, *Diversion of the Public Inebriate from the Criminal Justice System,* U.S. Department of Justice and Pennsylvania Governor's Justice Commission, 1973.

Table 3.2 Average time lapsed (between the date transcript is filed with clerk to disposition date) in months by type of disposition, by offense, 1973, Commonwealth of Pennsylvania

Offense	Average all cases	Disposed of without conviction					Convicted and sentenced			
				Acquitted						
		Total	Dismissed	By court	By jury	Other no penalty disposition	Total	On guilty plea	By court	By jury
Total	5.9	6.7	9.1	5.3	6.3	3.6	5.1	4.7	5.1	12.6
Part I offense, total	7.0	7.8	10.4	6.5	6.9	3.7	6.3	5.5	6.2	14.9
Homicide, total	15.0	12.6	20.0	6.5	8.7	6.3	15.7	12.0	12.5	23.2
Murder - first	14.0	8.6	1.4	2.7	16.4	—	16.7	9.4	16.2	22.9
Murder - second	15.5	10.7	14.7	7.7	8.5	6.3	17.1	13.3	13.8	24.4
Manslaughter - voluntary	13.0	22.6	43.9	3.9	2.4	—	9.9	7.3	8.3	16.6
Rape, total	7.6	6.4	7.3	5.3	5.6	17.2	8.5	7.1	9.1	9.4
Rape	7.7	2.9	3.5	1.8	4.3	—	11.9	14.4	5.1	11.6
Rape - assault	7.6	6.8	7.3	5.5	5.7	17.2	8.3	6.7	9.1	9.2
Robbery, total	7.7	8.7	11.6	6.8	7.8	5.7	7.2	6.2	7.3	13.1
Robbery - armed	7.8	8.9	11.5	6.9	7.8	5.7	7.4	6.4	7.6	13.1
Robbery - unarmed	2.5	27.2	27.2	—	—	—	1.1	1.3	0.2	13.0
Robbery - other	3.6	2.2	2.7	1.3			3.8	3.8	3.0	7.9

Table 3.2 Average time lapsed (between the date transcript is filed with clerk to disposition date) in months by type of disposition, by offense, 1973, Commonwealth of Pennsylvania (continued)

		Disposed of without conviction					Convicted and sentenced			
				Acquitted						
Offense	**Average all cases**	**Total**	**Dismissed**	**By court**	**By jury**	**Other no penalty disposition**	**Total**	**On guilty plea**	**By court**	**By jury**
Aggravated assault, total	7.0	7.9	10.1	5.7	6.1	3.6	5.8	5.2	5.5	11.0
Aggravated assault and battery	6.5	9.2	9.9	5.3	5.9	3.2	5.0	4.6	4.8	10.0
Assault with intent to kill	7.8	7.8	9.4	6.3	5.2	6.9	7.8	7.3	7.5	12.4
Assault - other serious	7.4	11.5	13.0	4.7	8.5	4.7	5.4	4.9	4.9	11.8
Burglary, total	6.5	7.9	10.5	6.1	6.8	4.3	5.7	5.4	5.6	12.6
Burglary	6.6	9.8	11.0	6.1	6.8	4.7	5.7	5.4	5.7	12.5
Burglary - other	6.0	8.7	8.7	6.0	6.3	3.5	5.3	5.1	5.0	13.2
Larceny, total	5.8	7.0	9.9	6.6	5.2	3.3	4.5	4.4	4.6	8.2
Larceny	5.7	6.9	9.9	6.4	5.4	3.3	4.5	4.3	4.5	8.4
Larceny - other	7.0	8.4	9.8	10.2	2.2	3.7	4.9	4.5	6.4	5.3
Auto theft	7.2	10.9	9.5	9.1	3.8	3.4	6.7	5.8	6.4	11.2
Part II offenses, total	5.7	6.4	8.7	4.8	5.8	3.5	4.7	4.4	4.7	11.1

Source. Pennsylvania Criminal Information System (PACIS) Pennsylvania Criminal Court Disposition, 1973. Pennsylvania Department of Justice, Harrisburg, Pennsylvania, 1974, p. 26.

Table 3.3 Volume and time lapsed between the date the transcript was received by clerks of court and final disposition, by offense, 1973, Commonwealth of Pennsylvania

Offense	One month or less	Two months	Three months	Four months	Five months	Six months	Seven months	Eight months	Nine months	Ten months	Eleven months	Twelve months and over	Unknown
Total	7,226	11,001	13,038	7,352	5,288	3,874	2,869	2,133	1,615	1,306	1,024	8,455	10,921
Percent of total	9.5	14.5	17.1	9.7	6.9	5.1	3.8	2.8	2.1	1.7	1.3	11.1	14.4
Part I Offense, Total	1,300	2,230	2,765	1,895	1,432	1,248	866	802	548	479	386	2,480	3,008
Homicide, Total	50	53	43	53	37	36	35	39	25	30	22	300	84
Murder - first	4	—	1	5	4	3	1	2	0	1	1	15	4
Murder - second	35	36	24	34	29	26	29	29	20	23	17	253	52
Manslaughter - voluntary	11	17	18	14	4	7	5	8	5	6	4	32	28
Rape, Total	32	23	27	24	25	24	22	32	14	7	7	3	35
Rape	1	1	1	2	—	2	1	2	—	—	—	3	—
Rape - assault	31	22	26	22	25	22	21	30	14	7	7	48	35
Robbery, Total	118	223	289	280	237	256	177	160	111	92	74	559	435
Robbery - armed	117	222	284	276	235	255	177	158	111	91	74	554	275
Robbery - unarmed	1	—	1	1	—	—	—	2	—	—	—	4	151
Robbery - other	—	1	4	3	2	1	—	—	—	1	—	1	9

Table 3.3 Volume and time lapsed between the date the transcript was received by clerks of court and final disposition, by offense, 1973, Commonwealth of Pennsylvania (continued)

Offense	One month or less	Two months	Three months	Four months	Five months	Six months	Seven months	Eight months	Nine months	Ten months	Eleven months	Twelve months and over	Unknown
Aggravated assault, Total	164	361	465	293	122	181	109	103	73	69	52	376	511
Aggravated assault and battery	110	234	341	172	154	97	56	58	35	37	17	206	279
Assault with intent to kill	38	80	70	86	63	70	34	36	24	26	15	116	133
Assault - other serious	16	47	54	35	44	14	19	9	14	6	10	54	99
Burglary, Total	471	816	851	664	564	444	293	289	189	168	118	894	965
Burglary	379	646	648	547	469	359	245	249	157	144	100	760	871
Burglary - other	92	170	203	117	95	85	48	40	32	24	18	134	94
Larceny, Total	438	741	938	502	374	249	176	140	107	93	89	554	918
Larceny	417	717	897	459	340	226	165	125	102	86	84	514	837
Larceny - other	21	24	41	43	34	23	11	15	5	7	5	40	81
Auto Theft	27	135	152	79	73	58	54	39	29	20	24	154	60
Part II Offenses, Total	5,926	8,771	10,273	5,457	3,856	2,626	2,003	1,331	1,067	827	638	5,615	7,913

Source. Pennsylvania Criminal Information System (PACIS), Pennsylvania Criminal Court Dispositions, 1973, Pennsylvania Department of Justice, Harrisburg, Pennsylvania, 1974, p. 26.

Moreover, a heavy volume of cases must not be confused as the only source, or even the prime source of delay in *every* court system. The public may delay reporting a crime, the police may require extended investigation prior to an apprehension, the witness may be reluctant to file a complaint, or he may be reluctant to testify. Certainly defense attorneys are in no rush either to prepare a case with full vigor or to bring it to a conclusion, particularly if their fee is not assured, or if they have more lucrative clients to represent in another court at a conflicting time.

There is a myriad of structural variables that contributes to the enormous complexity and dissimilarity of criminal justice systems throughout the United States quite beyond the traditionally identified decision makers in the system or the volume or type of cases being processed. In smaller metropolitan courts, part-time prosecutors and defense counsel may prefer long recesses between trial sessions in the criminal court calendar to build up their private, civil practices. Yet many small urban systems have a continuous trial calendar and full-time prosecutors and public defenders. In large metropolitan courts with high volumes of serious cases pressuring the prosecutor's office and trial courts, intensive plea bargaining is a standard characteristic of the system, as any student of the court knows.

Yet, many urban high-volume systems also have large numbers of trials and relatively *moderate* degrees of plea bargaining when compared to lower-volume courts.[5] We are not entirely sure why this is true. Certainly mandatory sentences will reduce a defendant's propensity to plead guilty, since the prosecutor cannot recommend a lighter sentence, although he can plea bargain a charge. States having mandatory sentencing will probably experience larger numbers of trials and possibly higher rates of dismissals if trial resources are overtaxed. But by no means is volume the only important system variable; judges may wish to reduce delay periods prior to trial, but they may be unable to identify where and why in the system excessive delays are taking place. Or chief administrative judges may be concerned with an unusual number of continuances granted particular attorneys, or with long periods of "dead time" served by defendants awaiting trial who could not raise bail. Informing these concerns of judges and prosecutors in most urban court systems may depend on computer- based data filing and information retrieval systems as well as on a court administrator to analyze and provide timely data.

Other structural variables that contribute to the complexity and dissimilarity of court operations include the trial calendar, alternative sentence dispositions

[5] Milton Heumann, "Plea Bargaining Systems and Plea Bargaining Styles: Alternate Patterns of Case Resolution in Criminal Courts," unpublished paper, American Political Science Association, 1974, pp. 9-12. Heumann uses comparative data from nine trial-level courts in Connecticut.

available to judges, and jury and witness notification and selection procedures. These variables only hint at the rich diversity of administrative practices and criminal law and procedure in the states, counties, and judicial districts throughout the United States.

Consequently, caution should be exercised by any student of the criminal justice system seeking to generalize about its interactive relationships. Each system has its unique qualities, and each reacts differently to stimuli such as an increased volume of cases, a fact that troubles (or should trouble both theory-building social scientists interested in determining behavioral consistency and those who attempt to describe a singular system for a national readership. Each variable's systemic, interactive impact may be measured on an individual system, but the enormous diversity of each system makes it extraordinarily difficult to draw generalizations from one system to another. In short, criminal justice confronts the system analyst with a labyrinth of idiosyncratic variables that alter inputs, decision-making patterns, outcomes, and feedback characteristics.

But systems theory in criminal justice supports the hypothesis that sheer numbers of cases in large, urban courts may have altered the accusational or adversary system of justice that formally distinguished American due process from the European continental system. Crowded dockets or simple administrative efficiency do influence court personnel to lessen the conflict inherent in an adversary system to produce a cooperative, smooth running operation. On the other hand, some scholars have questioned whether the adversary system ever did operate vigorously in our past.[6] Whether historically true or not, it is likely that contemporary American justice, as an informal administrative system, operates more under the assumptions of an inquisitorial system than is usually admitted. That is, police and prosecution have original investigatory powers, a presumption of guilt is actually borne by the defendant, and considerable discretion is allowed police, defense, prosecution, and the judge in determining the disposition of defendants.[7]

The systemic impact of caseload screening affects the correctional subsystem as well. For example, "diversionary" programs—pretrial probation or other forms of "nonstigmatizing" intervention—have proliferated as federal monies have encouraged "innovative diversionary" programs. There are three reasons for the rationale behind the diversionary program. First, it is believed that diverting offenders, particularly youthful, first offenders, from the official processes of the court system averts the "labeling" of otherwise socially acceptable individuals

[6] Heumann provides evidence that the adversary system of heavily relying on trials is a "lower court myth" in American history, but research in this area is very limited. Ibid., pp. 7-9, 13-15.

[7] That police and prosecutors presume guilt on the part of arrested individuals is well documented. Abraham Blumberg, *Criminal Justice* (Chicago: Quadrangle Books, 1967), Chapter 2; Jerome Skolnick, *Justice without Trial,* (New York: Wiley, 1967), p. 241.

who, by some contingency, have run afoul of the law. That is a favorite theme of the interactionist sociologists who argue, with considerable force, that deviancy is the product not merely of insulated impulses on the part of a "deviant" actor, but the product of how individuals are labeled, processed, and taught to play a "deviant" career. This same theme also has a popular humanitarian constituency with its own clichés: prisons are "schools for crime" and correctional institutions are "bankrupt." With such an assumption, it follows that the more young offenders who are diverted from the contamination of local lockups, jails, and prisons, the less crime we will have. The third reason mixes the above assumptions with an economic motif. Reverting to our public intoxication example in Erie, Pennsylvania, every intoxicant not arrested by a police officer theoretically saved the department, the courts, and the local jail considerable expenditures of time and human resources.

Federally funded programs have also encouraged improvement in police apprehension techniques. An interesting impact of this increase in police activity on diversionary programs was suggested by one experienced urban public defender. The pressure on police to arrest more offenders, particularly drug offenders, has increased the number of "junk cases"—cases that would not have resulted in an arrest years ago, such as possession of a reefer or lifting cheap jewelry from a five-and-dime store. The district attorney does not want to prosecute these cases, so he recommends them for a pretrial diversionary program. The denouement of diversionary programs, consequently, may mean diverting offenders whom the police did not routinely arrest in the past!

Systemic "screening" for correctional placement can work in the other direction as well. There is a maxim whose truth is reluctantly admitted by correctional program "innovators": "Good programs are victims of their own success." That is, judges who are knowledgeable of "good" correctional programs will contribute to a program's downfall by sending too many offenders into the program; This reduces the ratio of staff to offenders or adds to the difficulties of the program by referring disruptive individuals to a nonsecurity-oriented family center.

THE SYSTEM'S FOUR FUNCTIONS

There are almost as many system models for criminal justice as there are systems theorists. For purposes of description, I will use a simple structural functional analysis for four functional subsystems within the operational boundaries of the criminal justice system. The first is the *regulative* subsystem.[8] Its boundaries lie between the commission of a crime and the formal charge levied by the officer

[8]The terms "regulation," "resolution," and "disposition" are borrowed from Winfield S. Bollinger, "Toward a Theory of Criminal Justice", (Vol. 1, unpublished dissertation, Syracuse University, 1968, pp. 17-19. Bollinger's original conceptualizations have been altered, however.

at the preliminary arraignment before a magistrate. Police decision making, however, does not come into play unless the offense is brought to the attention of a law enforcement official either by a citizen complaint or by the official's own knowledge. The term *regulative* connotes the fundamental function of police decision making—that of social control. The decisions to arrest and to charge, which screen out many cases from the system, are influenced by a wide variety of variables that will be discussed in Chapter 6. However, the principal function performed by the officer is to order maintenance and social control.

Once the charge is formally made by the officer, the district attorney's office dominates the complex of *resolutional* decision making. Prosecutors also respond to a large number of variables, but their major function is to decide whether or not to prosecute, and how vigorously to bargain those cases that pass through the regulative police screen. The term *resolution* is used because the prosecutor must resolve the conflict between both the defense attorney and the weight of the court docket on the one hand, and the demands of the community, police, and state for a determination of innocence on the other hand. Questions of legal guilt (*mens rea*), police-defined guilt, or probable cause, the seriousness of the crime, the available resources of the prosecutor, and evidentiary difficulties of each case, all of these factors influence the prosecutor's decision to *nolle prosequi* or dismiss cases, negotiate a guilty plea, or go to trial. Clearly, prosecutors must face a different set of questions and problem definitions than those formulated by the police, a fact that explains the unavoidable tension and suspicion that separates the police department from the district attorney's office. The boundaries of this prosecutorial-dominated decision-making network normally lie between preliminary arraignment and trial.[9] Like the police function, the discretionary decisions of the district attorney are not highly visible and, therefore, are susceptible to internal administrative priorities within the district attorney's office.

Conversely, decision making during trial is very visible. The presiding judge, representing the complex of legal rules that guide the trial, is the principal decision maker. His primary function is to *adjudicate,* with the assistance of a jury, if there is one, or without their assistance if it is a trial before a judge. The option is the defendant's. There is still room for negotiating a plea during trial, but the process is more visible and thereby more restrained with the judge as primary arbiter. Although national court statistics from distinct local and state criminal justice systems are not easily aggregated, generally 11 percent of all felony cases that reach the court go to trial.

A fourth functional subsystem, corrections, may be characterized as largely *dispositional.* Traditionally dominated by the trial judge through sentencing, the disposition decision is now diffused between the judge during sentencing, parole

[9]If a citizen complaint is initially brought to the prosecutor, however, he controls the decision to charge, not a police officer. In this event, the boundaries stretch to the moment the complaint is made.

boards that may replace parole for the incarceration period to be served according to the sentence, and administrators in correctional institutions who may allow time off for good behavior. Alternative dispositions such as weekend or weekday furloughs, community-based treatment center placement, work release, education release, and pretrial diversion or probation programs have considerably diluted the sentence-related, dispositional function of the trial judge. Still, the initial disposition—to suspend sentence, to place on probation, or to incarcerate—remains under his control, and the fate of offenders sentenced to local jails is largely determined by him.

As is true with the police officer and district attorney, the influencing factors behind correctional decision making reflect different goals that exist in adjudicatory decision making. Guilt or innocence are not at issue; security, recidivism, and rehabilitative possibilities are. And these are only the *formal* goals of correctional decision makers. Like the police and the courts, correctional bureaucracies have a plethora of unwritten, institutional objectives; these objectives compete with police, prosecution, and court institutional objectives, not the least being reflected in an annual battle for larger budgetary outlays before the state legislature, the state planning agency handling federal funds, and units of local government. Each institution has its own constituents in the social-political system at large to support its policies and programs. The systemic function of *regulation, resolution, adjudication,* and *disposition* by no means exhausts the functions of decision making or describes the complex network of intervening variables from the broader social-political system.

CRIMINAL JUSTICE AS A NONSYSTEM

Repetitively, the criticism is heard from political reformers and criminal justice professionals that the criminal justice system is a "nonsystem." As an empirical observation, the statement is absurd; offenders are arrested, adjudicated, convicted, dismissed, and the like. As a normative observation the statement makes more sense; it generally refers to the lack of overall direction, cooperation, and coordination between the interdependent subsystems and their police courts and corrections and their components.[10] The key normative assumption in such criticism is, of course, that the subsystem *should* have unified goals, cooperative attitudes, and central direction.

As Chapter 3 argues, each subsystem's functions are performed in separate environments with differing objectives due to contending problem definitions,

[10] Daniel J. Freed, "The Nonsystem of Criminal Justice," from staff report to the National Commission on the Causes and Prevention of Violence," *Law and Order Reconsidered* (Washington, D.C.: U.S. Government Printing Officer, 1965), pp. 265-284, especially pp 266-270.

distinctively diverse roles played by criminal justice personnel and political interest group members, and our constitutional system. Lack of central direction, cooperation, and coordination are reflections of the politics of crime in the sense of conflict of interests among the actors, as well as a reflection of our constitutional system of separation of powers and individual rights. Such conflict-producing problems are not likely to be fully resolvable, although incremental improvements can be made.

For example, the reformist-deprecating reference to the nonsystem character of criminal justice often refers to the fragmentation of criminal justice organization and process. Police jurisdictions such as those of the FBI, state police, and city police all overlap and result in duplication of effort. The danger of state police, village police, and the county sheriff converging into one another at an intersection while rushing to the scene of the same accident is a standard quip among police officers. The spectacle of undercover narcotic agents from the U.S. Drug Enforcement Agency, state police narcotics divisions, and city drug squards arresting one another is frequently an embarrassing reality, but it reveals the jurisdictional jealousies that have often prevented separate narcotic units from sharing their information, their undercover agents, or their newspaper headlines. Yet suggesting a consolidation of police forces to rural and suburban police is like urging the National Rifle Association to support abolishing the Second Amendment. Planners in state and federal Safe Streets funding agencies have been continuously perplexed by the intensity of opposition they have experienced in attempts to consolidate police departments of fewer than 10 men.[11] In the Commonwealth of Pennsylvania such fragmented departments, often relying on part-time personnel, represent over 75 percent of the approximately 1400 police agencies in the state.[12] Each small department either duplicates supervisory personnel, criminal records and files, expensive communication systems, training programs, civilian clerical staff, and purchasing procedures, or it does without. Mostly they do without. Small departments normally cannot afford to provide detective services, training, computerized or microfilmed records, specialized service, and law enforcement units to deal with crisis intervention, sexual assault units, organized crime specialists, and the like. Yet the chiefs of these departments, and the citizenry, prefer fragmentation of police services. A bewildered young bureaucrat from a state planning agency, referring to 11 police departments along a 20-mile suburban strip paralleling the Susquehanna River in Pennsylvania, put it this way: "Each chief would prefer to wear the brass on his hat,

[11] Conversation between the author and a member of the Pennsylvania Governor's Justice Commission staff.

[12] Pennsylvania Governor's Justice Commission, *The Comprehensive Plan for the Improvement of Criminal Justice in Pennsylvania* (Harrisburg, Pa.: Pennsylvania Department of Justice, 1973), pp. 95-96.

than trade his high community status for a higher salary and better police service!"

The fragmentation that frustrates the tidy world of the planner is a reflection of competing goals within the suburb or town that opposes police consolidation. Modern law enforcement and its prerequisites—training, crime laboratories, higher pay, data processing, modern communications—is expensive, and suburban political jurisdictions often prefer low taxes to professionalized police, even when this means untrained, perhaps elderly citizens wearing the badge and toting a .32 magnum pistol on a part-time basis. Moreover, suburban and rural communities may not want impersonal professionals handing out a surplus of traffic tickets and summonses to local residents; they may prefer a more commodious, first-name relationship with the local law.

Police, courts, and corrections are all distinct jurisdictions with separate budgets, supervision, public functions, and political constituencies. There is no hierarchy of command, no centralized directing hand over the system. Mayors have some leverage over the police but very little leverage over the courts or corrections. Correctional personnel, except perhaps probation officers who are usually supervised by a trial judge, are more responsive to a state bureau or department of corrections or parole board. District attorneys, whose decisions to charge are relatively independent of the court, and trial-level judges, particularly if elected to their office, often have a county bar association or party organization as their political base; they are considerably insulated from either city or state political influence. Chicago's Mayor Richard Daley's ability to influence, until recently, the nomination and election of state district attorneys and judges generally represents an anachronism in local politics. Moreover, in an age of data retrieval systems and professional court management, no mayor, governor, or legislator, however powerful, can easily influence, in a systematic way, the delineating decisions for large numbers of criminal cases.

Fragmentation, rival overlapping jurisdictions, lack of centralized administration, planning and budgeting, separation of function between courts, corrections and police, and multiple constituencies—these all represent the complex labyrinth of criminal justice structures. Moreover, as we have previously argued, the structure is different in important ways from county to county, state to state, and region to region. The reason for the *non*system is not simply an absence of professionalism, or lack of planning, or political corruption, or even conflicts of political interest, although each of these arguments has some proportion of merit. Instead, the system was designed, to use James Madison's language, to "let ambition counteract ambition."[13] Countervailing influences have muddied the

[13] James Madison, "Federalist #51," in *The Federalist Papers*, ed. Clinton Rossiter (New York: The New American Library, 1961), p. 322.

waters of ciminal justice for at least as long as Lord Coke's resistance to Henry VIII and, considering our recent political scandals over Watergate, the countervailing powers between judiciary and executive seem to be well worth some loss in efficiency and clarity. Again we may usefully quote Madison: "In framing a government which is to be administered by men over men, the great difficulty is this: you must first enable the government to control the governed; and in the next place oblige it to control itself."[14]

POLITICAL LIBERTY AND THE WEB OF LAW

Our formal, constitutional system requires that power be divided between executive police power and judicial tribunes that administer justice. There are at least two justifications for the separation of power with respect to criminal justice. The first is obviously to insure objectivity in any court hearing for the accused. The defendant's accusers, the police, or prosecutor are by formal function not of open mind, while the judge is, at least formally, a neutral observer and rule-interpreting participant. The second justification is more subtle and more infrequently considered today than in the eighteenth century. The separation of power is to maximize objectivity of the courts by partitioning executive (police) and adjudicative (court) functions. Together with criminal procedures, such arrangements are presumed to protect the rights of the innocent, to get at the truth of what happened, to minimize feelings of vengeance by objectifying the court atmosphere, and to maintain a monopoly of force within the framework of law. Obviously, these objectives, particularly the first two, are inconsistent at many junctures. Moreover, behaviorists and lawyers alike continue to debate the extent to which each objective is realized in the criminal justice system's actual operation.

But the system is not designed solely to provide justice for traditional crime. It also functions to prevent the machinations of a temporary regime in power, at whatever local, state, or federal level, from illegitimately abusing the machinery of criminal justice to proctect or promote its partisan concerns.

American history provides a rich legacy of political trials in which political executives played a principal role: the trials of John Peter Zenger and Aaron Burr; *Luther* v *Borden;* The Alien and Sedition Cases; the prosecution of Tom Mooney; the trials of the IWW, Eugene V. Debbs, Sacco and Vanzetti, and the Doherty Brothers of Tea Pot Dome; and the numerous trials of war resistors and draft evaders during World War I. The Harrisburg-Berrigan trial,[15] the Angela Davis homicide trial, the Chicago and Seattle Conspiracy trials,[16] the Pentagon Papers

[14] Ibid.

[15] "The Berrigans: Conspiracy and Conscience," *Time* (January 25, 1971), pp. 13-17.

[16] Noam Chomsky et al. (eds.), *Trials of the Resistance* (New York: Vantage Books, 1970).

trials,[17] the conspiracy trial of Dr. Spock,[18] and the Watergate trials, perhaps the archetype of them all, are a continuation of that legacy. Prosecution may often reflect executive policy, particularly at the federal level, initiated not to enforce the law as much as to dampen opposition to domestic or foreign policy. On the other hand, the Watergate conspiracy represents the importance of judicial review of executive obstruction of vigorous prosecution and investigation, and the importance of an independent judiciary's vitality.

In this context it is important to challenge the prevailing myth of journalism that Watergate was single-handedly revealed by the press.[19] The crimes and corruption associated with Watergate, from the Agnew payoffs to the actual break-ins, were unraveled primarily by FBI investigations, federal prosecutors, grand juries, civil litigation, and Congressional investigative committees.[20] The persistence of U. S. Attorneys in Maryland, using plea bargaining and grants of immunity, exposed Vice-President Agnew. The Democratic National Committee's civil suit against the Committee for the Re-election of the President and the General Accounting Office's investigation forced Republican officials to disclose information about campaign contributions and provided publicity and indirect information that commenced to unravel the illicit financial web of the CRP. Ultimately, protracted but deliberate litigation in the federal courts forced release of the White House tapes. When White House Counsel John Dean convinced Jeb Stuart Magruder to lie to a grand jury, and Magruder's perjury was corroborated by former Attorney-General John Mitchell and others, the prosecutors were temporarily delayed from making a case against the "Big Enchiladas," as White House Assistant John Erlichman put it, in the White House transcripts. The lid on the cover-up was not pried open by the *Washington Post,* but by Judge John Sirica, the grand jury, and the Ervin Committee in the U. S. Senate, working in tandem. Judge Sirica made it clear to the Watergate defendants that long sentences loomed unless they cooperated with the Ervin Committee. The judicial pressure imposed prior to sentencing was effective in producing fruitful testimony from James McCord, whose letter to Sirica implicating Magruder, Dean, and Mitchell broke the wall of conspiracy surrounding higher members of the White House. While McCord's initial testimony was only hearsay, skillful handling by federal prosecutors of other defendants convicted for the Watergate break-in, particularly G. Gordon Liddy, helped to entice John Dean and Jeb Magruder to plea bargain and reveal the cover-up conspiracy in the course of negotiations for immunity from prosecution.

[17] Martin Shapiro, *The Pentagon Papers and the Courts* (Scranton, Pa.: Chandler Publishing, 1972).

[18] Jessica Mitford, *The Conspiracy Trial of Dr. Spock* (New York: Vintage Books, 1969).

[19] For example, see Barry Sussman, *The Great Cover-up* (New York: New American Library, 1974), Chapter 4.

[20] Edward Jay Epstein, "Did the Press Uncover Watergate," *Commentary* (July 1974), pp. 21-24.

The role of the press in all of this process was not to elicit information; in every case, the press published information already cold in the hands of investigating institutions. The Watergate case was cracked by traditional political and legal institutions—civil and criminal courts, Congressional committees, police investigation, and prosecutorial plea negotiation. That the criminal process was delayed from June 17, 1972, to the spring of 1973 was not the fault of those institutions. After all, the President of the United States was directing a conspiracy to suppress the investigation. The vital role of the press was to publicize that information and to provide an atmosphere of support for the traditional institutions to do their job (the FBI does not customarily investigate the White House!) and to shape public opinion for this historic, political event leading to the impeachment inquiry in the House of Representatives.

Politicized trials will remain an integral part of American politics. They are dangerous but inevitable in a legal culture such as our own, where the clash of powerful interests occurs within civil framework of law, and conflict is tempered by juridical symbols and formal definitions of right and duty. Not all political trials are the product of executive or prosecutorial abuse of discretion. Political figures, including dissenters, may be guilty of conspiracy to riot, kidnap, or murder, violation of national security classification requirements, obstruction of justice, and perjury, and they must be prosecuted. But Lenin was at least half correct when he said that "law was politics by another name." The dangers of partisan injustices in the name of criminal justice demand the elaborate procedural safeguards that can be utilized in full measure by organized political groups.

The excruciatingly delicate *voir dire* proceedings to select the Watergate juries and the endless appeals of the convicted conspirators may rattle the American left who raise righteous objections that only the rich and powerful may obtain the full measure of criminal justice. And, in part, the objection is well founded, although not particularly relevant to Watergate. But the extended appeals and successful reversals of convictions for Dr. Spock and his fellow "conspirators," or the Chicago Seven, or the sit-in demonstrators of the 1950s and 1960s may equally rattle the American right. The full panoply of legal procedure certainly reflects the advantage of the very wealthy. What is more defensible is that it also reflects the protection of political minorities who are well organized, whose cause is well know, whose litigation is highly visible and well publicized, and whose case is defended by the political bar—the NAACP (National Association for the Advancement of Colored People), the American Civil Liberties Union, and private defense funds solicited by the members of various political causes. The latter funds are used to support attorneys whose litigation strategy merges with the partisan politics of those who seek individual or collective redress through the courts. And the partisans are not necessarily underprivileged minorities or unpopular ideologues peddling unpopular ideas. As this chapter is written, eight New England governors have initiated a civil suit to enjoin President Ford from attaching a tax onto imported oil; this would place a financial burden particularly against state officials and the governor's constituents, and would place a political burden on the state houses involved. Nor do "respectable" political groups seek partisan advantage through the civil law alone. In state politics the astutely timed, subtle threat of indictment of state officials or politicians is an ever-present instrument and technique in political negotiations. Although it may be infrequently employed, it is frequently mentioned, particularly under circumstances involving accounting, fiscal accountability, or nonfeasance of office, when one group has control over a district attorney or comptroller's office.

Reconsideration of due process protections has frequently been produced as spin-off from political movements. Our own era has experienced the indirect effect on civil liberties that resulted from the conspiracy trial of members of the American Communist Party in the 1950s, the antiwar movement, the emergence of poverty as a political issue and, most important, the Black Social Revolution of the 1950s and 1960s. Of recent vintage is the feminist movement (the movement is as old as the 1840s,[21] but its impact on culture is now growing rapidly); the movement has provided a climate influential in producing the abortion case *Roe* v *Wade*[22] and alterations on the rules of evidence regarding rape in a number of states. Politcal groups have vigorously acted to establish legal rulings favorable to their cause and their leaders, rulings that restructured and limited discretionary judgments of prosecutors, police, and judges, correctional officials and the criminal law itself for all individuals accused of crime. Clarification of Fifth Amendment privileges, prosecutorial limits of criminal conspiracy and criminal association with subversive organizations, the constitutionality of capital punishment, the admissibility of confessions, the rights of the indigent to defense counsel at public expense, to a jury of peers free from discriminatory jury selection procedures, and freedom from police coercion are only a few areas where the rights of the criminally accused have been strengthened and expanded (and occasionally contracted); this has occurred as an incidental consequence of litigation accompanying political movements and interests whose agendas were otherwise only peripherally related to criminal justice.

Each of these advances has been made possible, in part, because court decisions were an important part of larger political agendas developed by broadly supported political groups representing economic, racial, and ideological minorities. The NAACP has been particularly active in the movement to abolish capital punishment; it has sponsored research linking race discrimination with those sentenced to death for rape and homicide. While race discrimination was not the

[21]We date the feminist movement in the United States from the aborted American Anti-Slavery Society in New York in 1840 and the World Anti-Slavery Convention in 1941. For discussion see Tyler, *Freedom's Ferment* pp. 443-462.
[22]*Roe* v *Wade* 410 U.S. 113 (1973).

commanding reason for striking down the death penalty—the principal argument was that it was administered so capriciously and arbitrarily that it represented "cruel and unusual punishment"—race was a major factor.[23] Justice Douglas drew specific attention to evidence of arbitrary discrimination (Table 3.4).

Table 3.4 Race of the offender by final disposition

Final	Negro		White		Total	
Disposition	N	%	N	%	N	%
Executed	130	88.4	210	79.8	340	82.9
Commuted	17	11.6	53	20.2	70	17.1
Total	147	100.0	263	100.0	410	100.0

$X^2 = 4.33$; P less than .05

Source. Furman v *Georgia* 408 U.S. 296 (1972), p. 2732.

Corporations have long defended Fifth Amendment privileges and limiting subpoena powers to protect their business against prying legislative and judicial inquiries and the eyes of competitors or unions. The American Civil Liberties Union was organized to counter the excesses of the Palmer raids against "subversives" following World War I; it has been particularly active in supporting incorporation of the federal Bill of Rights and federal procedure, by the Fourteenth Amendment, particularly on First Amendment issues. Of course, evolving criminal procedure is equally the product of the litigation of appellants who are not ideologically or politically involved, but policy judgments of appellate courts are particularly affected by appeals from groups having broad-based political resources who either directly represent clients or file *amicus curiae* briefs in some group's behalf.

To summarize, both criminal procedure and law evolve within the framework of a pluralist society. And the system operates, however haltingly, within the diversity of mulitple jurisdictions, relecting American local traditions, federalism, and a diffusion of political power. Formal organizations in criminal jurstice must be understood in this context. Moreover, the dysfunctional character of the police, court, and correctional subsystems is not entirely amenable to improvement or reform; its conflict reflects the institutions of American politics with its distrust of centralized decision making and its insistence on separating judicial and executive roles and power. Where improvements in criminal justice are made,

[23] *Furman* v *Georgia* 408 U.S. 296 (1972).

they will be incremental changes related to existing political institutions. To expect more radical change over a short period of time may be to consign oneself to the frustration of no change at all.

4

THE POLICE IN ORGANIZATION

Policy is often secreted in the interstices of administrative procedure.
Loren Beth[1]

Few citizens have serious contact with police officers, beyond receiving an occasional traffic ticket or asking for directions from a courteous officer during the daytime hours. For those who are poor, members of racial minorities, or outsider subcultures, police contacts are likely to be considerably less pleasant. For members of the lower class, the policeman is not "Officer Friendly," but may more commonly be perceived as "The Man" or the enemy. Paul Chevigny relates an acerbic class-oriented encounter in New York City.

> *On the wife's night off, they [a Harlem window washer and his wife, a barmaid] were having drinks in a bar where she worked, and at the end of the evening she went out into the street to hail a cab. A policeman, mistaking her flashy clothes for those of a prostitute, ordered her to move on. A vituperative argument ensued, and the wife was knocked down with a punch in the eye. When the husband ran out of the bar with a friend to protest, he was also knocked down. The wife was charged with assault and the husband with disorderly conduct.*[2]

From the police officer's perspective, however, an unaccompanied woman from Harlem with flashy clothes outside a bar is easily associated with prostitution. The indignation of the wife is misrepresented as resisting the request of a police officer

[1] Loren P. Beth, *Politics, the Constitution and the Supreme Court* (Evanston, Ill.: Row, Peterson, 1967), p. 28.
[2] Paul Chevigny, *Police Power* (New York: Vintage Books, 1969), p. 28.

to move on. To a civilian outsider, the officer's activity appears racist, authoritarian, and intolerably abusive.

Although police abuse is clearly represented here, the officer's behavior originates more from an authoritarian role as part of the peace-keeping function of the department than it does from any authoritarian disposition of personality. There is little evidence that police recruits are psychologically different from other young men and women of similar socio-economic background.[3] The police force continues to serve as a vehicle for lower-middle-class social mobility, however, and low-income minority groups—the Irish, Italians, Jews, Poles, and now blacks—have each served in their historical turn. Ethnic and class characteristics, no doubt, have affected police behavior, although to what extent is not clear. But the principal influence on the behavior of police officers has not been an *a priori* psychological disposition prior to their joining the force. Young recruits are not more authoritarian in disposition than other young men of similar background. Instead, police behavior reflects the uniqueness of the department's organizational structure and function. Even more important, it reflects the diverse role expectations of the courts, of vocal, interested groups in the general public, and especially of police colleagues. Police role expectations interact with the departmental command and missions and with the policeman's working environment to produce a police perspective of the problems of crime. This chapter is concerned with the police department, its organization, and its function; the remaining influences on police behavior will be discussed in a subsequent chapter.

POLICE RECRUITMENT

Police chiefs or civilian commissioners are normally appointed by a mayor, city manager or, rarely, a city council or other board. Commonly, the chief serves at the pleasure of the appointing executive or group and is, therefore, sensitive to political pressures. Some newer chiefs, however, have insisted on and received contracts of five years or more prior to accepting a position. A long-term contract insulates the chief from the mayor or city commissioners, and protects the integrity of his administrative authority over his men. However, such an event is unusual and normally occurs after a political scandal has forced a mayor to "clean up" the department and hire an outside professional.

In most urban departments today, police are employed and promoted after taking competitive civil service examinations, which usually consist of both written and oral components. Civil service testing for police is of fairly recent vintage, emerging around the late 1930s, the product of progressive reformers from an even earlier era. Prior to competitive exams the ranks of the force were filled by

[3]The literature is reviewed in Arthur Niederhoffer, *Behind the Shield: The Police in Urban Society* (Garden City, N.Y.: Doubleday, 1969), Chapter 5.

the patronage needs of the party who controlled City Hall. Traditionally, police work was an avenue of upward mobility for the lower-class immigrant. Germans, Irish, Italians, Poles, all provided, in turn, sons for keeping peace in the inner city. It was not until the decline of the city political organization, or at least an alteration of its political style, that the patronage system was replaced by a civil service system based on examination and merit.

There is one subtle exception to the decline of political judgment as a factor in police recruitment. That is the unique case of the black candidate who, today, is actively sought, often under the pressure of a court order, as a new addition to the force. The irony lies in the fact that modern reform of city machine politics successfully destroyed the patronage system, under which many, but not all, minority groups were given their share of government jobs, and government services were personalized and humanized for immigrants and the poor in an alien society. Patronage was replaced by civil service testing and advancement was supposedly based on merit. Of course, the black community was generally excluded from the spoils, as they were excluded from political life. When the black community did achieve black power through electoral politics, it was too late to "provide the spoils" in traditional fashion. In 1960 when Congressman Adam Clayton Powell demanded that a black police captain be assigned to Harlem, a black section of New York City whose local political organizations and elected offices were at that time completely controlled by black people, the Irish police commissioner for the city had to inform the congressman that Tammany district leaders (which Powell also was) no longer appointed police captains. The Civil Service decided those matters and the next man on the list would be appointed.[4]

In the very recent past, black Americans were denied police positions because of their color. The legacy of the peculiar institution of slavery produced racial discrimination both under color of law, within the social structure, and between individuals. Racial discrimination in recruiting police officers, once blatant, has in contemporary times followed the more subtle and perhaps unconscious choices based on cultural bias within the social structure. An example of the latter is provided by a suit alleging racial discrimination in the Philadelphia police department. Tables 4.1 to 4.3 illustrate "factors" cited by the plaintiff alleging discrimination and used by the police department to reject or accept applicants based on a background check. The tables are based on a random sample of candidates for the Philadelphia police department between 1969 and 1970 who were rejected after a background investigation. A separate group had been rejected based on a written examination. The plaintiffs in the suit identified the derogatory factors appearing in the background checks for black and white applicants and

[4]Daniel P. Moynihan, *Maximum Feasible Misunderstanding,* (New York: The Free Press 1969), p. 110.

Table 4.1 Probabilities of rejection given factor on background exam (table developed by plaintiffs' expert)

Factor	**White** (%)	**Black** (%)
Conviction	66.2	90.5
Arrests	72.0	93.0
Police contacts	40.5	83.3
Traffic offenses	32.4	67.5
Juvenile delinquency	81.5	91.2
Juvenile arrests	54.2	84.6
Court martial convictions	86.7	94.7
Summary offenses in military	50.0	83.5
Military arrests	50.0	100.0
Military discharge	75.3	94.4
No valid driver's license	57.8	89.3
Falsification of application	63.1	87.4
Fired	74.5	94.2
Job problems	70.3	89.4
Unemployed and/or on welfare	38.2	75.0
Bad credit	68.8	89.7
Education: academic problems	52.3	85.8
Education: discipline problems	59.9	91.9
Born out of wedlock	36.3	66.7
Divorce	67.9	79.4
Illicit or immoral conduct	64.7	90.0
Alleged threats or violence	81.9	95.5
Improper conduct of friends or relatives	41.8	71.5
Bad appearance	45.3	77.2
Other	52.9	79.2

Source: Commonwealth v O'Neill 348 F. Supp. 1084 (1972), p. 1105.

Table 4.2 Probabilities of rejection given a given number of factors (table developed by plaintiffs' expert)

Number of Factors	White (%)	Black (%)
1	11.0	29.5
2	15.9	24.6
3	26.8	53.7
4	41.6	70.4
5	56.6	87.0
6	74.4	93.0
7	76.9	90.6
8	88.6	92.9
9 or more	92.2	94.1

Source: Commonwealth v O'Neill 348 F. Supp. 1084 (1972), p. 1105.

Table 4.3 Incidence of factors by race (table developed by plaintiffs' expert)

Factor	White (%)	Black (%)	Black%White%
Convictions	6.3	9.0	1.4
Arrests	11.6	18.2	1.6
Police contacts	1.7	1.7	1.0
Traffic offenses	26.8	22.5	.8
Juvenile delinquency	5.1	8.0	1.6
Juvenile arrests	13.7	20.1	1.5
Juvenile police contacts	6.0	3.9	.7
Court martial convictions	.6	2.7	4.5
Summary offenses in military	15.5	21.5	1.4
Military arrests	.4	1.5	3.8
Military discharge	3.0	5.1	1.7
No valid driver's license	4.2	9.3	2.2
Falsification of application	41.3	67.3	1.6
Fired	13.5	27.0	2.0
Job problems	15.6	29.3	1.9
Unemployed and/or welfare	22.3	23.7	1.1
Bad credit	18.8	19.2	1.0
Education: academic problems	19.3	23.8	1.2
Education: discipline problems	13.8	19.0	1.4
Born out of wedlock	4.5	3.4	.8
Divorce	3.2	4.8	1.5

Table 4.3 Incidence of factors by race (table developed by plaintiffs' expert) (continued)

Factor	White (%)	Black (%)	Black%White%
Illicit or immoral conduct	9.7	29.4	3.0
Alleged threats or violence	3.0	6.2	2.1
Improper conduct of friends or relatives	18.5	35.1	1.9
Bad appearance	24.3	40.1	1.7
Other	56.3	78.7	1.4

Source: Commonwealth v O'Neill 348 F. Supp. 1084 (1972), p. 1105.

the probability of rejection associated with each factor (Table 4.1). The frequency of each factor being noted in the applicant's file for each racial grouping was then compared to the probability of rejection (Table 4.2). Although white candidates clearly had fewer derogatory factors in their dossiers (Table 4.3), race discrimination remains when both accumulated factors and isolated factors are held constant. Medical and physical reasons for rejection were found to have no impact on the court's finding of race discrimination.

Under pressure from federal and state agencies and armed with a profusion of state and federal statutes, executive orders, and appellate court rulings, blacks are vigorously recruited, but for a number of reasons are not responding with any enthusiasm. One reason is that the black community retains extremely negative feelings about police work. It is also true that bright, educated blacks who can do well on the civil service test have ample opportunity today to obtain higher pay and more pleasant working circumstances elsewhere. At the same time, black youngsters who are left behind are much more apt to have criminal records and do poorly on entrance examinations.

Civil service testing has frequently been criticized as a culture-bound instrument that does not measure the actual skills necessary for police work; the courts have required, at times, either suspending or replacing a particular test with one that does measure what skills police officers require.[5] The task of meeting the latter requirement of the courts is of protean dimensions, as we will discover later. The courts have also ruled that only convictions, not merely arrest records or "rap sheets" may be used to deny an applicant a position on the force.[6] The irony

[5] *Commonwealth* v *O'Neill* 348 F. Supp. 1084 (1972); *Human Relations Commission* v *Tullio,* et al., April 24, 1973, slip opinion. The district court decisions regarding the recruitment of police officers are based on Appellate and Supreme Court decisions prohibiting testing not related to actual job performance. See *Griggs* v *Duke Power Company* 91 S.Ct. 849 (1971); *Carter* v *Gallegher* 453 F.2d 315 (1971).

[6] *Human Relations Commission* v *Tullio,* Civil Action No. 30-73, Erie, slip opinion stipulation.

is, however, that the winds of reform that promote affirmative action in police recruitment practices may do so by sweeping aside both the fruits of earlier reformers as well as the abuses of the civil service examination.

There is a lesson in democratic politics to be discerned by the careful observer here. Patronage has its twentieth-century parallels—in the Democratic 1972 National Nominating Convention's quota system, in the administration of the Equal Employment Opportunity Act, in jury selection, and in police recruitment. The police are too sensitive an agency *not* to represent the community. The mayor, the courts, and the chief of police have a function to resolve community conflict and accommodate values. It is standard democratic politics to perform these functions by distributing jobs in proportion to the political activity and support of each faction in the political community. To be sure, the rise of the professions and the growth of the unions and the civil service have altered the dynamics of accommodation in city politics, but they have not altered the need for representativeness and accommodation. With the possible exception of Chicago, power in the city is more diffused today. The mayor's power to dispense or retract a large number of jobs and the sanctioning control that power gave to his office and party have given way to new centers of power. Among these are the "professional" associations and unions, which lobby for certification and licensing requirements at state and city levels to restrict competition and assure a training period that will make new members ideologically consistent with the political aims of the group. The latter efforts are particularly characteristic of public school teacher associations. The unions that dominate the civil service and public service are also enhanced because of the indispensibility of their role.[7] Life in the city jars to a sudden stop when subways and buses cease to run; public health is immediately imperiled when garbage is not picked up.[8]

Minority groups are part of this formula, too. Each year, larger concentrations of black Americans are found in major American cities. Black Americans already constitute a majority in Newark, Washington, D.C., and Atlanta. But the path to political power for most urban blacks has not simply been through the electoral process, professional associations, or unions. In fact, union seniority, family and ethnic solidarity, and racism have represented impediments. The road to jobs has also been blocked through effective use of the courts, utilizing existing civil rights legislation and the constitutional doctrine of the federal government.

Balancing community representation has always been a vital political objective in the restructuring of the modern police force that goes far beyond the frequently stated interest in equal employment opportunity. The challenge is how to have

[7] A. H. Raskin, "Why New York Is 'Strike City,'" in *Cities in Trouble,* ed. Nathan Glazer (Chicago: Quadrangle Books, 1970), pp. 67-83.

[8] I have no interest in embroiling myself in the debate over urban power structures here. I wish only to emphasize that police departments are under considerable pressure to be representative and that this pressure is not singular to only police departments in the city. For a review of the literature on the urban power structure debates see Edward Keynes and David M. Ricci, eds., *Political Power, Community and Democracy* (Chicago: Rand McNally, 1970).

community representation in police perspectives without returning to the practices of political hackery. Resolving conflict and providing for accommodation is also a question of providing multiple community perspectives among officialdom in government. This is particularly true in law enforcement, given the low visibility, discretionary authority of the police officer who needs community assistance to do his job. Apart from sheer political considerations, at best, community representation on the police force means that police officers will have cultural rapport with racial and ethnic minorities. In resolving conflict and preventing crime, as well as in trying to find out what happened after the commission of a crime, rapport with and knowledge of a minority subculture is an obvious asset. However, these talents are not usually measured in a written test.

On the whole, the Civil Service merit system has served us well. Other than a few holdover political officials from an earlier era, no one wants to return to the pre-1883 Pendleton Act days when nepotism, corruption, patronage, and incompetency were common in government. But simplistic appeals to professionalism and credentialization will not do either. Some modifications can be made in determining qualifications based on actual job performance. There is no reason why a computer specialist need be 6 feet tall, have 20-20 vision, or come up through the ranks. There is every reason to require him to have experience in systems analysis programming. Competition for such a job should not be limited to members of the force, but should be open to all.

THE DEPARTMENT

In large police departments of 200 men and women or more, formal organization is quite specialized. Usually a clear division is made between detective work and patrol assignment. Detective work is performed by senior officers in plainclothes after the commission of a crime and after a cursory investigation by a patrolman. The mythological detective of television fantasy is an independent soul who carefully interviews citizens in the neighborhood, uses the crime lab extensively, combs through criminal mug books and records at headquarters, and finally cracks the case. Even police science courses that stress criminalistics and investigation techniques sometimes unwittingly reinforce the myth. But the fact is that only a handful of cases, usually very prominent ones, are solved by intensive investigation. Normally the detective has very meager information on which to base an investigation and precious little time to run down what leads he has. Most cases for which there is no eyewitness are not solved at all. The cases that are solved normally are the result of an offender being apprehended for another crime. The offender may reveal he has committed the unsolved crime, or he may be identified by witnesses in a lineup or, much more rarely, by fingerprints.

Since most convictions depend on a police witness to the criminal event or a patrolman arriving at the scene in time to find a witness, some have argued that the organizational distinctions between detectives and patrolmen should be removed except in traditional areas such as homicide or narcotics. It is further argued that patrolmen who are familiar with the neighborhood may be at least as effective as a detective in dealing with potential witnesses.

Detective work usually means long, frustrating hours for veterans of the force. However, there are benefits for detectives that patrolmen do not share. The assignment is more interesting, requires imagination, and is rewarding in that detectives often see a case through, developing evidence, while the patrolman may be shunted aside shortly after discovering a crime.[9]

Moreover, the detective is not as exposed to danger as is the less prestigious foot patrolman. The element of danger exists not merely in situations where the patrolman is apprehending suspects. Many officers fear family crisis intervention assignments as potentially more dangerous, where internal family emotions are unpredictable and extreme. Still other veterans caution that apprehending a citizen for a routine traffic violation can result in injury or death to the careless officer. The tragic statistics of officers killed in the line of duty (Figure 4.1) bear out the truth of the veteran's counsel about both patrol work and crisis intervention assignments.[10]

The obvious danger to which police officers are exposed in enforcing the law and in maintaining public order mandates some degree of military organization, a chain of command, disciplined responses to orders, and training for appropriate responses to standard situations. However, the police officer is not a solider. The rule of civilian law requires commanding officers to be outwardly responsive to the outside constraints of court rulings and statutes, which establish standards of conduct that cannot easily be reconciled with martial law or military operations in a state of belligerency. The fact that we are a government of laws and not a government of arbitrary decision making by a military commander responding to the exigencies of the day (thankfully) complicates maintenance in a democratic society.[11]

There is the added difficulty, of course, that there are few standard situations for patrolmen, who must use individualized judgments concerning when to use force, when to arrest, and when to decline any action. Charged with maintaining both order and law within a pluralist value structure, the patrolman's use of personalized authority and discretion[12] to exercise it becomes inevitable.

[9] Niederhoffer, *Behind the Shield,* pp. 62, 82-85.

[10] In 1973, 26 percent of all assaults on police officers in the United States occurred while officers were responding to family quarrels, man-with-gun warnings, and other disturbance calls; the same percentage of assaults occurred during attempts to make an arrest. 1973 FBI Uniform Crime Reports, Table 64, p. 172.

[11] Skolnick, *Justice without Trial,* pp. 6-12.

[12] The personalized nature of police discretion and authority is documented throughout the literature. For a concise discussion see Wilson, *Varieties of Police Behavior,* pp. 32-48.

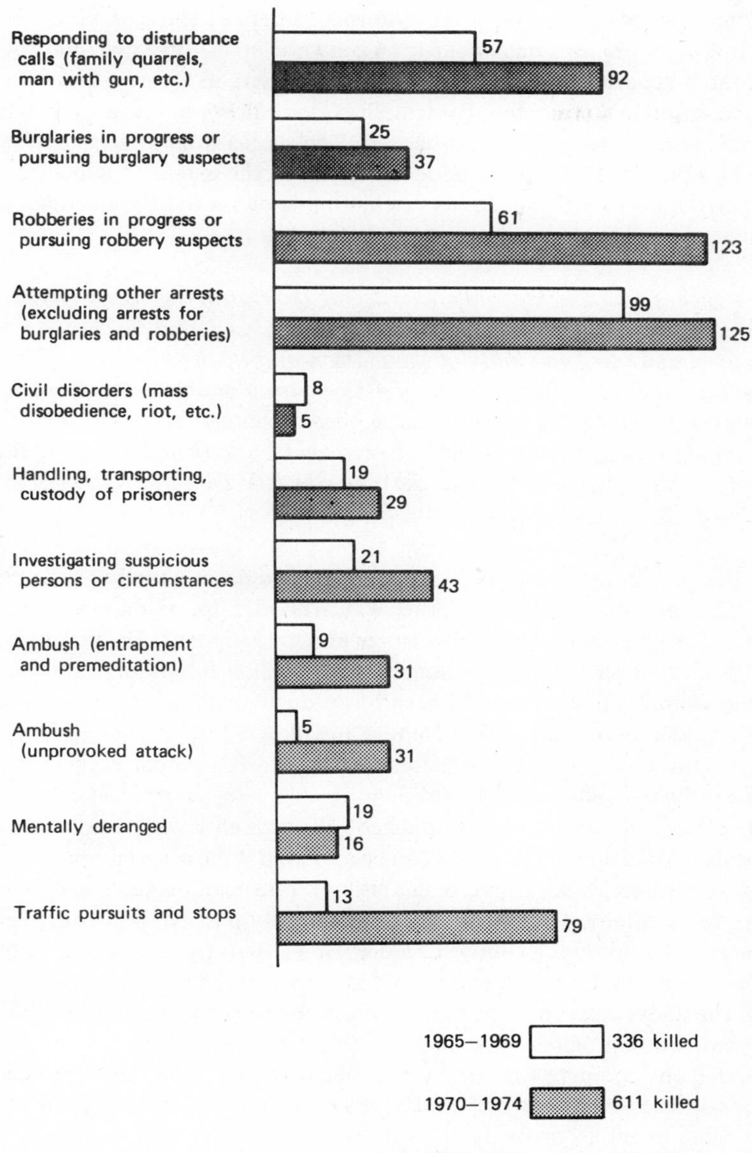

Figure 4.1 Law enforcement officers killed, by type of activity, 1965-1974. (Source. *FBI,* Uniform Crime Reports, *1974.*)

Although police routine with its uniforms, orders of the day, chain of command, and daily line ups has about it an outward image of strict military discipline, a more accurate characterization would be with a "quasi military" degree of regimentation and command control. Superior officers cannot simply bark out commands and expect them to be obeyed. The sergeant and lieutenant in command of a squad or platoon are perfectly aware of the extent to which they rely on the patrolman's initiative. In his fascinating book on the Philadelphia police, Rubinstein describes the interdependent relationship.

> *The sergeant's and lieutenant's exercise of their authority is tempered by an understanding of their own dependence on the goodwill and cooperation of their men in maintaining the unity of the platoon and the achievement of its goals. They know they can always get rid of a recalcitrant or dangerous man, but they do not want to antagonize their men, or encourage them to seek transfer. Every time a man leaves, a new man must be broken in, and their is no guarantee that the replacement will be as good as the man who left. They must also worry about the possibility that an angry man will betray them.*[13]

Betrayal, or "dropping a dime," can come from officers directing their charges toward those beneath them or the other way around. Supervisors provide a loose leash for their men, but every supervisor who "gives a man a break, lets him off without a sick check, allows someone to go home a few hours early without deducting from his pay, accepts 'Christmas money' or goes 'on the take' knows there is a possibility of being betrayed by his men."[14]

Low-level, low-visibility decision making by the patrolman is inevitable. To some extent low visibility can be raised, and patrolmen's discretion can be structured by a supervisor in "professionalized" departments with ample resources. Activity sheets and complaint forms can be reviewed, follow-up complaint reports can be reviewed and filed, traffic ticket citation rates can be kept, and clearance rates can be maintained. All of these are technically possible procedures and, in some cases, they are being followed. Complaints, arrests, and crimes known to the police are normally recorded in most large police departments today. Moreover, all the above data may be computerized for retrieval, review, and analysis by the commanding officer.

The social environment that surrounds the decision to arrest or to use coercive force cannot be conveyed on a form. Experienced superior officers know this and act or decline to act accordingly. The actual social setting surrounding a patrol-

[13]Jonathan Rubinstein, *City Police* (New York: Farrar, Staus and Giroux, 1973), pp. 42-43.
[14]Ibid., p. 43.

man's decisions is considerably distorted by the simplistic meaning conveyed by official report categories. For example, larceny might mean theft of a bakery donut by a 10-year old, or it might mean theft of a diamond ring; traffic tickets may be routinely put in a circular file by superiors for downtown officials, a fact known by patrolmen who fear reprisal; and accurate clearance rate maintenance (e.g., demonstrating that 1 out of 10 burglaries results in an arrest clearing the burglary) makes embarrassing material for the local press. Consequently, petty thefts, auto break-ins, and burglaries are frequently not reported.

SPECIAL DETAILS

Victimless crimes such as gambling, sex violations, and drug use and sale usually require specialized training and knowledge for undercover officers and arresting officers and require specialized assistance such as laboratory analysis of seized drugs and police legal advice for drawing up search and arrest warrants. Apprehension usually depends on the undercover officer's ability to provide opportunity for the offender to make a drug sale, place a bet on a number, or offer sexual favors, while still avoiding Fifth Amendment entrapment restrictions that prohibit a law enforcement official from enticing a citizen into criminal behavior. In the area of drug enforcement, often the only cooperative witnesses are informers who themselves frequently have criminal records for drug offenses. Therefore they are not always effective witnesses; their characters will be impeached by defense counsel during trial. Furthermore, undercover agents are very difficult to supervise, and careful questioning by a supervising police officer of an unsavory undercover agent is required to sift fact from fiction, gossip from hard evidence. This is particularly true since informants are under considerable pressure to deliver information to the police officers for whom they work. Consequently, special training, often on site through veteran officers, in criminalistics, procedure, and interrogation and apprehension techniques is required for vice and drug squads.

Entirely different sensitivities are required of the policemen and women who compose modern rape squads and family crisis intervention units. Rape investigation requires advanced training in criminalistics; state law, although it varies, often requires evidence of penetration, semen, and violence. Moreover, both police units are unique in one respect: they are victim oriented. The assaulted female must be treated with dignity and concern; she must be counseled to have an immediate physical exam and interviewed for facts concerning who assaulted her and where he might be, all with sensitivity and compassion. Here concern for human suffering obviously demands a psychological perspective quite distinct from the public order orientation of vice and tactical squad personnel.

Similar characteristics of sensitivity, civility and understanding are essential for crisis intervention squads. Taking pride in the demeanor of his crisis intervention officers, Chief Sam Gemelli of the 240-man, Erie, Pennsylvania, police department said: "My men can walk into a kitchen where Momma is threatening the old man with a butcher knife, sit calmly down, light up a cigarette and say, 'Now, what is all this about?' without flickering an eyelash."[15] The object is not to make an arrest, but to prevent an injury or save a life by defusing human emotions.

POLICE AS TECHNICIANS

Large police departments are employing, in increasing numbers, personnel with technical specialties in data processing, planning and analysis, laboratory criminalistics, and similar skills. The modern police administrator who must supervise uniform crime reporting, deploy officers for stake-outs, trouble spots and traffic control, or simply decide on priorities to determine which patrol car will be dispatched to which crime requires technical assistance. Most large departments have planning offices, although each office varies in levels of technical competency. Some departments have microfilm, data processing, or highly sophisticated record-keeping and retrieval systems. Still others have computerized dispatching systems that queue calls and referrals to squad cars based on the call's seriousness and the probability of other cars being available to respond to future serious calls. Virtually all police departments have at least limited access to crime laboratories and state or federal criminal data banks that contain arrest records, conviction records and, perhaps, additional information in court procedural decisions, criminal histories, and automobile licenses and registrations. The increase of criminal data banks at geometric rates has raised serious questions, to be dealt with later. But there is no question that it has elevated the technical level of police work and criminal justice research.

The change has not been without opposition from groups such as the Fraternal Orders of Police and police unions that represent the rank and file of the department. A common clarion call for union and intradepartment opposition has been the possibility of *lateral entry,* a term referring to employing highly paid personnel who do not come up through the ranks. To many men, bringing on the force a university graduate or former IBM employee as a high-ranked systems analyst or planner is equivalent to making the military historian and pacifist, Walter Millis, a four-star general.

Opposition to lateral entry often strikes the public as the antediluvian struggle of encrusted traditions, but rank-and-file concerns reflect not merely conservatism. Police work is insular and parochial by character. Survey research demonstrates that few officers expect significant assistance or understanding from the general public or even from personnel in other subsystems of the criminal justice

[15] My conversation with Chief Sam Gemelli, Erie Police Department.

system. Officers respond to perceived public indifference and insensitivity by insulating their feelings and behavior and keeping police matters within the department. Civilian review boards, civilian commissioners, government agencies, and academics—all those who have not been initiated into the complexity of police work and are not "sensitized" to what officers are "up against"—represent a threat. So it is with neophyte employees who are retained by lateral entry.

In summary, the modern police are members of a quasimilitary organization, with specialized tasks and functions. Unlike the military, the chain of command is very fragile; the patrolman operates within the framework of personalized discretion and authority. The roles and perceptions he will have in the field are not, in the main, shaped by any basic training, they emerge from the crucible of contending forces of the political and social environment within which he works.

5

THE POLICE DILEMMA

Once we know what the police should do and can do, then we can address the three critical problems of police recruitment, training, and leadership. As matters stand now, we do not know what we are recruiting men for, what kind of leadership we ought to be developing.[1] *Miami Chief of Police Bernard L. Garmire*

As with education in the 1950s, reform of the police is frequently linked to "professionalism," the assumption being that every difficulty—rioting and corruption,[2] race discrimination, and hostility toward the police—is, at least in part, attributable to the lack of professional training. The urgent need to upgrade the training of police officers has been implored by nearly every modern Presidential commission, agency, and administrator in law enforcement and criminal justice. The 1973 National Advisory Commission on Criminal Justice Standards and Goals statement on training echoed this concern. Citing a 1967 study by the International Association of Chiefs of Police that showed that the average policeman received less than 200 hours of formal training, the commission compared that figure to other professional training, and found that "physicians received more than 11,000 hours, lawyers more than 9,000 hours, teachers over 7,000

[1] Bernard L. Garmire, "The Police Role in an Urban Society," in *The Police and the Community,* ed. Robert F. Steadman (Baltimore: Johns Hopkins University Press, 1972).
[2] Robert A. Mendelsohn, "Police Community Relations, a Need in Search of Police Support," *American Behavioral Scientist* (1970) 13:747-748.

hours, embalmers more than 5,000 hours and barbers more than 4,000." No reasonable person would contend, argued the commission, "that a barber's responsibility is 20 times greater than a police officer's."[3]

Such bold comparisons provide little illumination for answering questions of police role and function. For what tasks are police officers to be trained? What are the roles that police are expected to perform? Are they primarily to retrieve cats from trees, protect civil liberties, promote racial harmony, direct traffic, and protect commercial establishments from burglary and larceny? Are they to be well-disciplined soldiers who follow orders in circumstances of public disorder and riot instead of responding to individual initiative and personal anger? Or should they be prepared for the discretionary demeanor that characterizes the policeman on patrol, trained to be community relations oriented, encouraged to reflect on human behavior in organizational settings, subgroup cultures,[4] and knowledgeable about criminology generally?

Some degree of realism has to be introduced in any discussion of the relationship between police training and reform of the criminal justice system. After all, the apparently low average-hour rate of training for American police is primarily a consequence of town and suburban departments under 20 men, many of whose personnel are part time. Town fathers are not looking for crime fighters. They are more interested in low-cost constables to keep the peace and issue traffic tickets, preferably to people from out of town. Extensive training is dysfunctional to these interests; even if it is financed by a Safe Streets grant, the officer must have a temporary replacement. Moreover, once he has been upgraded in education, he is likely to leave for a more professional position, ask for more money, or both.

The multiplicity of police roles and functions is frequently discussed in the literature, but with little consensus. And very little of the literature is concerned with the lack of linkage between experienced police perceptions of the problems of crime, how they actually perform their jobs, and police training. Nonetheless, educators and the Law Enforcement Educational Program of LEAA have promoted the virtues of education and training, quite oblivious of the distinctions between them. Since 1969, millions of dollars have been awarded by LEEP to colleges and universities to assist students in criminal justice curriculums and large sums have been awarded under LEAA action grants for training programs,

[3]National Advisory Commission on Standards and Goals, *The Police,* U.S. Department of Justice (Washington, D.C.: U.S. Government Printing Office, 1973), p. 380. On the other hand, the 4000 hours of barber's training is more apparent than real. See Clyde Woods, "Students without Teachers," *The American Behavioral Scientist* (1972) 16:15-25.

[4]William A. Westley, "Learning to Love the Police," *The New York Times Magazine,* November 15, 1971, p. 41.

primarily for police officers.[5] How this major effort has contributed to professionalizing the police is unclear. As Charles Tenney[6] suggests, police work is not comparable to traditional professional characteristics, including a defined set of conduct norms, a method of self-policing, independent practice, and licensing feature.

Tenney's survey in 1971 identified three categories of criminal justice curriculums: training, professional, and social science curriculums. Training curriculum is directed primarily to mastery and application of particular rules, developing particular mechanical skills. Examples of a training-type subject matter might be cleaning a revolver, patrol procedures and techniques, driving while in pursuit, internal discipline, and making out forms. Such material is often offered at the police academy or at brief training sessions sponsored by the state police agencies.

Rarely is any time at the academy devoted to questions of policy to guide the very broad use of discretion characterizing the patrol level. Police discretion is inevitable, even desirable but, as Kenneth Davis has reminded us,[7] discretion, unstructured by policy guidelines, means arbitrary law enforcement; structured discretion means appropriate review, administrative control, and precedent-setting guidelines for the future. The need for policy guidelines was also urged by the Kerner Report.

> *There are guidelines for the wearing of uniforms—but not for how to intervene in a domestic dispute; for the cleaning of a revolver—but not for when to fire it; for use of departmental property—but not for whether to break up a sidewalk gathering; for handling stray dogs—but not for handling field interrogations.*[8]

Of course, one might add that guidelines for such policy questions may never be clear when policy authority and discretion are diffused and personalized due to environmental variables such as danger and diverse community values.

The second curriculum category seeks to promote professionalism, to develop internalized standards of behavior objectively determined on the basis of agreed on goals, and to develop a foundation of expertise. On the other hand, the third category, the social science curriculum customarily offered by liberal arts colleges and universities, is designed to teach *about* a subject; it offers background and is not specifically oriented toward work preparation, as are the training and profes-

[5] U.S. Department of Justice, LEAA 1st Annual Report (Washington, D.C.: U.S. Government Printing Office, 1972), p. 230.

[6] Charles W. Tenney, Jr., *Higher Education Programs in Law Enforcement and Criminal Justice* (Washington, D.C.: U.S. Department of Justice, 1971), p. 4.

[7] Kenneth Culp Davis, *Discretionary Justice* (Baton Rouge: Louisiana State University Press, 1969), p. 99.

[8] Report of the National Advisory Commission on Civil Disorders (Washington, D.C.: U.S. Government Printing Office, 1968), p. 313.

sional curriculums. It is part of a general education in the social sciences focusing on one aspect along with other disciplines, such as sociology or political science, as another thrust of the curriculum. Of course, many criminal justice programs are a composite of these categories, a compromise between contending views of what functions the police are expected to perform. The somewhat vague and contradictory hope is that the proper "mix" of subject matter will upgrade the police.

POLICE PROFESSIONALISM AND REFORM

We cannot be sanguine that effective police reform waits on professionalism, although a popular assumption with American reform groups, particularly with educators, is that "the heart of the police problem is one of personnel."[9] The police professionalism position, suggests Susan White, is an argument for a certain kind of control of police behavior. Given the existence of unacceptable behavior by officers, we need to impose controls (i.e., a professional code) to change the officers' perceptions of what constitutes acceptable behavior on the job. But the criteria for police effectiveness are not clear and the exercise of discretion, which is central to police work, is often at odds with professional principles.[10]

Niederhoffer suggests nine principles that characterize professions generally: high standards of admission; a special body of knowledge and theory; altruism and dedication to the service ideal; a lengthy period of training for candidates; a code of ethics; licensing of members; autonomous control; pride of members in their profession; and publicly recognized status and prestige.[11]

Few of these criteria are capable of being adhered to after the most vigorous training or education, considering the contradictory roles and behaviors that police officers must perform in the line of duty. One indication of how police must apportion their resources is the proportion of citizen complaints. Wilson[12] found that only 10 percent of all calls to the Syracuse Police Department could be

[9] Charles B. Saunders, *Upgrading the American Police* (Washington, D.C.: The Brookings Institute, 1970), p. 7. Certainly the position that "upgrading police personnel and giving them the dignity and respect which they deserve" by formal training will improve morale and aid recruitment is difficult to argue with. See statement of Patrick V. Murphy, "The Improvement and Reform of Law Enforcement and Criminal Justice in the U.S.," *Hearing before the Select Committee on Crime,* House of Representatives, 91st Congress, first session, July 28-31; August 4-7, 11, 12; September 17-18, 1969, p. 220.

[10] Susan White, "A Perspective on Police Professionalism," *Law and Society Review* (1972) u:61-85.

[11] Niederhoffer, *Behind the Shield,* pp. 18-19.

[12] Wilson, *Varieties of Police Behavior,* p. 18.

classified as law enforcement oriented.[13] State police officials in Pennsylvania have indicated to me that approximately 90 percent of their policing hours is devoted to traffic control and assisting accident victims.

Psychologically, such conflicting role expectations for police officers take their toll,[14] increasing fatigue and lowering morale. Miami Chief of Police Bernard Garmire provides a useful illustration.

> *Here is the kind of thing that we expect of today's police officer:*
> *At 9:00 p.m. he responds to a robbery in progress and upon arrival exchanges gunshots with a suspect.*
> *At 10:00 p.m., after he has made a report of the incident, he receives a call of a violent family brawl. He is white, they are black, and the suspect with whom he just exchanged gunfire an hour earlier was black. The officer is expected to handle their marital problems effectively and dispassionately, but he also has to return to radio service quickly because it is Saturday night and two other calls are waiting for him. Need more be said? Do we really believe that one man can do this night after night, month in and month out? Granted, the officer is not fired upon or assaulted every night. But the potential is there and he knows it: witness the frequent news reports concerning the ambushes, snipings, and other offenses directed against police. Is it not time that we took notice of the realities of policing and admit that one man or one group of men cannot intellectually and psychologically do all this?*[15]

Nor can professional criteria readily be imposed by "reform" police chiefs or commissioners through a hierarchical chain of command, although under exceptional circumstances this can be done.[16] Police have vast discretion to arrest or not, to hassle or not, to investigate, and to use their discretion judiciously according to variables of public perception and the social setting. Such are the community political and perceptual constraints on police exercising or not exercising law enforcement authority. But there are multiple variables affecting police discretion to arrest or not that relate to his ability to exercise social control, to enforce the law, to maintain reasonably good relations with his peers in the department, and simply to stay alive as well. Moreover, these variables are grounded in a bewildering array of subcultures and disparate communities within which policemen make decisions. For these reasons there are sharp limits on the degree of control that administrative command and policy can exercise on

[13] For a review of this literature see Jesse Rubin, "Police Identity and Police Role," *The Police and the Community,* pp. 23-25.
[14] Ibid., pp. 25-39.
[15] Garmire, "The Police Role in an Urban Society," *The Police and the Community,* p. 5.
[16] James Q. Wilson, "Police Morale, Reform and Citizen Respect: The Chicago Case," *The Police,* pp. 137-162.

patrolman and detective discretion. Police organization is unique in that policy initiatives are often inverted. They originate from the bottom of the police hierarchy instead of the other way around. Indeed, some scholars have suggested that the higher the police salaries, the greater their educational attainment and, consequently, the keener their support of unionization, the *less* will be the control of supervisory personnel and the greater will be the officers' insulation from public accountability.[17]

The conflict between formal professional roles and functional roles of the police reflects the confusing array of contending mind-sets and interests in the political community. By and large, distinctions between criminal justice education "curriculums" and "training programs" reflect burning political issues, yet unresolved, as to what performance is expected in police work.

FOUR PERCEPTUAL EXPECTATIONS OF POLICE BEHAVIOR

From police curriculums, from the professional literature of police administration, and from the reform-oriented literature frequently critical of present police behavior, four perceptions of police work may be discerned: police as *law enforcers;* police as *subordinates to due process;* police as *maintainers of public order;* and police as *dispensers of social justice.* Obviously, none of these categories is exclusive of the others. It is possible to have vigorous law enforcement, adhere strictly to due process, preserve order, and do justice to all. But in the real world the four perceptions of police work are frequently linked to contending role expectations[18] and incompatible ends[19] in the police officer's mind, and to contending ideologies of political constituencies that support or oppose police practices.

The *law enforcement model* is the clearest representation and has received frequent comment. This perspective is dominant in police academies and police science curriculums. Its goals assign high priority to vigorous and efficient enforcement of all the criminal law by professionally trained officers. Supporters of this perspective often criticize "service" responsibilities of patrolmen—retrieving cats from trees, assisting in family crisis situations, accompanying drunks to their homes—as distracting and time-consuming tasks that divert patrolmen from their "real" law enforcement functions. Administrative unstructured discretion to

[17] Steven C. Halpern, "Police Employee Organizations and Accountability Procedures in Three Cities: Some Reflections on Police Policy-making," *Law and Society Review* (1974) 8:561-580.

[18] Peter K. Manning, "The Police Mandate, Strategies and Appearances," in *Crime and Justice in American Society,* ed. Jack D. Douglas (Indianapolis: Bobbs-Merrill Company, 1971), pp. 149-193.

[19] James Q. Wilson, "The Police and Their Problems: A Theory," *Public Policy* (19) 12:189-216.

make an arrest or not is also deplored as deterring police from their professional responsibilities: enforcing the law.

An early and influential article on criminal justice by Herbert Packer distinguishes between two parallel models in criminal justice: the *due process model* and the *crime control model*. According to Packer, the due process model stresses "legal guilt" according to logical procedures formulated by constituted authorities in the legislature and on the appellate courts. Thus, a suspect who appears clearly guilty, but whose conviction is involved in a violation of procedural criteria, is legally innocent.[20] The due process perspective is dominant among the legal professions, civil libertarians and, until recently, among professors of public law. It remains the preemptive perspective, as it must, for the appellate courts, although there are sharp differences of view regarding the scope and meaning of due process.

Packer's *crime control model* emphasizes factual guilt. Its output is directed toward the efficient administration of justice, a "capacity to convict, and dispose of a high proportion of criminal offenders whose offenses become known."[21] However, Packer does not distinguish between *law enforcement,* the perspective of professors of police science, and *public order,* the perspective of street-wise officers in the field and, not infrequently, the general public and local newspapers as well. Within the *public order* perspective, the veteran member of the force understands his task to be that of peace officer[22] as much as the needs of public order may require discretionary enforcement of the law. A clear example was provided to me by a member of the 1968 security team for the presidential nominating conventions in Miami Beach. A solitary police officer was guarding an entrance to the 1972 Democratic Convention. His orders were to prevent gate crashing, although his particular duty was compounded by taunting but otherwise friendly young demonstrators blowing marihuana smoke in his face. Needless to say, the officer stayed at his post and made no arrests.

In the law enforcement perspective, success is still measured in terms of arrests, although not in terms of sheer numbers; not everyone who violates the law is apprehended or rigorously investigated. Police have very little chance of apprehending a suspect for breaking and entering when he is not identified, and normally the investigating officer will merely file the complaint until a *modus operandi* pattern can be determined from a series of burglaries. But police will vigorously pursue those who, in their judgment, violate public order and count the arrest as a "good pinch." For example, a law enforcement officer may evaluate

[20] Herbert L. Packer, "Two Models of the Criminal Process," *University of Pennsylvania Law Review* (1964) 112:1-68.

[21] Ibid., p. 10.

[22] Albert J. Reiss, Jr., *The Police and the Public* (New Haven, Conn.: Yale University Press, 1971), p. 17.

the success or failure of a prosecutor by his conviction rate, particularly for those defendants who have been "troublemakers" for the officer. In this case, value is allocated either to the police who have charged an offender with a crime and is "guilty" in the eyes of the police, or to the defendant whose attorney has demonstrated to the prosecutor and judiciary that he is innocent or that he cannot be easily convicted without unrealistic commitment of prosecutorial resources. Maintaining public order is the perspective of the patrolman. He assumes "reform" means catching and convicting more offenders who are criminal or disruptive in his eyes and must be removed from the streets or otherwise deterred.

A fourth perception of what police ought to do is common to the perspective on criminal justice decision that emerges from a more general social critique of American politics. It is the view that police are to be evaluated as dispensers or negators of social justice. Frequently the major thrust of this view is that street crimes (robbery, burglary, assault, and the like) are characteristic of lower-class behavior, and white-collar crime (embezzlement, consumer fraud, income tax cheating) is characteristic of middle- and upper-class behavior. Given assumptions about middle- or upper-class dominance of the power structure, he is likely to conclude that conviction and punishment are more certain and severe for the former class than the latter class, and that crime reflects not a universal condition, but a relative social reality as defined by elites who have power. The instruments of that power are trained, organized law enforcement officers, although they are professionalized and depersonalized. In this second example the value allocated is punishment and denial of the fruits of certain behaviors labeled criminal, as contrasted with nonpunishment and encouragement of other behaviors formally labeled criminal (white-collar crime) but differentiated from street crime in vigor of enforcement, prosecution, and sentence. The model is class conflict and the assumption is that law enforcement is political, a product of social injustice, reform, and an attempt to prevent class discrimination and promote civil liberties through altering the social structure. The units of measurement are class characteristics as variables on the social control targets of the criminal law, and on decisions made at various substages in the criminal justice system. The key variables or root causes are likely to be inequitable income distribution, racial and sexual discrimination, and family instability resulting from poverty, poor housing, differential opportunity, or relative deprivation—the latter a consequence of upper-class affluence communicated to the lower class through the mass media.

Each perspective has played a prominent part in discussions between police officers, between intellectuals, and between other members of the criminal justice community, but rarely among all three groups. Each position has its own grounding in reality, but its own limitations.

Perhaps the position *least* analyzed in systematic fashion by those in official capacities in government is the law enforcement perspective. Rarely are the theoretical contradictions explored by those who hold the law enforcement myth.

Yet the incongruity between providing few social services while expecting the cooperation of the community in gathering evidence of crime is quickly apparent. Even more important is that decisions to arrest and charge are not based simply on the technical issue of probable cause. Instead the decision to arrest is related itself to social service functions and to the social management and control function of the police. There are numerous occasions when an arrest will result in disorder.

There is a persistent myth that the responsibility of a police officer is narrowly prescribed by statute and that the police are, in effect, ministerial officers committed to enforcing the law without fear or favor. The statutes of a number of states, for example, leave no ambiguity on the question of whether, having learned of a criminal offense, a police officer is free to do anything other than initiate a criminal prosecution. At least one jurisdiction (the District of Columbia) goes so far as to make it a criminal offense for an officer to fail to make an arrest.[23] That there is considerable attrition of potential offenders as they are processed has been commented on earlier. In an early study of attrition in the legal process,[24] Ennis found that police screened out 74 percent of all cases in which citizens had notified the police of a crime (Figure 5.1).

Clearly, law enforcement is not the only interest of the community. After all, contemporary policemen are a surrogate service agency on call 24 hours a day. Moreover, their service function cannot easily be separated from their primary historical role, still being performed, which is the maintenance of public order. Ordinarily ranked in terms of time expended, patrolmen spend more than 90 percent of their time on traffic control and accidents, fights, and public disturbances of a minor nature that do not result in a formal charge.

Silver's research indicates that the law enforcement function of contemporary police is recent in England, and the same could be said for municipalities in the United States prior to the Civil War. In "unpoliced society," police functions were performed—if at all—by citizens rotating in local offices (sheriffs, constables, magistrates) or acting as members of militia, posses, yeomanry corps, or watch-and-ward committees.[25] Their responsibility was to maintain order, usually for the benefit of the dominant class who made up the militias. At the same time, riot and disorder, according to Silver, provided an outlet for protest and redress by "the dangerous classes" whose message was not lost on the elite. As

[23]American Bar Association, *Standards relating to the Urban Police Function* (New York: Institute of Judicial Administration, 1971), pp. 117-120.

[24]Phillip H. Ennis, *Field Surveys II, Criminal Victimization in the United States,* A Report of a National Survey, The National Opinion Research Center (Washington, D.C.: U.S. Government Printing Office, May 1967), p. 49.

[25]Alan Silver, "The Demand for Order in Civil Society," *The Police,* p. 9.

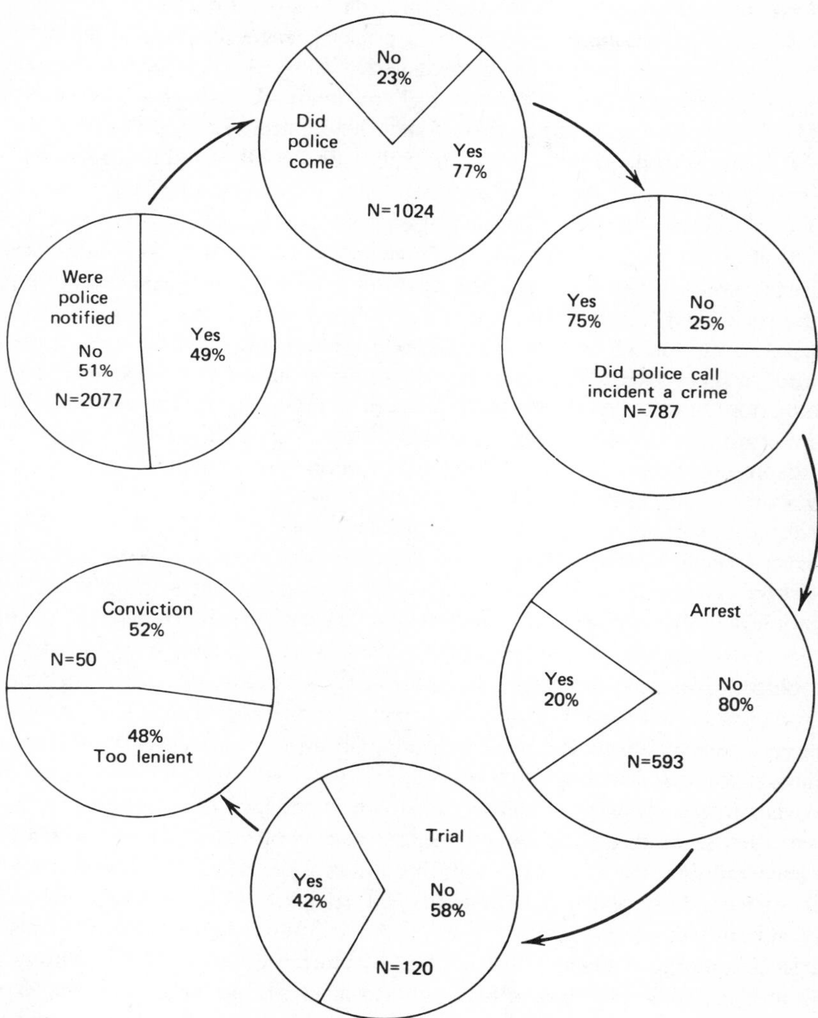

Figure 5.1 Attrition in the legal process. (Source. *Phillip H. Ennis,* Field Surveys II: Criminal Victimization in the United States, *A Report of a National Survey, National Opinion Research Center (Washington, D.C.: U.S. Government Printing Office, May 1967), p. 49.*)

we have seen, the experience of urban Boston was no different.[26] Enforcement of laws by a professional, bureaucratic police force developed along with an increasingly interdependent, industrial order, a sharp increase in democratic institutions more responsive to working- and lower-class demands, and a rising standard of civility.[27] Reiss and Bordua[28] have pointed out that police do not act on behalf of individual complainants, but on behalf of public order. In fact, veteran officers are inherently suspicious of complainants, a perfectly reasonable demeanor for the officer, although often resented by the irate victim. Police officers must be sensitive to private vengeance masquerading as a complainant against a serious offender, the police must not invoke the vengeance monopolized by the state (and it is that, at least in part) in behalf of private parties, but only in behalf of the public at large who may be threatened. The officer must also be mindful of the department's own limited resources and of the presence of serious justification, *in terms of public order.* Instead of invoking the complex machinery of the criminal process, the skilled officer will encourage a private resolution for the dispute between victim and perpetrator, as is often the case in family arguments or barroom altercations.

Young police officers are consigned to suffer an unenviable role conflict between enforcing the law with an arrest, and exercising their discretion not to make an arrest. There are innumerable reasons why arrests are not made after a violation that clarify but do not resolve the officers' dilemma. To begin with, penal law is notoriously vague.[29] For example, what constitutes "disorderly conduct," "keeping a disorderly house," "desecration of the flag," "trespass," or "public intoxication" is left largely to the officer's judgment. Judgment in such gray areas is exercised according to the need for public order, not the necessity of punishing criminal behavior.

A second reason why arrests are not made is the lack of resources. No police department can afford to assume the initiative in rooting out bigamy or eliminating prostitution. There is a long-standing practice of many state police organizations of frequently giving warnings instead of tickets for traffic offenders when they are understaffed. Conduct involving a community subgroup may also be overlooked by the police. Illicit gambling by church groups, private Sunday beer sales at a veterans' picnic, and black ghetto residents carrying knives have been historically overlooked. As is true with federal and state regulatory agencies, to a certain extent, illicit behavioral patterns are defined by the regulated as much as by those who police.

[26] See above, Chapter 2.
[27] Silver, "The Demand for Order in Civil Society," *The Police,* pp. 9-21.
[28] Reiss and Bordua, *The Police,* pp. 29-30.
[29] Wayne LaFave, *Arrest:* The decision to take a suspect into custody (Boston: Little Brown, 1965) pp. 83-89.

Often arrests are not made because of a special relationship between the victim and the perpetrator. Officers will not make an arrest when the complainant is likely to "drop the charge." The local pharmacist does not want to prosecute a young shoplifter whose dad and mom are known to him; insurance companies will often settle damages from the theft of a car on an informal basis, preferring surreptitious settlement, both to avoid embarrassment for their clients and to avoid spending time in court; assault and battery or larceny are common crimes between a prostitute and her "John," but they rarely result in an official complaint. The prostitute cannot prefer charges for assault for fear she will be arrested for her profession. Similarly, the John who has been fleeced by his "date" for the evening does not want his wife or girl friend to be informed through litigation.[30]

In some "wide open towns" near armed forces bases or gambling centers, proprietors prefer a high tolerance of criminal activity. Galveston, Texas has a recent, ribald history of opposition to vigorous antivice campaigns on the grounds that the law would interfere with the tourist and military trade. When former Chief Justice Earl Warren was a prosecuting attorney in California, his efforts to end organized prostitution "were strenuously resisted by bankers, real estate dealers, and retail furniture dealers," business interests who profited by dealing with prostitution organizations at rates higher than those charged to ordinary citizens.[31]

In other more "respectable" communities, state and federal law enforcement officials may be unpopular in themselves, and good public relations demand a less than full enforcement of the law. State and federal police are outsiders to many municipal governments and police departments and any police, other than the tolerant campus variety, are resented on university grounds.

Finally, the demeanor of the citizen who is apprehended by the police officer is an important, if extralegal, variable in the decision to arrest, particularly in areas where police depend on respect for their authority to minimize conflict with those who might give them trouble. Peer-inspired bravado and truculence from a juvenile gang member directed in a threatening manner against an investigating officer is likely to increase the likelihood of arrest in order to save face and maintain authority. The drunk who insults the plainclothes policeman in ignorance, the truculent driver who objects to the traffic cop's admonishment for his driving, and the student demonstrator who taunts the police are liable for arrest, not for their activity, which may be legal, but for their public abuse of a law enforcement officer.[32] Often the police officer does not distinguish between chal-

[30] Ibid., pp. 114-124.

[31] Donald R. Cressey, *Theft of the Nation* (New York: Harper and Row, 1969), pp. 61-62.

[32] LaFave, *Arrest,* p. 146.

lenges to his authority's legitimacy in the eyes of street-corner society and threats to public order.[33]

On the other hand, the more deferential the accused, the greater the civility of the police—including the possibility of a warning being substituted for a formal arrest. It should not be assumed that such behavior on the part of the police indicates a love of power or authority. Skolnick points out that uncooperative attitudes, such as going limp or passive, especially provoke hostility in police. In this case the civilian's behavior is not viewed as a threat to authority, but it does generate physical labor and annoying work that the officer considers irrational and unnecessary—a citizen making an officer sweat to take him into custody.[34]

Arrests may also facilitate the investigation of another offense. This can assume two forms. Arrest may facilitate search, holding in custody a potential fugitive while giving the prosecution more time to investigate. Or the threat of arrest may be used as a means to recruit a suspect, often a prostitute, junkie, or receiver of stolen goods, as an informer. Arrests are then avoided or charges later dropped for individuals who are active police informers. Skolnick and Lindesmith report that this practice is particularly important to narcotic and vice squads where crime is victimless and informers within the deviant subculture are indispensible to making a sound arrest. A proprietor of a "respectable" pawn shop may inform on addicts, and the narcotic squad may not inquire into possible violation for possession of stolen goods. As Skolnick put it, "In general, burglary detectives permit informants to commit narcotic offenses, while narcotic detectives allow informants to steal."[35] How true this generalization is probably depends on the obviousness of the crime, the degree of specialization of the detective squad, and the quality of information that an informer is prepared to give. However, the practice is reportedly widespread in narcotic enforcement and has received considerable criticism from civil libertarians for at least three generations.[36] Criticism for all of these practices will not doubt continue unabated, as will the arrest to facilitate other police purposes, particularly since the Supreme Court has recently upheld the practice of arrest for minor traffice violations to facilitate search.[37]

Veteran officers may also decline to process charges when an arrest would lead to consequences that clearly outweight the desirability of apprehension. Family quarrels, which take up considerable time, rarely result in arrest, and trivial crimes (a stolen bicycle, a shoplifted trinket) might be passed over by the officer. Youthful, first-time offenders may "get off" with a stern reprimand or, in an earlier era, with curb-side justice—an informal physical threat or shake-up by the

[33] Carl Wertham and Irving Piliavin, "Gang Members and the Police," *The Police,* pp. 65-75.
[34] Skolnick, *Justice without Trial,* p. 88.
[35] Ibid., p. 129.
[36] Lindesmith, *The Addict and the Law.*
[37] *Cardwell* v *Lewis* 417 U.S. 583 (1974); *United States* v *Robinson* 414 U.S. 218 (1974).

officer. Whether the latter is properly categorized as "getting off" depends on one's point of view and whether or not one is innocent. I like to ask my own students which they would prefer—rehabilitation in a reformatory after a professionally proper arrest, or the indignity of an officer's extralegal abuse which, nevertheless, does not result in court referral. Police must and do decide whether or not any advantage to society is gained by arresting a youth with no previous record who is caught stealing minor items, or by arresting an adult who is involved in an incidental scuffle.

Discretion is not always exercised by declining to arrest a technical offender. There are times when an officer will make arrests when there is little or no possibility of prosecution and when certain types of conduct are declared criminal to alleviate administrative problems for the police.[38] For example, in Detroit so many patrolmen were repeatedly called into domestic disputes that the chief of police issued a directive that in the future an arrest was to be made in all such cases. Presumably, he felt this action would put an end to all such cases.[39] Thus, arrests were made to minimize the necessity of future police action. Hundreds of arrests of questionable legality were made in Washington, D.C. during the march on Washington after U. S. troops invaded Cambodia. A very close acquaintance of mine was arrested shortly after arriving in the city while in his sleeping bag in Lafayette Park. The offense was for charging a police barricade, but the function of his arrest and of hundreds of others was to reduce the number of demonstrators to manageable proportions in sensitive areas of the city. This occurred after some radical organizers had threatened to "shut Washington down" by staggered civil disobedience on the P Street Bridge, the Memorial Bridge, and 14th Street Bridge.

The suspension of civil liberties and the rule of law is not unique in democratic countries. Just prior to the May Day arrests in Washington, Prime Minister Pierre Trudeau of Canada formally suspended civil liberties and declared martial law for a 30-day period following the assassination of his Minister of Justice by radical French separatists. Although it is technically possible for the President of the United States to declare martial law as well, the same result was effected by administrative arrests on a large scale, assuming what is probably safe to assume, that former Chief Jerry Wilson of the Washington police was acting under White House directive.

Nor are extralegal arrests limited to political protests that threaten the social order. Arrests for public drunkenness or loitering, quickly followed by release, are common techniques used by police officers to break up an unruly congregation on the street corner or a heated atmosphere in a bar.

[38] LaFave, *Arrest,* pp. 125-143, especially 129.

[39] Ibid., pp. 144-145. The city attorney put an end to the order, apparently fearing the police would arrest individuals for offenses not committed or, at least, not committed in the officer's presence.

Organizational theorists have long raised a jaundiced eye on the formal goals of organizations, pointing instead to latent goals and unwritten agendas. Incrementalists further suggest that the actual priorities of organizations are not based on long-term goals at all, latent or manifest, but on the day-by-day needs of the actors. Police organizations represent no exception to this generalization, although they are unique in one respect. As I have stated, the agendas are established by the patrolman operating within the political culture as much as by the chief or mayor's officer. In terms of discretionary judgments concerning arrest and maintaining public order, patrolmen and detectives usually *are* the administrators, a fact that has considerably disturbed professors of administrative law and procedure.[40] As with other criminal justice organizations, internal administrative priorities[41] generally emphasize the values of efficiency and time and the self-interests of the actors in an organization.[42] In police and prosecution organizations, internal administrative priorities frequently conflict with due process of law and decision making oriented toward the protection of the rights of the criminally accused.

Legal rules formulated by the courts and police training in criminal procedure and in community relations do have an effect but, as we have seen, the rules are mediated by the organizational norms and perspectives of the police. The police regard due process protections for the defendant, in some degree, as administrative obstacles to maintaining public order or obtaining an important arrest. Police perception of what is right is often distinguished from what is lawful. Exploratory search of a room prior to an arrest,[43] Contrived search of a suspect by convenient arrest,[44] and illicit wiretapping by state-organized crime units are widespread practices of police in spite of Supreme Court decisions to the contrary.[45]

[40] Kenneth Culp Davis, *Discretionary Justice,* pp. 162-166.

[41] Robert P. Rhodes, "Discretion, Diminished Responsibility and Due Process: A Study of the New York State Youthful Offender Statute as a Variable in the Prosecution of Crime" (unpublished Ph.D. dissertation, Syracuse University, 1971).

[42] Amitai Etzioni, *Modern Organization* (Englewood Cliffs, N.J.: Prentice-Hall, 1964), pp. 5-12.

[43] Skolnick, *Justice without Trial,* p. 144. In the enforcement of narcotic laws, Skolnick found widespread unlawful exploratory search being used. One police officer commented on this general practice: "Of course, it's not exactly legal to talk about as a police technique. But if you find something, you back off and figure out how you can do it legal. And if you don't find anything you don't have to waste a lot of time."

[44] Search without a warrant is illegal unless it is incidental to arrest or justified by probable cause that the safety of the officer is imperiled. Since it is easier to find a probable cause for arrest than to obtain a warrant, the former practice is frequently employed to rationalize a search. Suspected violation of parole, disturbing the peace, furtive moves of a suspected narcotic user, and reasonable suspicion that a crime is about to be committed and a protecting officer put in danger may all be used as grounds for arrest or search, in anticipation that the search will reveal evidence to convict on a more serious charge.

[45] *Mapp* v *Ohio* 367 U.S. 643 (1961); *Terry* v *Ohio* 398 U.S. 1 (1968). *Terry* has been sharply modified by *United States* v *Robinson* 414 U.S. 218 (1974).

Additionally, there is evidence that recommendations for closer judicial review of arrest and search procedure[46] will not be very effective in discouraging entrapment or illegal search, although police practices may become more circumspect. The limited time that a police department can spend on a given case, the increasing number of cases, and the character of vice crimes between consenting individuals make entrapment and illegal search almost indispensable to enforce the law.

Vice crimes are especially time consuming for legal officers because there are no complainants to testify or point out violators of the law. There are large numbers of violators who operate in a social milieu that protects or, at the most, is neutral toward prostitution, gambling, or narcotics. As was true during prohibition, vice squads must plot ingeniously to gather evidence.[47] In this type of crime, detection frequently depends on informants who agree to purchase narcotics while police watch or on searches that reveal incriminating evidence to the point where the police must decide how to enter again legally.

Although administrative factors (time, numbers of cases, the nature of crimes without victims) influence vice squads to circumvent higher-court decisions and to be aggressive and imaginative, the patrolman on the beat actually exercises greater discretion concerning arrest. Apparently this is because the patrolman interacts with all sorts of people in his area and his contacts center on assisting citizens more than punishing a particular type of person. To use Stinchcombe's distinction,[48] the patrolman exercises discretion as a "peace officer," not as a "law officer." Thus, the policeman may advise a married man soliciting a prostitute to go home to his wife, convince a father to marry off his pregnant daughter instead of pressing a statutory rape charge, or put a drunk in a taxi instead of making an arrest for public intoxication.[49] In spite of police manuals and sometimes statutes exhorting police to arrest all violators of the law,[50] the patrolman continues to represent the largest screening agency of the legal process that determines guilt and innocence.[51]

Can we reconcile the disparate roles and missions that the body politic expects the police to perform? Can we professionalize police behavior?

To record questionable police behavior is, of course, not to approve of it. Training, education, higher salaries, and status will, no doubt, prevent some of the worst abuses of discretion. My conclusion is, however, that training, educa-

[46] LaFave, *Arrest,* pp. 495-496, 503-509.

[47] Edwin Schur, *Crimes without Victims: Deviant Behavior and Public Policy* (Englewood Cliffs, N.J. Prentice-Hall, 1965), pp. 135-138.

[48] Arthur L. Stinchcombe, "Institutions of Privacy in the Determination of Police Administrative Practices," *American Journal of Sociology* (1963) 69:150-160.

[49] LaFave, *Arrest,* pp. 63-140.

[50] Ibid., p. 76; Skolnik, *Justice without Trial,* pp. 112-115.

[51] President's Commission, *The Challenge of Crime,* pp. 91-123.

tion, and restructuring police departments—in short, reform—will have limited effects on organizational behavior as long as that behavior reflects problematic dilemmas for police rooted in differing expectations from community to community and vague, frequently unenforceable criminal statutes. Given the difficulty of reconciling the rule of law with due process when enforcing victimless crimes, given middle-class reliance on the police to maintain higher levels of public order in divergent communities or subcultures, particularly when the political climate is uncivil and armed, we may be asking of our police departments more than any human institution can deliver. Solutions to the problems of crime do not wait on professionalism for the most part. Instead, they require altering the political and cultural environment within which the policeman works so that the officer's mandate is clear, limited in scope, and can be realistically achieved.

6

LAWYERS AND THE CRIMINAL LAW

If I were asked where I place the American aristocracy, I should reply without hesitation, that it is not composed of the rich, who are united by no common tie, but that which occupies the judicial bench and bar.
Alex DeTocqueville

For at least 50 years the problems of criminal justice have been posed by legal scholars generally in at least one of three ways. Some legal critics argued that criminal courts were less than just due to an absence of fair and uniform appellate court rulings, faithfully followed by trial-level judges. The clear-rule advocates had their detractors in the legal realists, who objected that rule legalisms memorized in law school and parroted by the bench often disguised "burning questions" of policy.[1] What was needed, according to the rule skeptics, was an element of judicial pragmatism[2] in applying rules, "a consideration of social advantage" of judicial application of rules free from formalism. A second approach, that of legal fact skeptics, reflected the fascination of American society with depth psychology in the twentieth century and saw a lack of appreciation of social and psychological bias, inherent in court procedures, particularly in judges.[3] A third objection, the

[1] Olivier Wendell Holmes, "The Path of the Law," Julius J. Marke, ed., *The Holmes Reader* (Oceana Publications, 1964), pp. 48-49.

[2] Ibid. Perhaps the most famous statement for judicial pragmatism is that of Mr. Justice Benjamin Cardoza in *The Nature of the Judicial Process* (New Haven, Conn.: Yale University Press, 1921), particularly pp. 167-168.

[3] Jerome Frank, *Law and the Modern Mind* (New York: Doubleday, 1963), pp. ixx-xix.

apparent inability of the courts to handle increasingly heavy court calendars and otherwise properly administer the court, remains a principal criticism of the most contemporary of legal critics.

Regarding the first two problem definitions, since at least 1914, federal rules of criminal procedure have been criticized as inadequate and have been extensively amended by the U.S. Supreme Court. The Court chose to reform federal court rules through its own administrative power to supervise federal judiciary procedures in the absence of Congressional legislation and Constitutional interpretation. Evidence obtained by federal officers in violation of the Fourth Amendment was prohibited from being introduced at trial.[4] Even earlier it restricted compelling testimony or evidence in trials, grand jury investigations, and legislative hearings.[5] By 1938, the Court required that indigent federal defendants be provided counsel on request;[6] shortly thereafter, acting within their powers for judicial administration, the Court excluded the admission of confessions in court if the defendant had been detained by the police for an excessive period of time instead of being promptly arraigned.[7]

In a flurry of decisions, beginning in the early 1960s, the Warren Court began to apply existing federal procedural standards and new Constitutional interpretations to the nonuniform and frequently dated criminal procedures of the states. The Court guaranteed defense counsel for all indigent defendants facing possible incarceration[8] and protected their opportunities for appellate review as well;[9] authored the minute details outlining acceptable police procedures for interrogation and obtaining confessions;[10] applied the self-incrimination clause of the Fifth Amendment to the states;[11] attempted to delineate, not always successfully or for all time, the circumstances and requirements for arrest, search and seizure;[12] expanded the right of jury trial;[13] prohibited "invidious discrimination" in jury selection;[14] reasserted due process protections for youngsters before the juvenile court;[15] removed technical barriers that previously had made it difficult for state prisoners to sue collaterally in *habeas corpus* proceedings in federal district

[4] *Weeks* v *United States* 232 U.S. 383 (1914).

[5] *Boyd* v *United States* 116 U.S. 616 (1886); *Counselman* v *Hitchcock* 142 U.S. 547 (1892).

[6] *Johnson* v *Zerbst* 304 U.S. 458 (1938).

[7] *McNabb* v *United States* 318 U.S. 332 (1943); *Mallory* v *United States* 354 U.S. 449 (1957).

[8] *Gideon* v *Wainwright* 372 U.S. 335 (1963); *Argersinger* v *Hamlin* 407 U.S. 25 (1972).

[9] *Griffin* v *Illinois* 351 U.S. 12 (1956); *Burns* v *Ohio* 360 U.S. 252 (1959); *Douglas* v *California* 372 U.S. 353 (1963).

[10] *Miranda* v *Arizona* 384 U.S. 436 (1966); modified in *Harris* v *New York* 401 U.S. 222 (1971).

[11] *Malloy* v *Hogan* 378 U.S. 1 (1964).

[12] *Mapp* v *Ohio* 367 U.S. 643 (1961).

[13] *Duncan* v *Louisiana* 391 U.S. 145 (1968).

[14] *Peters* v *Kiff* 407 U.S. 493 (1972).

[15] *In re Gault* 387 U.S. 1 (1967).

courts;[16] entered the murky waters of capital punishment[17] and negotiated pleas;[18] and, in countless other areas, broadened and strengthened the procedural rights of the criminally accused.

Normally, the Court's Constitutional justification for those wholesale attempts to reform local law enforcement and court procedure was the Fourteenth Amendment's due process clause applied to the first eight amendments to the U.S. Constitution. But the Court did not depend on the majesty of the U.S. Constitution in the abstract. They had a real-life model in the Federal Bureau of Investigation. Many of the Court's decisions merely implemented constitutional guidelines for the states, which were based on procedures under which the FBI had been operating for several decades. This fact would have a considerable bearing on the actual impact of Supreme Court decisions on state law enforcement; the FBI as a model law enforcement agency was not always comparable to urban or rural police departments operating during the 1960s. For example, all FBI agents are highly trained attorneys commonly enforcing only serious felonies. Their discretion is considerably more constrained by close supervision, and agents do not venture out on patrol, as do city police, but work on assignment. An agent's decision to arrest or not to arrest is, of necessity, quite visible to his supervisor. Unlike his state and city police colleagues, errors of procedure or abuse of discretion are more apt to be highly visible, since a high percentage of federally accused individuals will have committed widely publicized crimes or be prominent personalities who will invoke the full panoply of due process. By contrast, local police in the 1960s were most likely high school graduates with little training but with wide discretion. Their primary function was (and is) peace keeping not, as is the case with an FBI agent, high-visibility law enforcement.[19] At least initially, the appellate rules and procedures, mirroring the perceptual world of the attorney, had limited impact on the low-visibility, personalist style of the local police officer.[20]

Nevertheless, the impact of the Supreme Court, particularly of the Warren

[16] *Fay* v *Noia* 372 U.S. 931 (1963).

[17] *Furman* v *Georgia* 408 U.S. 238 (1972).

[18] *McMann* v *Richardson* 397 U.S. 759 (1970); *Santobello* v *New York* 404 U.S. 257 (1971).

[19] Of course, a major responsibility of the FBI under J. Edgar Hoover was in surveillance and intelligence-gathering activities for the Community Party and other groups considered subversive. These activities were surreptitious, but they could hardly be classified traditional law enforcement. What extent of time the FBI spent on surveillance during the Hoover years remains to be documented by scholarship, but journalistic evidence suggests it was excessive. See Nicholas M. Horrock, "The F.B.I.'s Appetite for Very Small Potatoes," *The New York Times,* March 23, 1975, Section 4, p. 1.

[20] For example, Michael S. Wald, et al., "Interrogations in New Haven: The Impact of Miranda," *The Yale Law Review* (1967), 76:1521-1648; Richard J. Medalie, Leonard Zeitz, and Paul Alexander, "Custodial Police Interrogation in Our Nation's Capital: The Attempt to Implement Miranda," *Michigan Law Review* (1968), 66:1347-1422.

Court, has been considerable in nationalizing police conduct and court procedure, and in protecting the rights of the accused—particularly for the indigent defendant. Although there is no way of knowing empirically, requiring the state to provide defense counsel for the accused who cannot afford an attorney has, in all probability, dramatically humanized the system.[21] It is also interesting to speculate on the possibility that the Court's decisions, by reversing or remanding highly publicized convictions, may have been a major catalyst for generating pressure on local political decision makers to support police and attorney training and professionalism, and on Congress to draft a Safe Streets Act to pay the bill. Ironically, the same legislation included an attempt to limit the Court's appellate authority in the area of confessions.[22] On the whole, where police and court personnel have been professionalized and provided higher pay, better and more training, and appropriate supervision, the rules of the appellate court have probably been adhered to with more diligence than elsewhere, although there is no way we can know for sure.

The third traditionally lamented problem area of the criminal courts—sometimes referred to as the law explosion—refers to the consequences of overcrowded courts, delays, assembly-line justice, and excessive plea bargaining, which produce in many minds an insufficient deterrent against crime. Of course, the image of assembly-line justice can be used in the rhetoric of those who argue for due process and civil liberty protection. They argue that assembly-line justice is disadvantageous to the defendant and, in cases where the adversary system is minimized, this may be the case. But on balance, hurried adjudication and crowded dockets are a greater advantage to the defense. Prosecutors may feel pressure to keep the dockets moving and may concede more to the defense in plea negotiations. The other alternative of the prosecutor is to request continuances. But a delay resulting in witnesses losing interest, leaving town, or losing their powers of recollection is hardly a better alternative for the state's attorney. Consequently, some of the most vigorous critics of delay and negotiated pleas are normally found on the side of law enforcement.[23] Such critics are likely to point out the negative effect that court congestion may have on deterrence[24] and will cite evidence that justice-delayed results in higher recidivism.

Yet, it was the American Civil Liberties Union that argued before the New York State Legislature that delay discouraged victims and other witnesses from

[21] *Gideon* v *Wainwright* 372 U.S. 335 (1963).

[22] 18 U.S.C. §3501, as amended, 1968.

[23] For example, see letter to Senator Sam Ervin from Chief Judge Edwin Stanley, *Speedy Trial Hearings before the Subcommittee on Constitutional Rights of the Committee on the Judiciary,* U.S. Senate, First Session on S.895, July 13, 14, 20, September 14, 1971, p. 197.

[24] Testimony of Richard Kleindienst, United States Attorney General, *Preventative Detention,* Hearings before the Subcommittee on Constitutional Rights of the Committee of the Judiciary, U.S. Senate, 91st Congress, Second Session, May 20-22, 27, June 9, 11, 17-19, 1970, p. 73.

testifying and encouraged recidivism as well as violating the rights of the innocent defendant waiting in jail without bond or out of jail with considerable anxiety.[25] At the same time, Justice William Rehnquist, then Assistant U.S. Attorney General, testified against an early version of S.895, arguing that the bill would delay justice, not speed it up. Rehnquist communicated the Nixon Administration's concern that speedy trial requirements, short of additional court resources, would encourage defendants who under normal circumstances would plead guilty to insist on a jury trial and hope for a mandatory dismissal.[26]

The relationships between delay and conviction rates is an empirical question that will concern us later. For now we are interested in the general political questions that are fundamental to both rule reforms and efficiency reforms. How do we, as a political society, allocate legal resources? Who are the beneficiaries or the malefactors of that distribution?

THE ALLOCATION OF LEGAL SERVICES

As would be true for any public policy that depends on professional services, the availability of legal talent at a price acceptable to the public represents a fundamental limitation on court reform. The manner in which lawyers are politically and socially structured limits the degree to which either the rule reform or the efficiency reform can be consummated without sharply redirecting legal resources from lucrative, noncriminal private practices to considerably less lucrative criminal practice.

Moreover, the question is not limited to the personal resources of prospective clients. Criminal courts' budgets, calendars, physical plants, and human resources compete with the civil court calendar and its constituents. There is no certainty that either local publics or criminal justice policy-makers will permit a reallocation of resources from civil law to the criminal law to pay for the legal talent. To a limited extent, local politicians have reluctantly supported public defenders, the professionalization of police, full-time prosecutors, and support services, but frequently only after prodding by the U.S. Supreme Court, accompanied by Safe Streets grants from LEAA. At this time it appears that current federal attempts to limit by statute the permissible maximum period between arrest and trial will provide an additional prod to reallocating resources for the criminal courts.[27] And the trend toward no-fault insurance reform, which should

[25] Allen P. Rubine, "Speedy Trial Schemes and Criminal Justice Delay," *Cornell Law Review* (1972) 57:795.

[26] Testimony of William H. Rehnquist, Assistant U.S. Attorney General, Hearings before the Subcommittee on Constitutional Rights of the Senate Committee on the Judiciary, 92nd Congress, First Session, July 13, 14, 20, September 14, 1971, p. 113.

[27] The Speedy Trial Act of 1974 provides for a maximum of 100 days between arrest and trial of offenders at the end of a staged 5-year implementation process (HR 17409, S. 754).

reduce the competition for resources from the civil calendar with that of the criminal courts, already has some attorneys reassessing the potential of a criminal law practice. But few state legislatures have passed vigorous no-fault legislation. Attorneys continue to dominate the membership of state legislative bodies and are understandably reluctant to reduce a source of income from their own brethren who are trial lawyers.

Even if they were willing, local policy-makers are limited in reallocating resources; the trial and appellate courts possess authority independent of county executives or commissioners who may prepare court budgets for public defenders and prosecutors. Still, locally or state-financed computer information systems or microfilmed files, well-trained police investigators, well-staffed prosecutors, and experienced public defenders can make some difference in the efficacy of the efforts.

Nevertheless, assuming equal levels of due process protection for a 60-day maximum, from apprehension to trial as for a 180-day maximum, without financial support, there may still remain a political trade-off that local politicians must face between financing convictions and financing a reduction of delay.

Of course, with additional resources (judges, courts, etc.), both delay and dismissals may be decreased and, presumably, recidivism decreased. Such a policy would assume a relatively equal value for maintaining present conviction rates, protecting present civil liberty guarantees, and decreasing delay. What additional resources might be necessary and what outcomes on recidivism could be anticipated from alternative policy initiatives are discussed in Chapter 10. But there is little question that providing more refined procedural rules while at the same time reducing delay will require considerably more human and material resources than we have hitherto provided. And this requirement points to a political impasse in a politics of crime. There is a highly probable, although not inevitable, contradiction between the mind-set of the attorney and the mind-set of those interested in administering justice with minimum delay, as well as many systemic problems resulting from the law explosion. *The American Bar Association Project on Minimum Standards for Criminal Justice*[28] is replete with recommendations for expanding procedures *and* additional standards that, if followed in every particular, would increase resource allocations to a politically prohibitive level for local politicians, lead to dramatic increases in delay, or result in disbarment or lesser sanctions of considerable numbers of attorneys who, at the present, engage in practices in which the standards, however vigorously condemned by the ABA, are nevertheless almost universally practiced. A quick review of commonly used techniques by defense and sometimes prosecution to obtain continuances[29] sug-

[28] American Bar Association Project on Standards for Criminal Justice, *The Prosecution Function and the Defense Function,* pp. 11, 71-74.
[29] Ibid., pp. 71-74.

gests that ABA standards, in some instances, point to an ideal, not to reality. DeTocqueville was correct. The ethical and procedural concerns of the attorney have played an enormous role in protecting the rules of civil society. And the life of the law is procedure, as Justice Frankfurter so eloquently reminded us time and time again.

But legal analysis represents a political perspective that assumes the moral-political framework of the criminal law and the primary significance of procedural responsibilities for attorneys. The interests of witnesses, police, victims, and public policy are somewhat lesser concerns in this framework. Systemic problems, such as delay or secondary deviance resulting from criminogenic labeling, are not lawyerlike issues; they require the perspectives of the systems analyst in the former case and of the sociologist in the latter. The training and the incentive system for attorneys are not designed to generate either systems or sociological perspectives. How attorneys are recruited, trained, and rewarded to provide services to the criminal justice system is an important factor in a politics of crime.

RECRUITMENT OF ATTORNEYS

Although the mind-set of an attorney reflects training in law and court rules, most attorneys have little interest in criminal law. The reason is straightforward: with some notable exceptions attorneys who practice criminal law have neigher prestige nor monetary reward. The incentives of the law profession are simply structured to encourage activities other than a criminal law practice, judgeship, investigation, or public prosecution. In the sense that incentives and disincentives in the profession suggest a value-laden distribution of legal services, the social and professional structure within which attorneys move is not conducive to applying legal talent to criminal justice problems. Of course, how value is allocated by the legal system is a political phenomenon.

The structure of legal education is an excellent point of departure for describing the allocation of values in the legal profession. To begin with, law school is very expensive, normally attracting only students who are capable of making an annual educational investment between $3000 and $4000 and who are willing to forfeit any outside income during the 3 years they attend law school. For the most part, law schools do not permit students to engage in part-time employment. The few night law schools that do are still imposing for the student possessing both the baccalaureate and a sizable debt. More frequently, the student who continues on to study law has completed an undergraduate education from a prestigious university, is debt-free, and will join a student body who is as affluent as he or, more rarely, she.

Careers in the law were not always restricted to the wealthy. In fact, law was once an avenue to material success and politics for those of humble origins.[30] In the nineteeth and early twentieth century, most students became "learned in the law" only through apprenticeships or by sporadically attending an itinerant proprietary school, after which they might take a certifying examination. Specialized law schools with entrance requirements and an academic rather than a practicing faculty generally appeared only after 1870, as the increasing complexities of industrial and financial capitalism demanded a higher level of skill and expertise. Still, as late as 1936, fewer than a six states required candidates for the bar exam to hold college or law degrees and, of the 190 law schools in operation, only 94 were approved by the American Bar Association.[31] Prior to today's highly selective, credentializing requirements, many poor but ambitious high school graduates attended law school at night to prepare themselves for the bar and held full-time jobs to support themselves. Today, a few night schools do continue permitting students to earn a living while they attend. But study at night school requires 4 or more years, a considerable sacrifice of income for the law student of limited means.

A significant characteristic of professional education—whether it be teacher education, medicine, or social work—is that it provides a reinforcing ideology for the behavior of the profession. Curriculums at most law school are not uncharacteristic. Young students are trained to profess and practice activities that successful attorneys profess and practice. Law school faculties enjoy high status within the university, with which most schools are affiliated, practicing attorneys dominate the teaching about the law, and the curriculum reinforces the mind-set of future lawyers. The curriculum, the selection of cases, the consequences the professor considers when recommending legal action, and the kinds of legal remedies are influenced by the predisposition of the profession.[32]

The traditional curriculum of law schools reflects the lack of prestige and monetary rewards associated with the criminal law or, generally, legal services to the poor. Contracts, torts, property, and civil practice play a prominent role in the education of first- and second-year students. Tax law and corporate law are also principal courses, while criminal justice-related courses such as Constitutional Law, Criminal Procedure, and Jurisprudence are not treated as part of the essential core. Except in the most prestigious schools, the teaching staff is drawn from large law firms whose business is conducted with clients who are associated with established institutions.

Moreover, the bar exams assure that great attention will be devoted to the civil law by emphasizing questions most suitable to such clients. There are few questions of interest to future prosecutors and criminal trial judges, and little incentive

[30] James Willard Hurst, *The Growth of American Law* (Boston: Little, Brown, 1950), pp. 256-257, 272.
[31] Ibid., p. 272
[32] Henry Jacob, *Urban Justice* (Englewood Cliffs, N.J.: Prentice-Hall, 1973), p. 38.

to study subjects like criminal procedure and jurisprudence, to say nothing about legal and social policy. The student interested in passing the bar cannot afford to ignore the basic curriculum. And passing the bar is not a *pro forma* windup for law school. In the nation as a whole, only about 70 percent of all law students pass the bar the first time so there is little incentive for the intellectually curious.

In the last generation, there has been a great deal more public financial support for career, full-time public defenders and prosecutors, for legal assistance for the poor, and for public-interest law firms. If this support continues, it is conceivable that public law and social policy may receive more attention in law schools in the future. In some law school curriculums such changes have already appeared, but most law schools remain very traditional.

Herbert Jacob has pointed to two biases in legal education that favor the use of legal talent to preserve established institutions and the status quo.

> *Law as a system of relationships has an inherent bias toward stability and predictability. The legal system is a way of stabilizing social relationships to such a degree that people can deal with one another with confidence; they can predict what others will do because their mutual obligations are relatively stable. In addition American lawyers obtain most of their income from business clients. . . . To win financial security, attorneys generally must develop practices which predominately serve the business community. Therefore, to succeed as a lawyer is to be invited to work for a large firm and then to win a partnership in it. These circumstances are reflected in the required courses and in the courses that students elect in law school.*[33]

There is also little question, except for the careers of flambloyant trial attorneys such as Edward Bennett Williams, Melvin Belli, or F. Lee Bailey, that criminal lawyers have the least peer status of all attorneys. Most criminal lawyers do not practice in the criminal courts out of choice. If their civil practice has not developed to an acceptable level, young attorneys make a living until their private practice does develop, if it does, by accepting defense clients referred for their services by police officers, neighborhood acquaintances and, especially, those who sit on the bench.

Of course, status is not synonymous with effectiveness. There is little systematic evidence beyond speculative assumption[34] that high-status attorneys are any more effective in defending a routine case in criminal court than the court house lawyer. Indeed, there is some evidence to the contrary.[35] We have earlier commented on the importance of informal social relationships in negotiations for a

[33] Ibid., p. 39.

[34] William J. Chambliss and Robert B. Seidman, "Prosecution: Law, Order and Power," in *Criminal Justice in America,* pp. 246-251; Blumberg, *Criminal Justice,* p. 19.

[35] See this chapter, pp. 000-000.

plea, manipulating scheduling to enhance the possibility of a dismissal or *nolle,* and "judge hopping" to plead before the judge likely to be most sympathetic with your client. These defense skills require intimate knowledge of local actors, negotiating skills, and a sense of timing, but only a rudimentary knowledge of the law itself. The nationally renowned attorney may be at a disadvantage if he is not socially and professionally in contact with judges and prosecutors. His client may be at a disadvantage as well. National figures may be more interested in a splashy trial and in attendant publicity than would a local lawyer at a time when their client may be better advised to accept a plea. Of course, if a lengthy trial represents the best possible defense, it may be that the defendant would do well to seek a prominent trial lawyer.

Certainly, the financial capacity of a defendant to retain legal assistance for extended periods for investigation and appeals will result in a superior form of legal assistance, particularly in technical and complex areas such as conspiracy, fraud, or tax law. But even in these areas the salient variable is not the status of the attorney, but the financial assets of the defendant.

THE FAMILY ATTORNEY

It has been argued by some critics that the organizational structure of attorneys discriminates against middle-income families.[36] Most legal talent serves the business community, particularly in large metropolitan areas, where commercial opperations are concentrated. Rural areas are sparsely represented by attorneys, and even the poor have the services of public defenders and legal aid. Moreover, family attorneys of the middle class must, of necessity, be generalists, drawing up wills and mortgages, writing liens, researching titles, or defending an occasional client arrested for drunk driving.

Such comparisons must be viewed critically. Obviously business and government institutions in the large cities need attorneys more than the average family, and they are willing to pay handsome retainers. Continuous legal analysis and consultation is a necessary ingredient in managing large-scale organizations where conflicting interests are common. The concentration of legal talent is indispensable where human transactions are complicated or technical, and conflict must be minimized to maintain delicate social arrangements. Labor relations, commercial organization, and government are all such areas where decision making has a wide impact on society. The concentration of attorneys and law firms approximate to labor unions, corporations, and government departments and agencies is not unlike concentrating research and medical services near universities and city hospitals where social services are most needed and population is most concentrated. A disproportionate distribution of attorney services in

[36] Jacob, *Urban Justice,* pp. 40-48.

urban areas compared to rural and suburban legal services is not, in itself, an indication of the manner in which attorneys are organized.

For the politics of crime the critical question is not what sector utilizes the lion's share of legal talent. Instead, the question is, to what extent does the structure of rewards and incentives in the organization of attorneys divert talent, time, and material resources from the criminal justice system, thus preventing the system from achieving its objectives of protecting the innocent, convicting the guilty, keeping the peace, and minimizing victim suffering? Such a question may be raised when the incentives of legal organization become dysfunctional to the objectives of criminal justice. Is the quality of defense correlated with the income of the defendant, his race, or his socio-economic class standing? Is prosecutorial policy linked with political groupings or related to the ratio of case volume to prosecutorial resources, such as salary and the number of assistants? Is the quality of adjudication related to resource limitations in the courts, courtroom space, salaries of judges, or number of judges? Are criminal courts lacking in management and communication capabilities resulting from disincentives structured in the profession of law? And, in my value structure, does the emphasis on legal conceptualizations of crime divert resources from a victim-oriented policy?

It is not my intent to suggest that either the status stratification of legal talent or the geographic concentration of legal services in urban areas represent major variables diverting resources away from resolving the problems of crime. In fact, the social structure of the legal profession and the resource allocations of our legal system and the decision making of attorneys and judges may be topics of limited interest in describing and explaining a politics of crime and criminal justice policy. The more vital areas to examine are probably in the larger political system. And, in this sense, DeTocqueville's effusive comment about the importance of legal talent and judgment quoted at the beginning of this chapter may reflect an earlier age and a lack of appreciation for the attorney as an instrument of vastly larger political forces and groups, each contending for their own interests.[37]

Other interests may have more powerful claims to legal services or other protections that tend to divert resources or aggravate crime problems. No one would argue that the wheels of government and industry should grind to a jarring halt for want of legal uniformity and predictability as a result of legal incompetency—merely to upgrade criminal justice. Yet a crime policy must also compete for funds and talent in the political arena, with other policy claims whose consistency with the public good, to the extent that can be identified, is more vulnerable to impeachment. Sometimes the organized interests or political forces who put forth other claims are extraordinarily powerful. The National Rifle Association's

[37] For criticisms of social science's overemphasis on judges, courts, and attorneys as the shapers of policy, see Richard Hofferbert, *The Study of Public Policy* (New York: Bobbs-Merrill, 1974), pp. 73-74.

rallying role in marshalling opposition to hand-gun restrictions, the National Trial Lawyers' association's skill in drowning no-fault insurance with debilitating amendments in several states, the long and presently losing opposition of the highway lobby against restraints on horsepower, fuel tax, mass transportation, and emission controls—all of these lobby organizations and their objectives are sustained by politically active and skillful constituencies. As a system, however, criminal justice has no clear constituency in support of particular outputs or goals.

No social science of which we are aware, *qua* social science, can reach expert conclusions regarding the public good portion of promiscuous hand-gun ownership, adversary proceedings to determine liability in accident litigation, or high energy consumption and production patterns in the 1950s and 1960s. Such conclusions represent political judgment, not social science. But social science can empirically measure the consequences of all three, within the limits of available data, to the fulfillment of crime policy objectives. It can also describe what is not often described by a narrow, nonpolicy-oriented criminology: the web of political interests aligned against fulfilling crime policy objectives. It also can ask more relevant questions concerning how to fulfill realistic crime objectives, given present social and political realities.

The highway lobby provides a useful illustration of the political limits imposed by the broader dimensions of American politics on reform policy in criminal justice. Since 1958, $180 billion of superhighways enticed a dramatic change in freight and public transportation from trains to trucks, buses, and private automobiles. Originally rationalized as the National Defense Highway Act, ostensibly to transport troops from coast to coast, the legislation sustaining this immense effort provided a 90-percent federal subsidy from a trust fund for states to construct the highway network. Unitl 1974, the legislation has been shielded from serious alteration by a web of special interests touching virtually all areas of American public life. The automotive industry profited from larger cars that were marketed for the high-speed highways, and the growth of the Big Three auto corporations provided some of the highest paid employment, and strong political support, from the ranks of organized labor. The oil corporations benefited from vastly expanded sales, and ancillary industries such as cement and steel profited from the construction of the highway network. Local real estate interests, sometimes with advanced information from local politicians, grew wealthy from speculation on home sites. The travel industry, a miscellany of chain-operated motels, gas stations, and restaurants, mushroomed along exits joining interstate routes. Local legislators enjoyed the gratification of hometown contractors, speculators, suburban home owners, and businessmen, at least those whose businesses were not dislocated by superhighways and whose commercial operations were big enough to benefit from economies of scale that large-volume competition demanded. Smaller firms, inconveniently located for the American motorist, fell victim to the national chains of supermarkets, discount houses, department stores, auto supply firms, restaurants, and motels.

All of this seems far removed from criminal justice problems. Not until one considers the impact of superhighways on burglary and robbery patterns of escape and scope of operations, or the resource expenditure of state police in traffic control and accident response, or the inevitable increase of shoplifting associated with large self-service department stores and supermarkets, unattended except for a battery of cash register clerks, do the political allocations of values become clear. Public policy alternatives theoretically could make dramatic changes: the reduction of speed on the nation's highways during 1974 resulted in far fewer victims[38] and consumed countless fewer police man-hours than in 1973. But American politics, until recently, did not and could not produce such policy on its own. After all, land speculation and government-subsidized mobility have both been in the mainstream of American politics since George Washington's time. There was no significant constituency for any American political leader's commitment to an energy policy. Indeed, there is virtually no constituency today that supports resource conservation if that means taxes, higher prices, or less convenience. Remote sheiks and militant Arab nationalists were to be the unlikely architects of whatever American energy policy we had in 1973 and 1974. Even then, it was not a traffic policy, but an energy policy that, fortuitously, saved lives. Other problems in criminal justice are similarly immune to frontal assault short of a traumatic crisis of national importance. Their resolution, like that of a traffic policy, invariably involves much broader and more powerful interests in our political fabric than those in criminal justice.

RECRUITMENT AND SELECTION OF PROSECUTORS

The crucial actor in the court and in the resolutional system is the prosecutor. With a staff of assistants ranging from none in small jurisdictions to more than 30 full-time assistant district attorneys in large metropolitan systems, the prosecutor routinely dominates decision making in the disposition of all serious criminal cases between the stages of preliminary arraignment and the beginning of trial.

Although the district attorney's office is enormously powerful, it is not lucrative for the experienced, talented attorney. Commonly, prosecutors must tolerate modest incomes, compared to that of successful private attorneys, and they must thrive in emotionally charged, publicly pressured law offices. Many chief prosecutors in middle-level urban (100,000 to 600,000 population) or rural areas are

[38] Statistics from the National Safety Council show that there were 3.6 deaths for every 100 million passenger miles in 1974, a reduction of 16 percent from the 1973 rate. Moreover, as gas became more plentiful in mid-1974, both average speeds and the rate of accident deaths increased. Data supplied in private communication from the National Safety Council.

part-time and maintain a private practice concomitant with their public responsibilities. Their assistants are frequently part-time as well, assuming that there are assistants. For example, in Pennsylvania, as late as 1972, only 11 court districts out of 59 in the state had full-time prosecutors.[39] There are obvious conflicts of interest posed by such arrangements, not the least being the priority which a prosecutor places on building his own practice at the expense of public obligations. Faced with an alternative of devoting time to an affluent widow whose probated inheritance will earn him 10 percent or going to trial on a robbery case instead of accepting a plea to a reduced charge, a part-time prosecutor's commitment to public duty may be seriously tested.

The above illustration is oversimplified. Although there is some evidence that part-time prosecutors neglect their public responsibilities in favor of their private practices, most part-time prosecutors would prefer a full-time position, even at less income than they would make in a private practice. But many jurisdictions do not have the volume of criminal cases to merit a full-time staff. In a sparsely populated county, there may be fewer than five attorneys. However, in states where attorneys are appointed to state jurisdictions and are funded by the state, most of the criminal courts are funded, for the most part, by the county. Officers from moderate-sized counties tend to be fiscally conservative, are close to taxpayers, and are concerned primarily with budgets and tax rates. Although county officials may accept full-time positions, they may also refuse to provide sufficiently attractive salaries. For many years in the Commonwealth of Pennsylvania the salary of full-time, elected district attorneys was set lower than $13,500 for middle-urban counties. The lobby organization for county commissioners, the County Commissioner's Association, was opposed to prosecutors whose salaries were higher than those of each county's troika of three commissioners. It was not until the county commissioners' salaries were raised that the county commissioners relented and supported district attorney salaries mandated by the Pennsylvania legislature.[40]

If remuneration for prosecutors is slight, political rewards and future private advancement provided powerful incentives for the young attorney; the prosecutor's office is frequently a stepping stone to a judgeship or higher elected office. Glick and Vines found that more than half of all state judges have held a post such as state's attorney or district attorney.[41] The 94th Congress had 17 senators

[39] Pennsylvania Governor's Justice Commission, *The Comprehensive Plan for the Improvement of Criminal Justice in Pennsylvania,* p. 43.

[40] This illustration is based on interviews with officers of the County Commissioner's Association and members of the Pennsylvania legislature.

[41] Henry Robert Glick and Kenneth N. Vines, *State Court Systems* (Englewood Cliffs, N.J.: Prentice-Hall, 1973), pp. 49-40. See also Herbert Jacob, "Judicial Insulation—Elections, Direct Participation and Public Attention to the Courts in Wisconsin," *Wisconsin Law Review* (Summer, 1966), p. 811, indicating that more than three quarters of circuit and supreme court judges have held prior public offices.

and 58 members of the House with past experience as prosecutors.[42] And Raymond Moley's survey of members of Congress from 1914 to 1926 and of governors of the states in 1920 and 1924 discovered that 42 percent had been prosecuting attorneys early in their careers.[43]

It is often said that county prosecutors represent the "conscience" of the community, with its insistence on both justice for the innocent and *lex talionis* for the guilty. If conscience of the community means a sensitivity to community values, local prosecutors are appropriately socialized for their role. Unlike the elite members of the bar who, in large cities, work in prestigious firms for commercial clients, prosecutors tend to have local roots extending to family and neighborhood; they attend local, nonprestigious colleges and law schools. As Jacob categorizes many local prosecutors, "law is their profession, but politics is their career."[44] Sensitivity to community conscience values while deciding to prosecute or not prosecute pornography, prostitution, abortion, Sunday sales violations, gambling, and other vice crimes is an indispensible trait for the successful prosecutor, particularly if he is an elected official.[45]

There is lively partisan interest in which party controls a local district attorney's office. Often the election is critical to the party, or at least to its chieftans. In Cook County, Illinois, for instance, the loss of State Attorney Edward Hanrahan, a Democrat supported by Mayor Daley, and the subsequent election of a Republican to the post resulted in indictments against Mayor Delay's chief lieutenants. The irrepressible mayor did manage to maintain the sinews of the Cook County organization, as the primary in the winter of 1975 attested, in spite of the indictments of several persons around him. Cook County encompasses both Democratic Chicago and the Republican suburbs. When the Democrats win, they can use the office as an instrument to attack suburban Republicans.[46] Of course, a city-suburb political split is not a prerequisite to political partisanship in a district attorney's office. The usually Democratic New York or Philadelphia offices, containing no Republican suburb to harass, may nevertheless sit on cases embarrassing to the dominant party, harass the opposite party, or threaten hostile factions within their own party. And the character of partisanship is normally

[42] U.S. Congress, *Official Congressional Directory,* 94th Congress, First Session (Washington, D.C.: U.S. Government Printing Office, 1975), pp. 4-195.

[43] Raymond Moley, *Politics and Criminal Prosecution* (New York: Minton, Balch and Company, 1929), p. 35.

[44] Jacob, *Urban Justice,* p. 59.

[45] Prosecutors are elected by partisan ballot in 44 states. In two states they are appointed by the governor, in two others by the circuit court, and in one (Delaware) the office does not exist. Advisory Commission on Intergovernmental Relations, *State-local Relations in the Criminal Justice System* (Washington, D.C.: U.S. Government Printing Office, 1971), pp. 113-114.

[46] See p. 59, footnote, in Jacob, *Urban Justice.*

negative. Partisan pressures on prosecutors more commonly lead to a reluctance to prosecute friends of the party, not to any eagerness to deliberately harass political opponents.

Recruitment of assistant prosecutors is, however, openly partisan. After each new election for district attorney, most of the openings for assistant district attorneys are commonly treated as patronage by the victorious party. Political rewards may also be distributed in the form of detectives hired by the district attorney's office, although that is less common, particularly if detectives are simply assigned on a part-time basis to the district attorney's office on temporary leave from a police department.

Nevertheless, any image of long lines of eager office seekers, law degrees in hand, would be illusory. Typically, the victorious district attorney's offerings for jobs will be rejected by many attorneys who prefer less demanding and more lucrative law work. Moreover, Jacksonian democracy not withstanding, most urban district attorneys' offices retain, regardless of party, at least one experienced, senior attorney skilled in criminal law, and large urban offices retain several, to maintain administrative continuity, to handle on-going case preparations and appeals, or simply to provide sagacious counsel for newcomers.[47] While the Chief Prosecutor may handle highly publicized cases, make strategic prosecutorial decisions in volatile situations, and meet the press, the career prosecutors perform routine administrative tasks and line up cases for trial or plea.

In spite of the political environment surrounding the prosecutor's office, many young district attorneys are relatively apolitical. Their motivation to accept the assignment may be to tide themselves over financially and gain experience until they can develop their own practice. And the public exposure and news coverage of district attorneys' offices generates helpful publicity to a young lawyer in a profession where advertising is unethical and soliciting clients violates barratry laws. This is particularly true in smaller urban areas where there are few large law firms in which an attorney can be assured a living. Some young attorneys may, indeed, test the political waters, lose, and abandon politics as a consequence. They, too, leave the district attorney's office after a reasonable length of time and concentrate on their private practice.[48] A career prosecutor such as Frank Hogan, chief prosecutor for New York County, is an exception, and few attorneys who serve in the office will follow his example.[49]

[47] Duane P. Nedrud, "The Career Prosecutor," *Journal of Criminal Law, Criminology and Police Science* (1961) 51:343-353.

[48] Jacob, "Judicial Insulation—Elections, Direct Participation and Public Attention to the Courts in Wisconsin," p. 811.

[49] Richard L. Engstrom, "Political Ambitions and the Prosecutorial Office," *Journal of Politics* (1971) 33:190-194; Kan Ori, "The Politicized Nature of the County Prosecutor's Office, Fact or Fancy? The Case of Indiana," *Notre Dame Lawyer* (1965) 40:289-303.

FEDERAL PROSECUTORS

U.S. Attorneys may be partly motivated by a desire for a judgeship or for higher office, by partisanship, or simply by the challenge of an interesting position. It is doubtful that financial reward provides much incentive. In 1974, five federal judges resigned to assume much more lucrative law practice elsewhere, setting a 100-year record for resignations according to Chief Justice Burger. Federal district judges now make $40,000 and may retire on full salary.[50] State trial-level judges average approximately $30,000 per year.[51] Recruitment for U.S. Attorneys is a function of Presidential appointment and patronage. But the degree of flexibility in policy judgments and prosecutorial discretion exercised by the U.S. Attorney is considerably less than that of his local counterpart. Federal prosecutors are subordinates in a legal hierarchy administered by the Department of Justice. Recent judgments concerning whether or not and when to prosecute marihuana possession, organized crime figures, members of the Communist Party, antiwar activists, or draft evaders are likely to depend on centralized policy direction instead of on the intuition of local federal prosecutors.

PROSECUTOR DISCRETION AND CRIME POLICY

As I have previously mentioned, the prosecutor's systemic function is resolutional. In deciding how and if suspects will be prosecuted, the prosecutor must resolve the demands of the police for action with the resources of his office for vigorous investigation, negotiation, and trial. To a lesser extent, prosecutors must resolve the demands of victims for justice with their office resources. Remember that prosecutors are also obliged to follow a more exacting standard, "guilty beyond a reasonable doubt," for obtaining a conviction than the police. Police need only "probable cause" that a suspect committed a crime before making an arrest.

I have also also emphasized what is well documented, that prosecutorial discretion is very broad and the prosecutor's role in deciding whether to dismiss, to accept a guilty plea, or to go to trial is based on considerations far beyond technical questions of guilt or innocence. Prosecutors play a very prominent role at trial as well, but that is precisely why their treatment of each case is much more circumscribed by the presiding judge and the formal rules of procedure. As with the police, the greater the level of visibility, the greater the adherence to the due process model and exterior rules.

[50] Pat Chapin, "The Judicial Vanishing Act," *Judicature* (1974) 58:161.

[51] Ibid., p. 163. This figure is somewhat misleading as trial-level judicial salaries for industrial states such as New York ($50,000) and Pennsylvania ($40,000) are considerably higher than their judicial counterparts in less industrialized states. See ibid., p. 196, Table 2, Judicial Salaries in Appellate and Trial Courts.

Prosecutor discretion not to prosecute has been frequently criticized. Kenneth Culp Davis has argued vigorously against prosecutorial discretion unstructured by court review. "The discretionary power to be lenient is an impossibility without a concomitant discretionary power not to be lenient, and injustice from the discretionary power not to be lenient is especially frequent; the power to be lenient is the power to discriminate."[52]

The fear expressed by Davis concerns what might be called backhanded discrimination inherent in arbitrary nonprosecution. Subjective decisions *not* to charge some individuals who have, in fact, violated the law and for which there is evidence to convict; these decisions may discriminate against those who have violated the same law but who have been vigorously prosecuted.

Similar concern was voiced to me by several trial-level judges commenting on Pennsylvania's Accelerated Rehabilitation Disposition (ARD), a pretrial diversionary program. ARD permits, with the support of the district attorney, the temporary dismissal of charges against a first-time offender. After 2 years, the court record is stricken if the defendant has not committed an additional crime. In practice, ARD is applied for one set of crimes in one court, but for different crimes in another court. Several courts in Pennsylvania automatically apply ARD to driving under the influence, an offense that carries with it a mandatory sentence of one year in jail and a $100 fine. Other courts will not apply ARD to driving under the influence. The variability of one's drinking habits could well determine whether or not the intoxicated driver receives a felony charge accompanied by a year in jail. Worse, ARD may be applied to some defendants but not to others for the same crime, permitting racial or class discrimination. For any or all of these reasons, some judges in the Commonwealth have refused to accept motions for ARD, except under extraordinary circumstances.

On the other hand, the prosecutor's decision *to charge* has been subject to criticism as well, particularly when used to enforce community policies only peripherally and technically related to crime. For example, district attorneys, using their power of arrest, may utilize the seldom-invoked charge of fornication or bastardy against individuals who are reluctant to provide timely child support payments. Francis Allen provides a bitter example in an Eastern state where mothers of illegitimate children had been convicted and incarcerated for fornication, because it was cheaper to support mother and child in a reformatory than it was to maintain the family on the county welfare rolls.

> *Having been guided through the main structure of the institution—a rambling wooden building of Victorian vintage—I approached a rather modern brick establishment, located some distance away. As I entered the door, I suddenly discovered that I was standing in a nursery. On both sides of the room were rows*

[52]Davis, *Discretionary Justice*, p. 170.

of cribs, each crib occupied by an infant of an age ranging from three to eighteen months. These were children of women prisoners, born while their mothers were in penal custody. In almost every case the mothers were unwed and had been sentenced to the reformatory following conviction for some offense relating to extra-marital sexual relations. As I began to react to this spectacle, I was led to the obvious inquiry: Why are there so few infants here? Surely, these babies represent only the smallest fraction of the total number of illegitimate children born each year in this populous state. The answer to this question is significant and characteristic. These were unwed mothers without the financial resources to pay for the medical expenses of childbirth or the subsequent care of their offspring. True enough, the state had made funds available to local public agencies for the care of such mothers and their children. But these funds were not fully compensatory. Accordingly, some localities soon discovered that it was cheaper, when measured by immediate budgetary considerations, to proceed criminally against such women, thereby shifting the full burden of their provision and care from the locality to the state.[53]

PROSECUTOR DISCRETION AND THE YOUTHFUL OFFENDER

The law itself can encourage discrimination in prosecutorial decisions to charge or not. An ironic case is provided by our studies of the New York State Youthful Offender (Y.O.) Statute. Under the New York Y.O. Statute,[54] a Y.O. charge may be substituted for a criminal charge if the accused has not been previously convicted of a felony, is between the ages of 16 and 19 years, and is not charged with a capital crime. The intent of the statute is to erase any criminal record that would stigmatize a youngster after his return to civil society. Accordingly, upon court direction that a Y.O. will be so treated, the indictment is sealed, and all public scrutiny is prohibited. The State Department of Correction receives information on the offender, acquired at the time of arrest, but no other information centers are informed. The actual sentence is determined by felony standards, although the receiving institutions for youthful offenders are not general penal institutions that house adult offenders.

The absence of a criminal record for youthful offenders does fulfill its purpose, protecting youngsters from criminal stigma and job discrimination.[55] A Y.O. conviction for motor vehicle violation may not be recorded on a license or appear

[53]Francis A. Allen, *The Borderland of Criminal Justice* (Chicago: The University of Chicago Press, 1964), pp. 5-6.

[54]*McKinney's Code of Criminal Procedure,* §913-e to 913-r, as amended (1968).

[55]Op. Att'y Gen. 125 second case, cited in *McKinney's Code of Criminal Procedure,* §913-o, as amended.

on an accident report.[56] A Y.O. record may not be used to deny an applicant public or private employment, even in police work. Four dispositions are provided in the *Code of Criminal Procedure* for Y.O.s: (1) a sentence of probation; (2) a sentence of conditional discharge; (3) a sentence of unconditional discharge; and (4) a reformatory or an alternative local reformatory sentence of imprisonment. To determine the period of the sentence, the criteria to be used, the conditions to be imposed, the manner of revocation, the place of commitment and other such incidents of sentence, the sentences provided are governed by the provisions that would be applicable in the case of a felony.[57]

The privacy of Y.O. records appears to be a serious concern among the police, personnel of the court, and members of the bench whom I interviewed. There is, however, continuous inquiry into the records of youngsters from insurance companies, credit institutions, prospective employers, and especially the armed forces. However, several people interviewed believed the statute "vague" regarding the release of information. In one instance a district attorney revealed to an army officer the "general information" that a youthful offender had a "questionable record." The official did not believe he was violating the law in doing so.

The low visibility of Y.O. records, many of which involve serious crimes, especially increases the discretionary power of the prosecutor. A determination to invoke the Y.O. charge is up to the discretion of the court, but it usually follows a recommendation by the prosecutor and an investigation of eligibility by probation. Whether such discretionary power is exercised to influence a disposition based on the same criteria for factual investigation and due process used in adult cases was a major question that this study sought to answer by comparing the dispositions of stratified samples for Y.O.s and non-Y.S.s (Table 6.1). The study demonstrated that the protection that Y.O. status provides against stigmatized records may have its price. Y.O. defendants fared decidedly poorer than non-Y.O. defendants in both the adjudication process and at sentencing.[58]

Yet prosecutor discretion, properly structured, is an indispensibly flexible tool for both the administration of justice and public policy. The American Bar Association (ABA) has attempted to provide standards for the prosecutor's decision to charge to prevent abuses.

a. It is unprofessional conduct for a prosecutor to institute or cause to be in-

[56] *Cuccio* v *Department of Personnel-Civil Service Commission* 243 N.Y.S. 2d 220 (1963); *New York City Transit Authority* 4 167 N.Y.S. 2d 715 (1957). Affirmed 7 N.Y. 2d 194 N.Y.S. 2d 39 (1957).
[57] *McKinney's Code of Criminal Procedure,* §913-m, as amended, (1967). A new amendment, effective September 1, 1969, altered this disposition to allow sentences that correspond to the actual criminal sanction of the offense. This did not affect the study, since the data reflect only the older provision.
[58] Rhodes, *Discretion, Diminished Responsibility and Due Process,* pp. 156-163. For a noncomparative study of Youthful Offenders in New York State see Blumberg, *Criminal Justice,* pp. 172-176.

Table 6.1 Youthful offender and nonyouthful offender outcomes.

	Y.O. (%)	Non-Y.O. (%)
Percent of change[a] in mean seriousness of charge from original police complaint to final prosecutor charge prior to plea or trial	111 (N = 21)	73.2 (N = 29)
Percent pleading not guilty after indictment	0	24
Percent dismissed or acquitted	0	24

[a]Calculated as average incarceration possible for each crime type according to statutory minimum-maximum.

stituted criminal charges when he knows that the charges are not supported by probable cause.

b. The prosecutor is not obliged to present all charges which the evidence might support. The prosecutor may in some circumstances and for good cause consistent with the public interest decline to prosecute, notwithstanding that evidence may exist which would support a conviction. Illustrative of the factors which the prosecutor may properly consider in exercising his discretion are:

- **i.** the prosecutor's doubt that the accused is in fact guilty;
- **ii.** the extent of the harm caused by the offense;
- **iii.** the disproportion of the authorized punishment in relation to the particular offense or the offender;
- **iv.** possible improper motives of a complainant;
- **v.** reluctance of the victim to testify;
- **vi.** cooperation of the accused in the apprehension or conviction of others;
- **vii.** availability and likelihood of prosecution by another jurisdiction.

c. In making the decision to prosecute, the prosecutor should give no weight to the personal or political advantages or disadvantages which might be involved or to a desire to enhance his record of convictions.

d. In cases which involve a serious threat to the community, the prosecutor should not be deterred from prosecution by the fact that in his jurisdiction juries have tended to acquit persons accused of the particular kind of criminal act in question.

e. The prosecutor should not bring or seek charges greater in number or degree than he can reasonably support with evidence at trial.[59]

Formal standards and appellate court rulings can provide guides for prosecutor discretion and minimize arbitrary abuse of power. But many factors influence the decision to charge or not that do not follow the logic of positive law, but are closely related to social policy. Both judges and prosecutors frequently view present statutory punishment for nonviolent crimes as excessive and, for humanitarian reasons, they may reduce or dismiss charges. This intervention is not limited to prosecutors and judges. Ample opportunities for reduction or elimination of the length of a sentence, or even the sentence itself, exist after sentence has been passed. These decisions may be made by parole authorities, correctional program directors, or judges, depending on state law and procedure. Charge reductions may also be made by a prosecutor in return for information or testimony. Or certain "crimes" may be acceptable, even welcomed, by the community that the prosecutor represents. Finally, the number of crimes committed, the resources to deal with each crime, and the relative seriousness of each offense demand that the urban prosecutor establish priorities. Which cases will be vigorously prosecuted on the original charge, even if this requires, as it often does, going to trial? Which cases will be bargained for a plea to a lesser charge? Which cases will be dismissed?

ADMINISTRATIVE PROCESS AND THE GUILTY PLEA

It is stated in the scholarly literature of criminal justice with regularity that our legal system would be unable to operate without the frequent use of guilty pleas as an alternative to trial. In practice, guilty pleas account for roughly 90 percent of all convictions,[60] saving a considerable amount of time and money. But the frequency and low visibility of guilty pleas raise important questions for a politics of crime. To the extent that courts seek to supervise the behavior of police in areas such as search and seizure, eavesdropping, and confession, does the guilty plea function to insulate patterned operations of police and court officials that contravene due process? What are the behavioral patterns involved in guilty pleas and

[59] American Bar Association, *Standards for Criminal Justice Relating to the Prosecution and Defense Functions,* American Bar Association 1971. The ABA Standards are printed in 18 volumes. Price is $3.25 for a single volume; bulk order prices are $2.50 each for 10-24 copies of the same title, and $2 each for 25 or more copies of the same title. They may be ordered from ABA Circulation Department., 1155 E. 60th Street, Chicago, IL 60637.

[60] Donald J. Newman, *Conviction: The Determination of Guilt or Innocence without Trial* (Boston: Little, Brown, 1966), p. 8.

what are their sociological roots? Furthermore, what are the variables influencing a plea of guilty? Are they reliable, and would they be countenanced, if known, at the appellate level?

Blumberg found that the police are not responsible for a large number of confessions and guilty pleas. His study concludes that the defense counsel is the most reliable source; pressure from police accounts for only 5.94 percent of all confessions prior to indictments[61] and, by implication, such pressure tends to minimize the impact of the *Miranda* warning on guilty plea rates.[62]

The assumption that conviction rates would be drastically reduced if persons in custody are told of their constitutional rights to remain silent and to consult with an attorney was widely held by police administrators and by the Republican candidate for President in 1968, Richard Nixon. The policy controversy has not fully abated. The consequence of the *Miranda* warning has probably received more attention from scholars interested in impact analysis of court decisions that any other public issue. And the Constitutional debate remains lively, with the Burger Court incrementally shrinking the broad parameters of the earlier Warren decisions in *Escobedo* and *Miranda.*[63]

The assumption linking falling conviction rates with *Miranda* has been challenged by a report compiled by Chief of Detectives Vincent W. Piersante of the Detroit Police Department. Comparing conviction rates and confessions before *Escobedo* v *Illinois* with those after the implementation of the decision, the report concluded that the number of confessions had not significantly dropped while the conviction rate had remained constant.[64] Contrary hard evidence is revealed by a large Pittsburgh study,[65] reporting that the percentage of cases with confessions dropped from 54.4 percent to 37.5 percent after the *Miranda* ruling. As Seeburger and Wettick point out, the primary benefit from obtaining confessions from all participants in the crime is to avoid the hearsay rule that excludes the use of one defendant's confession against the other defendants. However, a defendant who

[61]Blumberg, "The Practice of Law as a Confidence Game," p. 33.

[62]The *Miranda* warning requires that a police officer warn a defendant "in clear and unequivocal terms" prior to interrogation that he has a right to remain silent, that anything he says "can and will" be used against him in a court of law, that he has a right to counsel prior to questioning and during interrogation; that if he cannot afford an attorney, one will be appointed for him prior to questioning, if the defendant so desires. *Miranda* v *Arizona* 348 U.S. 436 (1966) 1602.

[63]*Schneckloth* v *Bustamonte* 412 U.S. 218 (1973), sustained the consent of a person not in custody to a search of his automobile, even though the police had not informed him of his right to withhold consent; *Harris* v *New York* 401 U.S. 222 (1971) permitted a defendant's statements obtained in violation of the *Miranda* warning to be used to attack his credibility on the witness stand, if the original statements were not coerced or involuntarily given.

[64]Theodore Souris, "Stop and Frisk or Arrest and Search—The Use and Misuse of Euphemisms," in *The Impact of Supreme Court Decisions,* ed. Theodore L. Becker (New York: Oxford University Press, 1969), pp. 176-180.

[65]Richard H. Seeburger and R. Stanley Wettick, Jr., "Miranda in Pittsburgh—A Statistical Study," The University of Pittsburg Law Review (1967), 29: 2-12.

confesses and who will probably be convicted partly on the basis of his confession will normally find it advantageous to cooperate by testifying against the other defendants. Since the drop in confessions is partly due to the presence of defense counsel at initial police interrogation, Seeburger and Wettick's statistical study appears to challenge Blumberg's previously cited research based on sifted interview data, that criminal defense is a "confidence game" that mitigates against *Miranda* and *Escobedo,*[66] and that police influence was minimal in obtaining confessions and, thereby, encouraging pleas. Certainly we are in accord with his conclusions concerning the customarily cooperative role of the defense counsel as opposed to the existence of a vigorous, consistently adversarial relationship. Probably *Miranda* has reduced confessions. However, confessions must be corroborated. Any drop in confessions may occur from a pool of weak cases, minus corroborating evidence. The case for or against *Miranda* from a police and prosecutor's point of view remains to be demonstrated.

However much influence police have on confessions, they can and do assert influence with the prosecution to increase or decrease criminal sanctions. The kind of demand the policeman makes on the prosecution seems to depend on the historic relationship he has with a particular type of defendant. A speeding offense, for example, is applied differently to a member of an arrogant motorcycle gang than to a neighborhood youngster. Prostitutes who "scream and kick" when routinely picked up may be informally sanctioned for their uncooperative attitude. City health ordinances have been conveniently used as a sanction against unruly behavior, allowing a health officer to detain uncooperative prostitutes for 8 days, ostensibly for a V.D. check[67] but, in effect, denying the girls a week's income.

DEFENSE-PROSECUTION ROLES

Data tend to demonstrate the important role defending attorneys play in streamlining the production of criminal justice.[68] Although theoretically cast as adversaries in front of a neutral judge, the defense lawyer usually plays a cooperative role to keep the court calendar moving. As previously mentioned, the relationship between most defense attorneys and their clients has been described by Blumberg as a "confidence game."[69] The defense lawyer chooses strategies that will lead to working out a plea of guilty, assuring a fee, and yet maintaining his status as the defendant's agent in the eyes of the client. Skolnick's participatory observation research tends to support this view, although his conclusions do not imply,

[66] Blumberg, "The Practice of Law as a Confidence Game," pp. 16-17.
[67] Skolnick, *Justice without Trial,* pp. 107-108.
[68] Skolnick, "Social Control in the Adversary System," pp. 52-70.
[69] Blumberg, "The Practice of Law as a Confidence Game," pp. 20-21.

as do Blumberg's, that a cooperative role as opposed to a vigorous, consistently adversarial relationship necessarily means that effective defense is not provided. Skolnick describes the competent defense attorney as a "coach" who advises his client on the attitudes and behaviors necessary to get by in the legal system.[70] His major task is to gain the confidence and cooperation of the client. His skill as a coach depends on his own understanding of the interests of other functionaries (police, prosecution, judge) in the system and his capacity to fulfill those needs. But both the number of cases he represents and the working relationship he has with prosecutors and judges may make him all the more effective in defending his client, once the client has convinced the public defender of his innocence.

What are the interests of the other functionaries concerning the administration of criminal justice? Both the judge and prosecution must weigh administrative responsibility for keeping the calendar moving against the needs of "justice" and the pressures of public opinion. In some high-volume courts, pressure from the calendar is so great that one prosecuting attorney is in charge of tactical decisions concerning which cases to try. Reasonable guilty pleas are not often turned down, and back-up cases are always ready for trial in the event another case is dismissed by a guilty plea. The most popular cases for back-up are often those involving narcotic charges and assault. Apparently, this is because the witnesses are almost always police officers who can reliably be kept waiting to testify.[71]

Vilhelm Aubert has written that law has two basic and intimately connected tasks: to solve conflicts and to foster conformity to legal rules.[72] Certainly conflict is avoided wherever possible in relations between prosecutor and defense attorney in most cases. The prosecuting attorney wants a "good record of convictions," and the defense attorney is also concerned with his status as a competent lawyer. The prosecutor is equally concerned with his credibility in convicting those who are indicted, since victory eases the next job of convincing defendants to plead guilty. When the prosecutor achieves a quasimagisterial acceptance, he enjoys the countervailing advantage of a presumption of administrative regularity. Any conflict between defense and prosecution at the trial level endangers all of these interests. Consequently, whenever possible, conflict is restricted to secretive plea bargaining.[73]

In his book *Justice in Moscow,* George Feifer defines the Soviet trial as "an appeal from a pre-trial investigation . . . the closer the investigation resembles the finished script, the better."[74] Although it would be inaccurate to compare

[70] Skolnick, "Social Control in the Adversary System," p. 54.

[71] Ibid.

[72] Vilhelm Aubert, "Courts and Conflict Resolution," *Journal of Conflict Resolution* (1967) 11:40.

[73] Skolnick, "Social Control in the Adversary System," pp. 60-70.

[74] George Feifer, *Justice in Moscow* (New York: Simon and Schuster, 1964), p. 86. Feifer qualifies his comment considerably.

Soviet justice with the American legal system, there are striking similarities if one removes the formality and rhetoric. Certainly the theoretical formulations of how the adversary system should operate, articulated in *American Bar Standards,* do not always correspond to the realities of the criminal court. Any understanding of prosecutor behavior must include the social and organizational relationship among defense counselors, judges, and prosecutors that minimizes the operations of the adversary system.

As previously discussed, the prosecutor must also respond to systemic variables, such as heavy caseloads and limited prosecutorial resources.[75] One of the ways that heavy caseloads can be handled is by negotiating a plea to avoid trial. Systemic pressures on a prosecutor for negotiating a plea will frequently stretch the boundaries of formal standards. For example, a promise of sentence leniency by the prosecutor in return for a plea, although overtly not acceptable in several jurisdictions, is *de facto* permitted by the abundance of sentencing options available to the judge and by standards cues provided by the prosecutor in his sentence recommendations. Newman's study of sentencing concluded that "There is little doubt that, where possible, judges in all three states tend to show greater leniency in sentencing to the defendant who pleads guilty than to the defendant who demands a jury trial."[76] Apparent respect for the defense in front of his client on the part of courtroom personnel also enhances the defending attorney's powers of persuasion. That the attorney's actual relationship with his client is often less important than his relationship with the court may be suggested by the practice of judges postponing the case of an unbonded accused awaiting a plea for the purpose of encouraging payment for the attorney's fee.[77]

THE QUALITY OF PRIVATE AND PUBLIC DEFENSE

A defense attorney, particularly a public defender, has conflicting loyalties between court administrative processes and his client's anticipation of a vigorous defense. But it does not follow that this conflict, in itself, decreases his effectiveness in protecting the interests of his clients. In fact, his position in the court process may enhance his effectiveness. While it may be true that a public defender is more apt to plead his clients guilty than are retained counselors, this is probably explained by the fact that a public defender's client is either a repeated offender or an obvious offender. High-visibility crimes seem to be a functional aspect of poverty, and the public defender represents indigent clients exclusively. The

[75] See pp. 103-111 above.

[76] Newman, *Conviction,* pp. 60-62.

[77] Blumberg, "The Practice of Law as a Confidence Game," p. 30. The practice appears widespread as confirmed by my conversations with private attorneys as well.

professional offender is more discrete and usually has a private counsel.[78] It is also true, as Table 6.2 illustrates, that a public defender's client is more apt to be convicted and is less apt to go to trial or to be acquitted if he does. Again, these tendencies appear to reflect the character of the clients, not the abilities of the public defender. Skolnick[79] categorizes four general types of defense attorneys: (1) those inexperienced with criminal cases; (2) those hostile to the prosecuting attorney's office; (3) those private lawyers who are experienced and cooperative; and (4) public defenders. Concerning the second category of lawyers, Skolnick comments that they may provide a good defense for the innocent, but they do not represent their other clients adequately. This is because they tend to go to trial instead of engaging in skillful plea bargaining. Consequently, they either "win big" (acquittal) or "lose big" (receive a long sentence). Nor is the private lawyer's interest in going to trial symptomatic of his interest in a client. He may have a financial interest in going to trial unless there is a set fee for his services beforehand.

The inexperienced lawyer also tends to be distrustful of collaboration with the police and prosecutor's office and is, therefore, more willing to go to trial. He also does not have the rapport with court personnel that experienced criminal lawyers and public defenders have. His unpredictable behavior may appear contentious and uncooperative to the district attorney, who is more likely to press maximum penalties in retaliation.

Contrary to popular opinion, the public defender may be in a better position to defend a client he considers innocent than a private attorney. The public defender's comparatively modest talent is balanced by the large number of cases committed to his charge and by his personal relations with the prosecution. The prosecution recognizes the potential harm that a public defender can cause by insisting on jury trials for many of his clients, and this awareness is a vital factor in negotiated pleas. Moreover, he usually recognizes that public defenders do not press a defense hard unless they feel justified. For these reasons a defender who is well known may have more persuasive powers in bargaining than an "outside" attorney, counterbalancing his lack of legal experience and technical competence.

Popular clichés notwithstanding, the preponderance of research suggests that with some exceptions the public defender is nearly as effective as the private attorney under normal circumstances when socio-economic variables, crime type,

[78] By professional offender I refer to larceny and burglary conducted by highly skilled individuals whose profits are high and who view arrest and imprisonment as a "cost factor" in a business; or, members of organized crime, who are likely to have attorneys on retainer or at least selected prior to an arrest.

[79] Skolnick, "Social Control in the Adversary System," pp. 52-70.

Table 6.2 Comparative success rates for defense counsel[a]

	Los Angeles, 1968[b]	
	P/D (%)	R/C (%)
Guilty plea	(11,020) 77	(7,679) 72
Dismissal—*nolle*	(1,728) 12	(1,820) 17
Acquittal (trial)	(371) 3	(376) 4
Conviction (trial)	(1,185) 8	(819) 8
Total	(14,304)	(10,694)

	Commonwealth of Pennsylvania, 1972[c]	
	P/D (%)	R/C (%)
Guilty plea	(9,514) 44	(8,492) 36
Dismissal—*nolle*[d]	(5,045) 23	(6,130) 26
Acquittal (trial)	(2,341) 11	(4,247) 18
Conviction (trial)	(4,589) 21	(4,716) 20
Total	(21,489)	(23,585)

[a] The categories used in all of the research in this table were collapsed in some cases to eliminate unnecessary confusion. P/O refers to Public Defense; R/C refers to Privately Retained Counsel.
[b] *Source:* Gerald W. Smith, *A Statistical Analysis of Public Defender Activities,* National Technical Information Service, U.S. Department of Commerce, 1970, p. 56.
[c] *Source: Pennsylvania Criminal Court Dispositions, 1972,* Pennsylvania Department of Justice, Bureau of Criminal Justice Statistics, Harrisburg, 1973, p. 39.
[d] Includes other no-penalty dispositions.

and past records of clients are held constant.[80] Moreover, this is true at both plea bargaining and trial stages and for full-time public defenders and part-time public defenders.[81] A Denver study argues persuasively that the crucial variable between privately retained counsel (R/C) and public defender (P/D) dispositions

[80] Jean G. Taylor et al., "An Analysis of Defense Counsel in the Processing of Felony Defendants in Denver, Colorado," *Denver Law Journal* 50:43; Gerald W. Smith, *A Statistical Analysis of Public Defender Activities,* U.S. Department of Justice, Law Enforcement Assistance Administration, Washington, D.C., National Technical Information Service, Grant No. NI-081, p. 81.
[81] Robert P. Rhodes, *A Comparison of Effectiveness for Privately Retained Counsel and Public Defender, Erie County Court of Common Pleas,* Pennsylvania Governor's Justice Commission, November 1974.

is that the former are more often employed and considered good bail risks.[82] Indigent clients who are frequently unemployed and who have unstable family relationships are more apt to be denied bail or qualify for release on their own recognizance; their indigency makes it difficult for them to raise bail money. At the same time, there is general recognition that unreleased defendants are most likely to be convicted (Table 6.3).

Table 6.3 Acquittal rates for released and unreleased defendants while case pending (in percent)[a]

Custodial Status	Acquitted	Convicted
Released	19.4	80.6
Unreleased	10.1	89.9

[a]Sample of 2617 theft defendants in 1970 countywide felony defendant file.
Source. Rand Corporation, Prosecution of Adult Felony Defendants in Los Angeles County, March 1973, p. 50. Reprinted by permission of the publisher, from *Prosecution of Adult Felony Defendants: A Policy Perspective,* by Peter Greenwood, et al. (Lexington, Mass.; Lexington Books, D.C. Heath and Company, 1976).

The picture remains confused. The Rand study[83] of the Los Angeles District Attorney's Office partially discounts the relationship between high conviction rates, unreleased defendants, and public defenders.[84] Moreover, there is a burning question between civil libertarians and students of criminal justice as to whether or not the variables of unemployment and family stability are more strongly associated with probable guilt than nonrelease and an inability to defend properly against the contentions of the state. The Rand study found that released defendants whose cases were not vigorously defended (either plead guilty early or their defense rested on evidence at the preliminary hearing) fared no better than defendants who were not released. But those whose defense was vigorously pursued and were out on bail or released on their own recognizance fared decidedly better than those whose defense was equally vigorous but who were in jail.[85]

There are several reasons beyond social risk variables, which may explain the

[82]Taylor et al., "An Analysis of Defense Counsel," pp. 42-43.
[83]Greenwood et al., *Prosecution of Adult Felony Defendants in Los Angeles County: A Policy Perspective,* pp. 50-51.
[84]Ibid., p. 50.
[85]Ibid., p. 51.

success of freed defendants contrasted to the lack of success for detainees. Frequently, routine defendants find they much convince their own attorneys of their innocence before they face the court. The overwhelming number of defendants are, in fact, guilty. A defense attorney assumes that, and knows that going out of one's way, seeking witnesses and other evidence to build an exculpatory case for a client who is lying, does not represent a rational portioning of one's resources. However, if the defendant can convince witnesses to come forward with supporting evidence or with character testimony, or even encourage a more articulate relative to provide insight into what really happened, his day in court may be materially brighter. I remember a case in Washington, D.C., where an officer with a lacerated scalp charged that he was assaulted with a lethal weapon. Witnesses rooted out by the defendant testified that the "weapon" was a friendly snowball aimed elsewhere with an unintended jagged piece of ice. The case was dropped.

Prepared with additional facts, the defense attorney has both moral incentive and material assistance to build a viable defense and to go to trial if the disposition is not satisfactory. Moreover, the defendant who is out on bail tends to benefit from a greater delay period between the time of arrest and final disposition, a hiatus that can be used to keep out of trouble in order to convince the judge at the delayed hearing that he *can* keep his nose clean and maintain good, honest work. Of course, the incarcerated defendant does not have this opportunity.

Certainly a qualifier is in order regarding the optimistic conclusion I have reached regarding public defenders. No doubt there are numerous jurisdictions where public defender services are decidedly inferior, although I cannot document such an assertion. One could fairly conjecture that public defender services were inadequate in the past and existed not at all in many states prior to *Gideon* v *Wainwright.*[86] The same could be said of prosecutors in recent history. Perhaps prosecutor and public defender services improved only in the 1960s and 1970s, possibly as a result of massive LEAA spending or perhaps because of public and Bar Association attention. We may never know.

There is little question, however, that the public defender's office has assumed additional responsibilities which it was not obliged to meet in the past. The U. S. Supreme Court has insisted on a greater dimension of formal participation for defense counsel in juvenile and adult courts.[87] The public defender's office is

[86] *Gideon* v *Wainwright* 372 U.S. 335 (1963).

[87] *Gideon* v *Wainwright,* 372 U.S. 335 (1963), *Gideon* was expanded in *Argersinger* v *Hamlin,* 407 U.S. 25 (1972), to include the right of counsel for any person who may be imprisoned, absent an intelligent waiver; *Coleman* v *Alabama,* 399 U.S. 1 (1970) provided the right of the indigent accused to appointed counsel at preliminary hearings; *Miranda* v *Arizona,* 384 U.S. 436 (1966), among other things the inadmissibility of confessions where the defense counsel was absent during custodial questioning and required that the defendant must be appraised of his immediate right to counsel. *In re Gault,* 387 U.S. 1 (1967), held that a defendant in juvenile court has a right among other things to counsel at hearings and trial.

responsible for the bulk of cases in which a defense attorney is necessary, approximately 60 percent of all such cases nationally, [88] and it is the public defender's resources that are most heavily taxed by the new procedural resources of the court.

The pattern of caseloads handled by one metropolitan public defender's office confirms the multiplication of functions performed by the modern public defender. The type of adult criminal case that makes up the data for this study[89] represents only 57 percent of the entire public defender caseload. The remainder of the caseload was divided between juvenile hearings (23 percent), juvenile detention hearings (7 percent), mental health hearings (5 percent), and parole hearings (5 percent).

The National Advisory Commission on Criminal Justice Standards and Goals (1973) has recommended full-time and adequately compensated public defenders.

> *Many public defenders at present serve their office only part time and maintain an outside private law practice. This creates many problems. The attorney who serves as a part-time defender is compensated according to law at a fixed rate for his services. The total income of a part-time public defender, therefore, largely is determined by what he can earn in private practice.*
>
> *There is a significant danger that the defender will devote less energy to his public office. There is also a potential conflict of interest in such situations. As a public officer the defender must maintain formal relationships with the various law enforcement officials with whom he deals lest he compromise, in the eyes of the community, the office of public defender. At the same time, he must maintain informal relationships with those same officials as attorney for his private clients. This puts the part-time public defender in an awkward position. Often a part-time defender is justified when the caseload in the jurisdiction is not sufficient to warrant a full-time defender office. Where this is the situation, defender services should be regionalized so as to create an office with a large enough caseload to justify a full-time defender. The financial rewards of private law practice can be large. In order to attract qualified people, public office should hold reasonable financial rewards as well. Where defenders devote their full energies and resources to their office they should receive adequate compensation. The public defender is an important component of the criminal justice system, comparable to the prosecutor and the chief judge of the highest trial court of the jurisdiction. For purposes of salary, therefore, he should be treated in a similar manner.*[90]

[88] National Advisory Commission on Criminal Justice Standards and Goals, *Courts* (Washington, D.C.: U.S. Department of Justice, 1973), p. 267.

[89] Rhodes, *A Comparison of Effectiveness for Privately Retained Counsel and Public Defender.*

[90] National Advisory Commission, *Task Force Reports: The Courts,* p. 267.

Professional associations have joined with Standards and Goals in urging that public defenders assume even greater burdens. Moreover, additional responsibilities have been mandated by states.[91] Public defenders may be expected to represent indigent defenders on appeal, in collateral attack proceedings, in circumstances involving penitentiary disciplinary proceedings, and in parole revocation hearings. Moreover, their caseload has sharply increased in adult criminal court, juvenile court, and mental health hearings in which they have been obliged by law to represent the indigent. Obviously, these additional responsibilities may dilute the quality of defense of the public defender, if additional resources are not allocated to his office.

In conclusion, attorneys represent a critical elite in the criminal justice system. They see their function as preserving the rules of procedure and the decorum of civility. On the whole, they have performed that function well. Yet their professional training and recruitment patterns, incentives, and sanctions encouraged a mind-set not always prepared to raise questions of policy that go beyond professional standards and traditional procedures, or the "given" of criminal law as substantively nonpolitical. Training in the law is particularly irrelevant to public policy, although the political socialization that many attorneys receive is very helpful to sort out the feasibility of implementing a particular policy. Finally, training or professionalism may have limited impact on improving criminal justice, but often the self-interests of attorneys do not correspond to measures designed to reduce delay time or reallocate resources from commercial and governmental legal careers to a career in the criminal law.

[91] American Bar Association Project on Standards for Criminal Justice, *Standards relating to Providing Defense Services* (Chicago: American Bar Association, 1967); Commissioners on Uniform State Laws, "Model Public Defender Act," *Handbook of the National Conference on Uniform State Laws* (Baltimore: Port City Press, 1970). See also *Purdons* 16 §9960.1-9960.8 for examples of additional statutory requirements in the Commonwealth of Pennsylvania.

7

COURTS AND JUDGES

Until recently, legal scholars and social scientists have devoted most of their attention to judicial behavior, assigning to appellate courts, especially the U.S. Supreme Court, the preponderance of attention of rigorous, empirical research and traditional legal analysis. The weight of attention accorded the appellate courts, reflected in journals and college texts and curriculums, often encouraged without intending to the myth that upper courts are the focus for the crucial decisions in the criminal justice process. Lower courts of the first instance and trial-level courts received short shrift. Important as appellate courts are in establishing rules for the criminal justice process, they receive no more than a small fraction of cases that are appealed. Even courts of general jurisdiction handle generally no more than 10 percent of all convictions by trial.[1]

More recent research has examined court proceedings prior to trial, particularly its routines for decision making, including the lower-level courts. The picture that emerges from that research is one of complex, sometimes chaotic, processing of large numbers of vastly different criminal defendants whose fate, as the previous chapters have demonstrated, is determined by police interests, complainants, prosecutors, defense counsel, family relationships, occupational patterns, clerk-of-court management, and numerous other systemic factors, in addition to the seriousness of their criminal transgression.

The judicial role, although vital, is not primary to the system's operation. To be sure, trial-level judges are a vital component in the adjudicational process; they are the interpreters and guarantors of procedural rules, the arbiters of fundamental fairness in the system. But few felony cases ever reach the trial stage. In the absence of a trial, the only contact a judge of general jurisdiction courts has with a defendant is likely to be when an attorney moves in a hearing to dismiss, to plead

[1]The President's Commission, *Task Force Reports: The Courts,* p. 9.

guilty, to suppress evidence, or to quash an indictment, or when the judge presides over some similar legal maneuver. Although the judge theoretically reviews, consents to, or rejects decisions of the prosecutor, in practice, members of the bench are not close to each case and must rely on the district attorney's office to manage the docket, to separate serious offenders from nonserious offenders, and to negotiate charges. Judges are not very active at trial; they are expected to be neutral observers supervising the adversary contentions of prosecution and defense. Of course, in the perspective of most defense attorneys, judges are biased toward the prosecutor, a not unlikely possibility given the dependence judges have on the district attorney's office. But few members of the bench assume the aggressive posture of a Judge Sirica in the Watergate pretrial hearings and trials, independently questioning witnesses or prosecutors or defense counsel, and one suspects that posture would not be customary for Judge Sirica in less extraordinary circumstances. In fact, many states will not permit such intrusions, insisting, theoretically at least, on judicial neutrality. For the most part, the trial judge stays on the sidelines.

SENTENCING

Sentencing, however, remains the principal function of the trial judge. But even sentencing is no longer his function exclusively. The actual number of months and years that inmates spend in jails and prisons depends on the sentencing options of a particular state. If the offense has a *mandated sentence,* required by statute with no judicial discretion permitted, the judge has no latitude, except possibly to suspend the sentence or to permit the prosecutor to reduce the charge to a lesser offense. On the other hand, if the punishment permits a flexible minimum-maximum, the judge may assign a *flat sentence* of definite length, a decision totally dominated by the judge. Most states now have some form of *indefinite sentence.* That is, the trial judge may determine a minimum and a maximum, permitting the prisoner to leave at the minimum length, leaving the actual time determined by "good time" served by an inmate. The "good time" feature of sentencing is supported by prison authorities as well as by some judges who are concerned about the slippage of their traditional sentencing authority. The view of most prison authorities has traditionally been that the flexible minimum provides the necessary incentive for good behavior and proper prison management.

Virtually all of the states have some form of *indeterminate sentence* for some adult crimes and for juvenile offenses. The age of rehabilitation and therapy has provided the logic to remove the fixed sentence, with its connotation of retribution and punishment, with the indeterminate sentence. The indeterminate sentence was early hailed by reform penologists[2] in the late nineteenth century and accom-

[2] Enoch Wines, *The State of Prisons and of Child Saving Institutions in the Civilized World* (Cambridge University Press: John Wilson and Sons, 1880), pp. 641, 651.

panied the rise to the reformatory and the modern prison system. The sentence was expected to provide opportunity to save individuals from a life of crime[3] instead of merely taking punitive vengeance in proportion to the gravity of the crime by a traditional jail term. Zebulon Brockway, a leading professional penologist and reformer, summed up the logic of the indeterminate sentence in 1912. The task of scientific penology was the protection of society "by prevention of crime and reformation of criminals. . . . " Brockway's mind visualized the following humanitarian role for reformatories and prisons: "criminals shall either be cured or kept under such continued restraint as give guarantee of safety from further deprivations."[4] The indeterminate sentence may be distinguished from the indefinite sentence in that the trial judge sets neither a minimum nor a maximum, but leaves the decision for actual time served to be determined by "professional" penologists and their staff psychiatrists, psychologists, counselors, social workers, field parole officers and, most important, state parole boards that review applications for parole.

There is considerable evidence that there is more constraint than cure in the indeterminate sentence. The State of California represented in 1959 the cutting edge for corrections, particularly in institutionalizing the indeterminate sentence and modern correctional therapy. From 1959 to 1969 the mean time for inmates serving in prison serving an indeterminate sentence in California increased from 24 to 36 months, the longest in the United States.[5] At the same time, the number of persons incarcerated in the United States per 100,000 rose from 65 in 1944 to 145 in 1965.

There is little question that use of the indeterminate sentence removes the sentencing function, other than making the decision to incarcerate, from the judge and gives it to the professionals in corrections. And, quite clearly, general developments in correction toward community-based treatment, halfway houses, work-release and educational furlough require decisions to be made, not by the judge at sentencing, but by correctional personnel. The trend is away from judicial authority in sentencing. In short, the role of judge as decision maker in the criminal justice system has been overemphasized in comparison to attention paid to other actors—notably prosecutors, defense attorneys, and police. Although the judge may maintain closer supervision of bail decisions, plea bargains, dismissals, and *nolles* in smaller jurisdictions where caseloads are light, in larger systems he depends on the district attorney's office. There are some court systems

[3]Rhodes, *Discretion, Diminished Responsibility and Due Process,* especially Chapter 4. Also see Anthony Platt, *The Child Savers.*

[4]Zebulon Reed Brockway, *Fifty Years of Prison Service* (New York: Charity Publication Committee, 1912), pp. 389-391.

[5]A Report on Crime and Punishment in America Prepared for the American Friends Service Committee, *Struggle for Justice* (New York: Hill and Wang, 1971), pp. 91-92.

structured so as to require judicial involvement in plea negotiations, but these are the exception.[6] The primary activity of the judge is at sentencing and in presiding over the small minority of cases that go to trial.

The highly visible trial activities of the judge have, no doubt, contributed to misconceptions of judicial roles. The notion that all criminals are tried Perry Mason style certainly contributed to distorted perspectives of judicial importance; the public law training of reform-minded attorneys and political scientists also contributed to these false ideas, since their training emphasizes the high-level decisions and status of the bench, adjudication as a rational-legal process, and the trial as a forum of final reckoning. Still another factor in exaggerating judicial centrality is the tendency for reformers, academic and legal, to ignore routine court behavior and give their attention to the far more glamorous appellate courts. We do not suggest that the trial judge plays a minor role. The trial-level judge remains a major figure at one stage of the system, but shares decision making with many other figures of equal importance in terms of the power of deciding how to allocate values in criminal justice.

The power of the bench certainly is not limited to the criminal court; judges are very influential in local politics off the bench. They are dispensers of patronage on a sizable scale: clerks and assistants, tip-staffs, secretaries, receptionists, and white-collar employment in and around the courthouse. Before appellate court restrictions on jury selection, prospective jurors, frequently unemployed and welcoming a *per diem* juror's allowance, were drawn from lists of citizens supplied by local elected officials, including judges. Trial judges are also powerful members of the local bar, are apt to be senior members of local law firms, and normally contribute considerable years of service to their political party. There is not much question that for a politically ambitious attorney, a judgeship often symbolizes the summit of a political career, short of a nationally elected office. A position on the bench is considered an appropriate reward for past service to the party, a fitting environment of aloofness, perhaps even scholarly reflection if the position is in an appellate court, for retiring politicians who wish to leave the contentious life of partisan pressures. The length of partisan service appears to be related to the level of the judicial appointment or nomination; the state trial and appellate level judges and federal trial-level judges have the most years of political office holding experience prior to their assuming judicial duties, and federal appellate court judges have the least. This suggests that the assumption of Richard Nixon in 1968 and many others before and since, that experienced trial-level judges appointed to the U.S. Supreme Court would be more precedent-

[6] Donald McIntyre, "A Study of Judicial Dominance of the Charging Process," *Journal of Criminology and Police Science* (1968) 59:463.

oriented and less partisan, is misplaced. Whether experienced trial judges follow *stare decisis* with more fidelity than those who have not served on the bench has not been examined. But research has identified a high degree of partisanship in the background of sitting judges. Glick and Vines found that over 72 percent of all state supreme court judges in 1969 had held at least one nonjudicial political office.[7] Jacob also notes the close relationship between local social and political affiliation and recruitment of trial-level judges, particularly if partisan elections or the Missouri plan are methods for selection.[8]

REFORM AND JUDICIAL RECRUITMENT

Of all the themes to capture the imagination of citizens comitted to reform in the courts, none has loomed larger than judicial selection. As with many "good government" causes, however, reform movements frequently were characterized by a lack of empirical analysis of benefit distributions resulting from various selection procedures. Instead, reform-minded citizens, many of them attorneys, emphasized moral and professional standards—good character, legal ability, objectivity, and legal training at prestigious schools—for those selected for the bench. Superior personnel, not social or system change, represented the key to reform, and a salutary outcome was assumed once judicial reform was secured.

REFORM OF THE J.P.

Perhaps the most unambigous triumph of advocates for judicial reform had been in the reform of the minor judiciary.[9] The system of justices of the peace or lay judges was inherited from our colonial period. Forty-seven of the 48 states provided for J.P. courts in their constitutions as late as 1915.[10]

Justices of the peace may be distinguished as one kind of court among the lower or "inferior" courts in general. The line of demarcation is not always clear. Lower courts handle misdemeanors and summary and minor civil cases. J.P.s customarily are lay officials and usually are supervised in no more than a cursory manner. Until recently, J.P.s administered traffic fines, set bail, approved warrants for arrest, search and seizure, accepted fees for licenses, and sentenced violators for up to a year in jail for misdemeanors. Normally, there was no requirement for the J.P. to possess a law degree or even receive legal study beyond

[7] Glick and Vines, *State Court Systems*, p. 48, Table 3-4.

[8] Herbert Jacob, "The Effect of Institutional Differences in the Recruitment Process: The Case of State Judges," *Journal of Public Law* (1966) 15:107-108.

[9] Kenneth E. Vanlandingham, "The Decline of the Justice of the Peace," *Kansas Law Review* (1964) 12:389-403.

[10] Martin Mayer, *The Lawyers* (New York: Harper and Row, 1967), p. 465.

a cursory training program. Appeal was difficult from arbitrary judgments, record keeping was haphazard or nonexistent, and corruption was rampant, given the absence of supervision and review. A notoriously common practice was to drop charges for speeding or drunken driving for a "consideration," thus saving a license suspension for a desperate, well-heeled motorist; the J.P. split the bribe with the arresting officer. The official environment for this extortion was likely a restaurant booth, a rear room in a drug store, or a parlor in the J.P.'s home.

Of course, all J.P.s were not corrupt, but the J.P. was very responsive to local culture, suspicious and exploitative of outsiders. A common method of financing the J.P. encouraged exploitation; court frequently operated on a fee system where the J.P.'s income partially or wholly depended on his collection of fines.[11] Few acquittals were rendered under such an arrangement. Moreover, in traffic court, the arraignment promoted kickbacks between the J.P. and the police, who often channeled their charge to the most lucrative court. The sum of this iniquitous relationships of greed and conviction was that several generations of American government students were sardonically instructed that J.P. meant justice for the plaintiff!

Apart from its nativist bias and "red" fright characteristic of the age, the famous statement of Chief Justice Hughes early called attention to the plight of those in the lower courts.

> *A petty tyrant in a police court, refusals of a fair hearing in minor civil courts, the impatient disregard of an immigrant's ignorance of our ways and language, will daily breed bolshevists who are beyond the reach of your appeals. Here is work for lawyers. The Supreme Court of the United States and the Courts of Appeal will take care of themselves. Look after the courts of the poor, who stand most in need of justice. The security of the Republic will be found in the treatment of the poor and the ignorant; in indifference to their misery and helplessness lies disaster.*[12]

Although reforming the J.P. system did not have the drama and moral pageantry of a Supreme Court landmark decisions, it has had a profound effect on ordinary citizens, most of them the powerless and rejected—alcoholics, youthful traffic offenders, and debtors. Although serious criticism of the lower courts remains, eliminating the J.P. undoubtedly has increased objectivity of judgment, reduced exploitation of strangers passing through, improved records, and resulted in fewer embarrassing circumstances where the state police officer had to inform a rural J.P. that his fine or reading of the law was illegal. Contemporary members of the minor judiciary either are attorneys or must pass a rudimentary examina-

[11] In 1927 the U.S. Supreme Court ruled that a judge is disqualified in a misdemeanor case where his compensation for conducting the case depends on his verdict. *Tumey* v *Ohio* 273 U.S. 510 (1927).
[12] Cited in John A. Robertson, *Rough Justice* (New York; Little, Brown, 1974), pp. vii-viii.

tion; they are certified by the state, are paid a salary, and usually are under some administrative control within a unified court system.[13]

REFORM OF TRIAL AND APPELLATE STATE COURTS

Less clear-cut in result was the reform enterprise of removing "partisanship" and upgrading talent and "character" in the trial and appellate courts. A number of alternative selection procedures are periodically promoted to reform the judiciary of these levels, but the procedures themselves reflect contending images of the nature of criminal justice.

As Herbert Jacob suggests, "The selection procedures used to recruit judges reflect the confusion over the work that trial level judges perform."[14] Elite attorneys in local bar associations call for higher standards of intellectual capacity and character, while the customary activities of trial judges, according to some members of the legal profession, are routine, even dull, and not at all intellectually provocative.[15] Good-government groups combine with the civil bar to urge that "politics," that is, party partisanship, be taken out of the court.[16]

FEDERAL SELECTION

At the federal level, judges are appointed by the President with the consent of the Senate. However, 20 to 60 judgeships are available in a given year,[17] and the President does not conduct a personal review. A deputy attorney general is normally assigned to a preliminary screening of candidates, and the Attorney General makes a final recommendation to the President. Senatorial courtesy is respected, and a senator may reject a presidential nominee. This rarely occurs publicly, since senators from the party of the President and from the state where the vacancy occurs are consulted long before the final nomination. Senatorial influence is considerably less for appellate and Supreme Court justices, since the focus of attention is on both patronage for loyal party support, often to the senator

[13] For an illustration of a lower court recently purged of its justice of the peace, see Justin Green, Russell M. Ross, and John R. Schmidhauser, "Iowa's Magistrate System: The Aftermath of Reform," *Judicature* (1975) 58:380-389.

[14] Jacob, *Urban Courts,* p. 68.

[15] Maureen Mileski, "Courtroom Encounters: An Observation Study of a Lower Criminal Court," *Law and Society Review* (1971) 56:473-538, 524-525.

[16] Richard Watson and Ronald Downing, *The Politics of the Bench and Bar* (New York: Wiley, 1969), pp 7-14.

[17] Based on years 1964 to 1966. See Harold W. Chase, "Johnson Administration Judicial Appointments 1963-66," *Minnesota Law Review* (1968) 52:970-993.

himself, and on the allocation of values of a trial-level judge in cities and countries where congressmen derive their political base.[18]

The Selection System: Who Benefits?

The traditional perspective of legal reformers makes it difficult to answer the question of who benefits from various types of selection systems. After all, to what does the qualitative question of "character" in a judge refer? Does he take bribes? Are his judgements weighted with prejudice? Is he lazy and nondeliberative? Even if these questions are properly posed, they are not readily answerable by social science methodology.

Table 7.1. Initial adoption and change of judicial selection systems in the American states by historical periods

Method of Selection	Period			
	1776-1831	**1832-1885**	**1886-1933**	**1934-1968**
By legislature	48.5	6.7	0.0	0.0
Gubernatorial appointment	42.4	20.0	10.7	5.6
Partisan election	9.1	73.3	25.0	11.1
Nonpartisan election	—	—	64.3	11.1
Missouri Plan	—	—	—	72.2
	100.0	100.0	100.0	100.0

Source. Glick and Vines, State Court Systems (Englewood Cliffs, N.J.: Prentice-Hall, 1973), p. 41.

As Table 7.1 demonstrates, at present there are five selection procedures,[19] or combinations of these procedures, currently in use by the states. *gubernatorial appointment,* where the Governor selects judges on the basis of patronage, merit, or informal advice; *legislative election,* where selection is made by the legislature, with or without the Governor's influence, often with party patronage considerations; *nonpartisan elections,* where the judiciary is chosen without overt party support or labels, although informal support from party leaders influence the nomination and campaign; and *partisan election,* which is a product of the Jack-

[18] Ibid., pp. 995-999.

[19] The categories are somewhat arbitrary, given the variations of selection procedures that exist. They are taken from Glick and Vines, *State Court Systems,* p. 39.

sonian era's[20] passion for elected offices. The latter method is still used by major states such as New York. Judges run with party labels and participation by party organizations is a normal part of the election procedure. The *Missouri Plan* is the most complex and widely used selection system and has three essential parts. First, slates of candidates are chosen by a nominating commission of attorneys and laymen, chosen by the Governor. Second, the Governor chooses a judge from among the list of nominees. Finally, the electorate votes the Governor's choice either up or down in an open election. In some states the legislature formally "elects" judges after a recommendation by the Governor. In other states, the Governor appoints judges with the consent of one or both houses of the legislature. In practice there seems to be little distinction between the two methods. The political interest that is dominant is the Governor's, and he may use his appointment power to appoint individuals who are highly recommended by members of the local bar and prominent attorneys. More often, partisan supporters of the Governor in local areas urge one of their own for appointment. The individual appointed customarily belongs to the same party and also has political roots in the local community.[21]

Other states remain true to Jacksonian democracy and provide for partisan or nonpartisan elections for the judge. The distinction in actual practice between partisan and nonpartisan election is not very great, as even in the latter, word-by-mouth campaigns are conducted or subtle party endorsements are given short of violating the law.[22]

Moreover, the political route that attorneys take in securing a judgeship in states that require an election will not differ greatly from the route of gubernatorial appointment, particularly if judicial tenure is lengthy. There are several reasons why this is the case. Lawyers nominated and elected to coveted positions on the bench are apt to be older and die "in office" more frequently than other elected officials. In some states, there seems to be an understanding that elected judges will resign prior to the end of their tenure. In both cases, the vacancy is filled by appointment of the Governor. Once appointed, a sitting judge has an advantage at the polls, although the gubernatorial appointee does less well than judges elected on their own to a full term. Jacob found that every incumbent was returned to office between 1940 and 1963 in the Wisconsin trial courts, although only 9 of 17 gubernatorial appointees seeking a full term won their races.[23]

[20] James J. Alfini, "Partisan Pressures on the Nonpartisan Plan," *Judicature* (1974) 58:217.

[21] Jacob, *Urban Justice,* pp. 70-71; John E. Crow, "Subterranean Politics: A Judge Is Chosen," *Journal of Public Law* (1963) 12:274-289.

[22] Malcolm Moos, "Judicial Elections and Partisan Endorsements of Judicial Candidates in Minnesota," *American Political Science Review* (1941) 35:69-75; Sidney Ulmer, "The Political Party Variable on the Michigan Supreme Court," *Journal of Public Law* (1962) 11:352-362.

[23] Herbert Jacob, "Judicial Insulation—Elections, Direct Participation, and Public Attention to the Courts in Wisconsin," pp. 086-087, table on p. 806.

The Missouri Plan has been promoted and adopted in 21 states.[24] The plan was designed to remove the selection process from "partisan" emotions and nominate for the Governor's consideration only well-qualified candidates. But research indicates that the selections process substitutes one political process for another. Influence shifts from personalist or party organization to internal maneuvering in local and state bar associations and in the election of lawyer members of the nominating commissions.[25] Political cleavages that emerged within the bar often run along plaintiff-defendant lines.

Whether the character and talent of judges recruited under the Missouri Plan are superior to alternative methods of selection has not been and may never be reliably determined empirically[26] unless judicial wisdom can be operationalized. Does prestigious pedagogy help to adjudge the fate of a 19-year old, with his 17-year-old companion in illicit love, accused of statutory rape by the irate father of the girl? Will a legal education provide judicial wisdom for the ignorant worker who, failing to receive his anticipated weekly pay through the oversight of his boss who left hurriedly on a vacation, simply forges his boss's signature on a stolen office pad of checks? Anyone who has witnessed the sea of woes waiting outside a district attorney's office has to consider that social contingencies, webs of circumstances, and lack of social insight and resources are also "causes" of crime, and decent men and women of compassion have no business judging guilt or innocence in a merely technical fashion.

The problem is similar to that concerning Aristotle when he posed the question, Is politics a science or an art?[27] We may ask, Is judging the science of knowing or discovering the correct laws and deducing the appropriate application? Or is it artfully applying the collective wisdom of the body politic within a flexible, but lawful, framework? The highly qualified attorney may reflect the former; the politically experienced if less professional attorney may be most responsive to the latter. "The life of the law has not been logic," wrote Holmes, "it has been experience."[28] And experience in public life should, according to Holmes, lead to "considerations of what is expedient for the community concerned."[29] The judgment of guilt and innocence is partly a public policy function. This is not to suggest that elected judges have cornered all insight regarding the public interest.

[24] Alfini, "Partisan Pressures on the Nonpartisan Plan," p. 217.

[25] Watson and Downing, *The Politics of the Bench and Bar,* pp. 19-48.

[26] There is equal difficulty in determining beyond the level of plausible generalization, the influence of socio-economic background on judicial decision making. For a review of the literature see Walter F. Murphy and Joseph Tanenhaus, *The Study of Public Law* (New York: Random House, 1972), pp. 104-112.

[27] Aristotle, Ethica Nicomachea from *Introduction to Aristotle,* ed. Richard McKeon (New York: The Modern Library, 1947), pp. 308-543.

[28] Oliver W. Holmes, *The Common Law,* ed. Marck Dewolfe (Boston: Little, Brown, 1963), p. 5.

[29] Ibid., p. 32.

But the qualities that make up a successful attorney in private practice are not necessarily those that are requisite to judicial wisdom.

What, then, do judicial selection processes say about the politics of crime as I have conceptualized the subject? We do not know at the trial level if partisanship-nonpartisanship is related to civil liberty goals, or judicial objectivity and temperament, although Stuart Nagel has demonstrated some relationship between party affiliation and judicial bias for state and federal supreme court judges.[30] For example, Democratic judges were more likely to favor the defense in criminal cases, the administrative agency in government regulation cases, the broadening position in free speech cases, the government in tax cases, and so on. Correlatives were also found between ethnic background and judicial decision making.[31] But such findings are not necessarily indicators of political intrigue in the judicial process in need of reform. As Nagel suggests, "Regardless of judicial tenure and modes of selection, there probably will always be a residue of party-correlated judicial subjectivity as long as political parties are at least partly value-oriented and so long as court cases involve value-oriented controversies."[32]

Nor is there any body of research revealing that racial or other discriminatory attitudes against minority groups result from judges recruited from one selection process instead of another, although there are regional and cultural correlates with racism.[33] What criminal justice policy can do about racist judges being elected or appointed is very unclear. The elimination of racism is part of the agenda for a political movement, not merely a government agency. Of course, the political bar can represent the interests of minority defendants at both the trial and appellate levels, and appellate courts can establish judicial policy restricting invidious discrimination against minorities in judicial sentencing. Finally, we have no notion of linkages, positive or negative, between types of judges, their sentencing practices, and reductions of victim suffering. Quite possibly the most serious relationship between the politics of crime and judicial selection in need of inquiry is that between judicial administration, court management, the adequacy of judicial numbers and systematic outcomes, the number of trials, delay times, the decision to charge, and plea bargaining. As these past three chapters have indicated, important changes have been made. But for all the scholarly attention and criticism of the courts, attorneys, judges, and legal pro-

[30] Stuart S. Nagel, "Testing Relations between Judicial Characteristics and Judicial Decision Making," *Western Political Quarterly* (1962) 15:425-437.

[31] Stuart S. Nagel, "Ethnic Affiliations and Judicial Propositions," *Journal of Politics* (1962) 24:94-110; Stuart Nagel, "Political Party Affiliation and Judges' Decisions," *American Political Science Review* (1961) 55:843-850.

[32] Nagel, "Political Party Affiliation and Judges' Decisions," p. 850.

[33] Kenneth N. Vines, "Federal District Judges and Race Relations Cases in the South," *Journal of Politics* (1964) 26:337-357.

cesses, suggested new reforms in the structure of the legal profession and in the judicial selection process do not hold promise for any dramatic inpact on the problems of crime.

Part Two

CRIME AND POLICY

Part One examined the structure and environment of the criminal justice system as it affects the behavior of actors in the system. Essentially I argue that many crime problems are insoluble due to conflicts of interests that are often the function of organizational roles and contending perceptions. Crime and its problem definitions and solutions and the theoretical frame-work used by intellectuals as well as by criminal justice practitioners emerge from these contending perceptions, representing broader political agendas to reform the criminal justice system.

Chapter 8 picks up the theme that perceptual differences accompanied by contending interests and problem definitions frame the context for the politics of crime and make policy analysis a very difficult enterprise. It explores the problem of values in science, planning, and evaluation. Chapter 9 provides a brief overview of crucial issues and concepts for crime policy analysis and planning. It also reviews a number of techniques that will be explored in subsequent chapters. Chapter 10 discusses the possibilities of utilizing a victim-suffering index as a measure of crime seriousness for policy analysis.

Chapters 11 to 14 represent a broad assessment of the possibilities for crime prevention policies that could realistically be implemented by criminal justice agencies. Of course, the topics raised—sentencing, court delay, bail bond reform, drug control, victimless crime, and handgun regulation—are all immensely complicated taken alone, and each topic has an enormous literature. We cannot possibly do each justice, because the effort would have to be encyclopedic. Many important topics that were discussed in developing the politics of crime theme earlier—white-collar crime and organized crime, for example—are not extensively discussed for purposes of policy analysis. An author has to draw boundaries somewhere. The topics generally reflect areas where crime policy might be effective in reducing victim suffering for person-to-person and violent crime.

8

PLANNING, POLICY ANALYSIS, AND THE INSOLUBLE PROBLEMS OF CRIME[1]

Since the enactment of the Omnibus Crime Bill of 1968, there has been no lack of interest in "action" programs to solve our crime problem on the part of the federal government. The Law Enforcement Assistance Administration (LEAA), created by the act, has for fiscal year 1974 expended in excess of $480 million in block grants to the states and an additional $386 million in categorical grants and federally operated programs. Less than 5 percent of that appropriation was intended for research,[2] primary emphasis of the Administration being directed toward immediate action. Moreoever, LEAA has had considerable assistance in identifying what practical action ought to be taken. President Johnson's Commission on Law Enforcement and Administration of Justice produced nine technical task force reports on various problem areas, and President Nixon's Commission on Criminal Justice Standards and Goals published an additional five volumes of specific and quantitative recommendations that, it was hoped, would have an immediate practical value.[3]

Both commissions were badly needed, but neither commission could agree on what practical action to take or what goals to pursue. When it came time to spend the millions of dollars of Safe Streets grants they had been allocated, local and state officials could do no better. Most of the early allocations were spent on hardware and equipment; millions were simply unspent. To "move the money," in the vernacular of State Planning Agency bureaucracies, criminal justice plan-

[1] A shorter version of this chapter appeared in *Policy Studies Journal* (1974) 3:83-89. I am grateful to the Policy Studies Organization for permission to reproduce some of that material.

[2] National Council on Crime and Delinquency, *Criminal Justice Newsletter,* Vol. 4, No. 24 (December 1973), pp. 2-3.

[3] The President's Commission on Law Enforcement and Administration of Justice, *The Challenge of Crime in a Free Society* (Washington, D.C.: U.S. Government Printing Office, 1967); National Advisory Commission, *A National Strategy to Reduce Crime.*

ners were saddled with the irrational, if typical, task of bureaucrats in a grant economy: finding projects on which to spend their allocation before it lapsed and their budgets were slashed for next year.

The "action" money had little policy framework to guide its use. There was no crime theory linking specific actions with policy objectives on which scholars agreed. Instead, each interested component of the criminal justice system—policeman, county politician, judge, attorney, academic—who could influence the SPA substituted what *he* thought the money ought to be spent on.

And so it goes. LEAA is not the first federal funding agency with a vague mandate and it will not be the last. It is in the nature of democratic government to "satisfice" constituents first, paying attention to identifying a coherent set of objectives only as an afterthought. "Satisfice," in this context, means that Congress legislates only to the extent necessary to satisfy immediate pressures from constituents. Further changes are marginally made as pressures continue. For the most part Congress is institutionally incapable of long-range planning. After all, the function of a legislature is to represent, not to engage in long-range planning. To a lesser extent, even the executive must respond to immediate pressures, particularly when it is involved in promoting legislation. In 1968 when the Safe Streets legislation was passed, Congress was concerned about the summer riots of 1967 to 1968 and violent demonstrations against the Vietnam War. And so were local decision makers who wanted gas masks, riot helmets, bullet-proof vests, and subterranean communications. Constitutents were satisfied. Probably no other course of action could have been taken in those years. Criminal justice is overwhelmingly a local question involving county judges, local police, and mayors. For all the rhetoric in the 1968 Presidential campaign, the White House and Congress could do little about crime other than decry its increase and provide lots of money for locally initiated programs. But, if we wish to know the *results* of our expenditures, we must raise questions about the relationship between announced program objectives, resources committed to those objectives, alternative approaches,and their relative success. When such questions are raised, we begin to think about crime policy analysis.

THE FIELD OF POLICY ANALYSIS

There is little agreement about what constitutes policy analysis. The lack of agreement is not surprising, since policy analysis applies to very different subject areas and is thoroughly interdisciplinary in methodology. Some scholars are primarily interested in assessing the process of decision making in government and examine the variables that affect decision making. Others examine the "outputs" of public institutions—that is, cases decided by the court, laws passed by the legislature, budgets produced for state and local government—and try to identify the variables that produce comparative differences. Recently, social scientists have begun to explore the actual consequences of public policy or its impact. These scholars caution that consequences must be distinguished from policy outputs and intentions.

As an illustration, decision makers in the policy *process* might look for alternative renevue-producing measures to balance a state budget and settle on a cigarette tax. The tax is the *output*. If the tax is sufficiently high that it encourages illicit traffic in unlicensed cigarettes, however, the government may end up spending more money on law enforcement than they collect from the additional tax. The latter possibility raises fertile ground for impact analysis. There is a running debate over emphasis in policy analysis. Some argue that policy analysis should emphasize scientific generalizations and theory building, using comparative analysis to isolate particular socio-economic-political variables as they relate to public policy. Such critics shun analysis of applied policy as value laden and premature.

Other policy scholars have stressed describing and evaluating specific policy choices and programs, borrowing technical tools of measurement from wherever they can find them in the social and natural sciences. Program evaluation may proceed as follows: a rape crisis intervention program may have as a manifest (publicly expressed) *goal,* the prevention and deterrence of forcible rape. A latent goal of a municipal government that supports the program may be satisfying the demands of local feminists to replace *macho* police officers with more sensitive, female, rape squad personnel. The public *objectives* of the program are easily quantified and indicators of success applied: the number of arrests for forcible rape, the percent of clearances (arrests for forcible rape, compared to forcible rape situations known to the police), and the percent of convictions (a rough and partial measure of police competency in collecting evidence). Of course, the fulfillment of latent political goals will be evaluated by the political actors, not by the policy analyst. Finally, the *impact* of the program can be assessed by examining the relative reduction of forcible rape per 100,000 females, over projected rates that would have occurred if the special rape unit had not been implemented. Obviously, this is only a brief sketch of an evaluation design; it ignores major problems such as nonreporting and isolating the police procedure variable in affecting conviction rates, dismissal rates, and plea bargaining.

Neither a general theory approach to policy analysis nor applied policy is alien to the approch presented here, although it would not concur that applied policy analysis is always premature. Nor would it hold that the one is value laden, while the other is value free.

I assume that policy analysis must answer three questions: What are the goals of crime policy and how can those goals be translated into quantified objectives? What kinds of governmental interventions can be discerned? And what are the consequences of those actions in terms of fulfilling crime policy objectives? However important a critical comprehensive social analysis of crime is, and it is important, both causal and interactive analyses have great difficulty in answering policy questions short of vague references to preserving public order, resolving conflict, or reinforcing social norms.

There are three reasons for the paucity of policy analysis in criminological thought, as contrasted to its concentration on explaining social phenomena. The first is that a crime policy must be implemented by decision makers in the criminal justice system—judges, attorneys, policemen, parole officers, and the like. They are in no position to alter seriously the social realities that criminological theory explains are the root causes of crime—poor housing, poverty, broken homes, racism, and violent subcultures. A feasible crime policy must be relevant to the immediate concerns of the criminal justice decision makers who must carry out policy.

Second, if we have learned anything from several decades of social programs to provide decent housing, eliminate poverty, provide legal and social services to the poor, and attack mental illness, it is that social and behavioral scientists do not have an overabundance of expertise in solving these problems. And we must be chary of predicting consequences of government intervention. Most certainly, there is little evidence to predict that reductions of crime will inevitably follow programs that redistribute income, provide better housing, end racism, improve medical delivery to the poor, curb the power of corporations, or expand educational opportunites. My own political views are that a guaranteed income program designed to assist the working poor, to strengthen the integrity of the family, and to reduce chronic underemployment may have a major impact on reducing crime. More important, such programs have merit for reasons unrelated to reducing crime. I also believe that slavery and the later quasislave institution of Jim Crow left an incalculable legacy of violence and crime in the United States. But I cannot predict as a social scientist that my personal political agenda will reduce crime. Moreover, such social and historical generalizations do little to instruct the chief of police regarding how to handle a rash of burglaries; he needs more than a lecture on history or social stratification.

When crime is diagnosed, as it often is by criminologists, as resulting from the pecularities of the social structure, the most obvious appeal for a solution is to a social movement and political activism. Racism, sexism, and economic disparities all refer to injustices in the social structure that require political action beyond the criminal justice system. But social movements and political activism must be clearly distinguished from crime policy. The question of forcible rape provides a useful example. Very probably "consciousness raising" for men and women to end sexism will have a profound impact on the number of violent attacks and on the willingness of women to testify without shame against their attackers. The crusading journalism of *Ms.* magazine, the litigations and lobbying of the National Organization of Women, and the national publicity of the Joan Little trial all produce symbolic gains for women's liberation—translated into less exploitative sexual attitudes in men. But none of this provides analysis for police and court policy to prevent, arrest, convict, or deter rapists. Policy analysis must deal with the actions and consequences of rape squads, investigation and interview techniques, and evidentiary and procedural changes for rape cases in court.

Social analysis and calls for political action are not substitutes for policy analysis, although they provide the climate for its implementation. But such initiatives are inherently political judgments. Political strategy cannot be defined by social science theory. No social scientist can predict the consequences of public policy, although astute insights about ends and means that inform political judgment can be made by perceptive social scientists. In this latter role the social scientist is a consultant more than a policy analyst. The political variables that infuence the formation and execution of policy are too complex to permit social science theory to be conveniently plugged into the process with any predictability.

Policy is most acutely assessed *a posteriori.* Here the consequences of policy initiatives are examined after the fact and a determination can be made as to what extent the objectives of that policy have been reached. *A priori* policy analysis need not be precluded, but the expertise of the social scientist here does not have the power that is provided by a carefully designed evaluation of the extent to which an ongoing program has achieved its goals.

I must, therefore, disagree with those who argue that crime policy should be based on causal analysis and that its purpose should be to demonstrate how the social structure should be altered to reduce crime.[4] To begin with, criminologists differ on the causes of crime. Even if there were general agreement on crime causation, knowing what causes crime does not let us know what the government can do about it.[5] Of course, any analysis must depend on behavioral theory. Evaluational models depend on an understanding of the interrelationships that exist between relevant variables and an ability to extrapolate indicators that measure their variability. Certainly the fact that larceny and burglary go up at Christmas time is suggestive of the motivation for theft and of the need for preventative measures for that time of year. But to speak of basic causes of crime —poverty, subcultures of violence, lack of family affection or stability, and socioeconomic status—is to speak to areas where the entire political process is involved.

A crime policy grounded in causal approaches of necessity leads to proposals to alter the social structure. It is one thing to know what variables in the social structure are correlated with crime; it is quite another to suggest what the government can do about it. Causal analysis is not policy analysis. Short of Plato's *Republic,* no social scientist can propose policies to alter the social structure and expect that such policy proposals will be based on social science theory. They will

[4]Daniel Glaser, *Strategic Criminal Justice Planning, National* Institute of Mental Health, HM 3 42-73-237 (Washington, D.C.: U.S. Government Printing Office).

[5]James Q. Wilson, *Thinking About Crime* (New York: Basic Books, 1975), pp. 43-57.

be subject to the politics of competing bureaucracies, state and local government, the electoral politics: the web of government. After all, disagreements about income distribution, educational opportunity, privilege and deprivation (in short, the substance of structural distinctions) is what the whole of politics is all about. Social scientists have no corner on answers to such enduring questions. Police and courts cannot wait for major social change; they must respond with policy decisions about rape and murder now. A feasible, realistic crime policy must be relevant to the immediate concerns of criminal justice decision makers who carry out policy.

PLANNING

Definitional comments also should be made about planning; like policy analysis, the term is used in different ways. I define planning as the efficient use of limited resources to obtain stated objectives. Obviously, timing and mobilizing resources are important to the planner. If a county-wide communication system for the police is to be planned, cooperation from local police departments, budget allocations from county governments to pay for equipment, competitive bidding by vendors who provide the hardware, the purchase of local radios and other equipment, and the hiring of trained personnel must all follow in timely sequence.

Planning may also take on more sophisticated responsibilities by assessing alternate resources to obtain the same objectives by the most efficient means. Assume that the communication system's stated objective is to reduce injury and death caused by accidents and to facilitate the investigation and apprehension of criminal offenders by decreasing patrol response time. A reduced speed limit, improved roads and vital intersections, and a limited communications network on major highway arterials might serve the same purpose and be cheaper. When competing alternatives to reach similar objectives are assessed, planning becomes evaluative.

At the other end of the continuum, planners may assess the objectives themselves and develop priorities for dealing with the problems of criminal justice. Organized crime may be considered more important than person-to-person crime outside of organized crime, person-to-person crime may be considered more important than training police, and so on. Here the planner plays a major role in defining the objectives to be pursued instead of simply examining the means to get there. This third level, and to some extent the second level, have been referred to as "strategic planning,"[6] while the first level may be referred to as "tactical planning."

This latter emphasis can safely be referred to as a merger of planning with *a priori* policy analysis, an approach about which we have expressed reservations.

[6]Glaser, *Strategic Criminal Justice Planning,* pp. 3-10.

Whether tactical or strategic, planning that is related to feasible public choices will take place in a politicized atmosphere. To begin with, the self-interests and ideologies of the planners, the agencies for whom they work, and their constituencies in the body politic play important roles in any planning scheme. In fact, any alternative plan or alternative allocation of resources or ranking priorities begs a political decision. It affects jobs, bureaucratic power, status, and sometimes even elections. Therefore, actual planning decisions (apart from published plans or studies) will rarely have strategic objectives. Instead, they will be incremental steps designed to accommodate interests in the political community.

POLICY ANALYSIS AND VALUES

Finally, planning and policy analysis is performed within a political framework in the criminal justice system. Policy designs reflect the mind-set of various actors in the system and the alternative problem definitions and solutions that they possess. Problem definitions inevitably contain some distribution formula, delineating who gets what, when and how. For example, are arrests for armed robbery to be increased by concentrating patrols or impact squads in high crime areas? Certainly, this means a need for greater resource allocation to police in given areas, more protection for potential victims of armed robbery, assuming impact squads are an effective countermeasure (a proposition seriously questioned by recent research). It also will force a greater demand on the resources of the courts. If the courts are unable to obtain additional resources to handle their increased caseloads of robbery offenders, plea bargaining may increase and the "value" of vigorous prosecution may decrease. Political analysis is vital in identifying what problem definitions and solutions (or subgoals) presently exist in criminal justice, which variables help create such definitions (political culture), which solutions flow from the existent definitions, and how these solutions interact with other solutions.

It must be recognized that criminal justice personnel, policy analysts, and criminologists all have theoretical models from which they proceed, explicitly or implicitly, to evaluate what goes on in the criminal justice system. And, frequently, both theoretical orientations are value laden in terms of both goals and means. For precisely this reason, the plentiful proposals for reforming the criminal justice system, whether from the American Bar Association, presidential commissions, or learned treatises from academics, are frequently ignored or hostilely considered by various actors in and out of the system. The actors in the system are often psychologically conservative in that they reject the implicit values of the solutions proposed without articulating the reason for their opposition, without mentioning or sometimes even being aware of the value conflict in their goals. Such value conflict will probably continue to obstruct the definition of problem areas and any concerted attack on their resolution, so long as there is a paucity of political theory that can bare value differences and alternative objectives of contending evaluation models.

Consequently, while it is currenlty fashionable and accurate to characterize criminal justice planning and evaluation efforts as fragmented, eclectic, uncomprehensive, and without a theoretical foundation for public policy, this state of affairs is largely inevitable. Disjointed planning and evaluation efforts in criminal justice today reflect not merely uncertainty as to solutions, but powerful disconsensus as to the nature of our criminal justice problems.[7] If theory is, in some sense, concerned with means and ends (and current policy problem definitions in criminal justice imply the value of multiple outputs or ends for the criminal justice system), and if such ends are competing, as I think they are, the problem of criminal justice will remain insoluble, subject to incremental, approximate solutions at best. Policy analysis models that emerge from contending problem definitions will, for the most part, reflect the disconsensus.

POLICY THEORY AND PROBLEM DEFINITION

Competing problem definitions presently exist throughout the political community, among interest groups, among actors in the subgroups and organizations in the criminal justice system, and among academic groups, not excluding policy analysts. Disparate problem definitions emerge from mind-sets as evaluation models that are, themselves, the functions of contending organizational roles[8] and interest group perspectives of police, prosecutors, defense counsels, trial and appellate judges, civil libertarians, criminal justice planners, and the general public. Political interests formed by organizational roles and group behavior establish the parameters of policy, objectives, standards, and even indicators as measures of success for goal fulfillment. Examples of such evaluation models that emerge from mind-sets are due process models, administrative efficiency models, class conflict models, law enforcement models, and social control models. Of course, the most vigorous efforts of policy analysis to remain detached and objective will not avoid value conflict in policy analysis. Some conflicts of value in criminal justice are formally institutionalized, as in the adversary system; still others reflect social tensions that stretch far beyond the criminal justice system.

Social science can make a major contribution to criminal justice evaluation in three areas. First, it can measure the impact and consequences of government

[7] John A. Gardiner, "Research Models in Law Enforcement and Criminal Justice," *Law and Society Review* (1971), 6:223; James Q. Wilson, *Varieties of Police Behavior* (New York: Atheneum, 1973), pp. 227-236.

[8] Malcolm M. Feeley, "Two Models of the Criminal Justice System: An Organizational Perspective," *Law and Society Review* (1973), 7:407-425.

programs on securing the announced objectives of an agency or department.[9] Formally, this is the most common function of contracted research in policy analysis. Commonly, the process of research involves identifying goals of the contracting organization, a department of corrections, a police department, prosecutor's office, and the like, quantifying those goals, developing data indicators of success or failure, and measuring the results against some target or standard. Often the organization does not explicitly identify goals or indicators that are the operating parameters of the evaluation design. For example, management studies may examine personnel procedures with implicit objectives of facilitating harmonious relationships or clarifying the chain of command. The evaluator has a responsibility in this circumstance to help the organization identify its operating goals.

Second, a critical social science can measure, although with great difficulty, the impact of programs on informal objectives, the unwritten agenda of policy, such as income and budget redistribution.[10] Virtually all important legislation has an unwritten agenda of distributing values to one group and not another, undergirding the formally stated objectives in its preamble. The Safe Streets Act of 1968 was no exception. A major debate raged over the block grant concept whereby moneys would be distributed and administered by the state versus the categorical grant concept under which the LEAA gravy train would normally go directly to the cities, bypassing state government.[11] In 1968, most of the moneys went to the state and "units of local government," not necessarily to the large cities.

It is not news to students of American politics that city, county, and state governments serve different constituencies, are often controlled by opposite parties, jealously guard their sources of revenue from Washington, and are alert to fiscal allocations either by legislation or by administrative policy. Legislatively, in 1968, the states and suburban county governments won the greater piece of the pie, according to the allocation formula for Safe Streets funding,[12] although the large cities recouped somewhat in the Crime Act of 1970, which required the state plan to provide "for the allocation of adequate assistance to deal with law enforcement problems in areas characterized by both high crime incident and high law enforcement activity."[13]

[9] Moynihan, *Maximum Feasible Misunderstanding*, pp. 190-203.

[10] Leonard Merwitz and Stephen Sosnick, *The Budget's New Clothes* (Chicago: Markham, 1971), Chapter 9; Arthur Maas, "Benefit-Cost Analysis: Its Relevance to Public Investment Decisions," *Quarterly Journal of Economics* (1966), 80:208-226; Aaron Wildavsky, "Analysis, Systems Analysis and Program Budgeting," *Public Administration Review* (1966), 26:292-310.

[11] Normally, but not always, categorical grants benefit large cities rather than state government. State government can more easily control the distribution of block grants.

[12] 82 Stat. 198-203 (1968).

[13] 42 U.S.C.A. P3733, as amended, 1970.

The infighting over who gets the greater share of LEAA funds partly reflects the contending interests of police departments, most of which are within the jurisdiction of the cities, the courts, which are likely to be within the funding jurisdiction of either counties or states, or corrections, whose bureaucracy is subordinate to either state or county political jurisdiction or to a combination of both. But, for the most part, local and state governments have skillfully used LEAA funds to supplant and augment their general budgets by dressing up their standard services with "innovative" program labels. Of course, this practice is not unique to criminal justice. It is a standard ploy of planners and grantsmen in all institutions that depend on grants in aid. The practice is made particularly easy for grantsmen at local levels, given the broad categories that are identified as fundable by Safe Streets legislation[14] and the decentralization of funding decision making. Yet, given the fragmentation of criminal justice jurisdictions and the continuous manipulation of local budgets, it is difficult to see how centralized funding decision making could prevent budgetary supplantation with or without squadrons of accountants. Costly communications equipment and emergency street light signaling, used primarily by ambulances and fire engines, have frequently been purchased through LEAA moneys. Capital expenditures for court houses, computer centers, and municipal facilities need not service police and courts exclusively. Even if they do, such a large investment relieves the necessity of onerous local bond issues or new taxes. Even the education of many students reading this volume is financed by the Law Enforcement Education Program of LEAA under the rubric of training and education "in areas related to law enforcement or suitable for persons employed in law enforcement."[15] Obviously, the meaning of law enforcement has been stretched beyond its contextual meaning in the statute to embrace the more generalized needs of colleges and universities and traditional disciplines that are only peripherally related to police work. All these practices of supplanting other budgetary needs are carried out without serious difficulty and in full compliance with the letter of the law, if not the spirit, in spite of the statutory caveat accompanied by administrative directives that federal funds made available "will be so used as not to supplant State or local funds, but to increase the amounts of such funds."[16] One might conjecture that a tacit recognition of this practice was one of the factors motivating the Nixon administration's Law Enforcement Revenue Sharing Act of 1971.[17]

This short digression about LEAA Safe Streets funding is not intended to be

[14] 82 Stat. 201 (1968).

[15] 42 U.S.C.A. §3746, as amended, 1970.

[16] 82 Stat. 201 (1968).

[17] Congressional Record, U.S. Senate, March 2, 1971, S1087, introduced by Senator Roman Hruska; Presidential Message to the Congress, March 2, 1971, regarding special revenue sharing in criminal justice.

critical of LEAA. Most federal programs adopt a life of their own apart from their frequently vague statutory origins as they attempt to meet the needs of their clients and, particularly, the needs of the funding organizations and government planning or service agencies whose existence depends on the federal dollar. The planning of expenditures does not relate to a "rational plan," at least not in the sense that the planner has a clear objective, lists every possible choice of action, and identifies all the consequences for the planning objective that will flow from each choice. Instead, planning tends to be *ad hoc,* incremental, and opportunistic.[18] A program to be planned does not proceed from a *tabula rasa,* be it a housing project, a social service program, or a criminal justice management information center. Any planner is faced with "givens," old boundaries well established by statute, existing state and local initiatives or opposition, and "clients"—politicians and interests who will be affected. Generally, a plan is a document for survival for all concerned, and new directions are approached carefully. Social scientists who attempt to describe or analyze the unwritten agenda policy obviously have a difficult task. But it is a vital task for independent scholarship, because the most important portions of the policy agenda are the least articulated.

Finally, a theoretically conscious social science can bare the competitive mind-sets now in use for policy analysis by both practitioners in criminal justice and social scientists. The third of these contributions, the focus of this chapter, is crucial in a subject area as value laden as criminal justice; the clarification of problem definitions, value assumptions, and goal inconsistency in various perspectives is preliminary to identifying conflicting mind-sets in dialogue concerning criminal justice reform. I believe this will be a thankless task; the basic value structures within competing theoretical perspectives command tenacious loyalties in all of us. However, theoretical consciousness[19] of inevitable value bias in policy analysis is necessary to reveal the difficulty of problem definition in criminal justice.

Those who are explicitly interested in a general political theory of criminal justice have largely ignored the area of policy analysis. Some of the general theory literature, often sociological, calls for major reordering of the social structure, an alternative as vague in its program and consequences as it is unlikely to occur.[20] There is also an exploding literature involving the politics of crime at a descriptive level.[21] The theoretical point of departure for this literature is either

[18] Edward C. Banfield, "Ends and Means in Planning," in *American Politics and Public Policy,* ed. Michael P. Smith (New York: Random House, 1973), pp. 159-166.

[19] William E. Connolly, "Theoretical Self-Consciousness," *Polity* (1973) 6:5-35.

[20] Richard Quinney, *The Social Reality of Crime* (Boston: Little, Brown, 1970), pp. 11-25.

[21] Jacob, *Urban Justice* pp. 1-3; James Eisenstein, *Politics and the Legal Process* (New York: Harper and Row, 1973) pp. 4, 307-323; James R. Klononsky and Robert I. Mendelsohn, eds., *The Politics of Local Justice* (Boston: Little, Brown, 1970); George F. Cole, *Politics and the Administration of Justice* (Beverly Hills, Calif.: Sage Publications, 1973), pp. 15-20.

David Easton's much quoted definition of government as "the authoritative allocator of values in society,"[22] or Harold Lasswell's equally recognizable definition of political study as inquiry into who gets what, when and how.[23] What does seem in short supply are critical assessments of policy outputs, their impact, and the implicit values attached to the measurement techniques that evaluate the achievement of policy goals.

DATA AND VALUES

The problem is not lack of data alone, although anyone who has engaged in criminal justice evaluation recognizes the data problems to be anything but minor. Criminal justice agencies and departments are swimming with data, but many of these data are useful only for internal administration, official reporting, and public relations. Systematic data collection must be undertaken for evaluation purposes, but the conceptualization of what data to collect, what they are to measure, and for what objectives requires a value judgment and reflection about the nature of the problem.

For example, traditional uniform crime reporting is a useful indicator of police activity, but it is misleading as an indicator of actual criminal behavior that often goes unreported. Data generated by current efforts of the Law Enforcement Assistance Administration to measure criminal behavior through victimization surveying generally avoid the problems of crime that goes unreported to the police by relying on survey techniques. Although victimization surveying is generally a valid and reliable measure of legally defined criminal acts,[24] it is not necessarily an accurate measure of the seriousness of crime from the aggregate perspectives of the victims who suffer.[25] Nor do any of these indicators reflect the more generalized perspectives of the public, which is more apt to respond to a publicized incident in the newspaper than to a statistical formulation. Obviously, the public perspective is immeasurably more important to the local police chief and mayor.[26] Finally, systematic data collection of legal decisions at crucial stages in the courts is essential to evaluate systematic management problems such as crowded dockets, delay, or excessive workloads. But if it is not offender based (i.e., identifies offenders by name or code), no control can be applied to past offenses to compare defense counsel effectiveness or to analyze discriminatory practices. If data are offender based, their use may interfere with juvenile justice,

[22] David Easton, *The Political System* (New York: Knopf, 1960), Chapter 5.

[23] Harold Lasswell, *Politics: Who Gets What, When, How* (New York: McGraw-Hill, 1936).

[24] Anthony Turner, "Victimization Surveying—Its History, Uses, and Limitations," Unpublished paper, National Institute of Law Enforcement and Criminal Justice (July 1972).

[25] See Chapter 9 for an extensive analysis of victimology and its limits for policy analysis.

[26] Wilson, *Varieties of Police Behavior,* p. 228.

with its emphasis on sealed records, or with the rights of privacy. As a practical matter, data processing and retrieval systems may be quietly opposed by local law enforcement because they will interfere with efforts by the police to clear the streets of prostitutes and pickpockets by extralegal sweep arrests or hinder attorneys who rely on low-visibility decision making to minimize adversary conflict and maximize efficiency.

Different types of data imply valued objectives to be measured and cannot easily be applied to disparate problems for which they were not conceived. The problem is not simply technical; it represents the conundrum of the fact-value dichotomy with which policy research must persistently struggle. Different facts often presuppose particular values and social objectives within an explanatory paradigm.

POLITICAL PARADIGMS IN CRIMINAL JUSTICE

Currently, there is a wide variety of political paradigms that measure the allocation of values in criminal justice. Some are conscious, scholarly attempts to model behavior. With others, theoretical awareness about implicit concepts, goals, and indicators of value vary in sophistication. Nevertheless. a wide variety of models, *weltanschauungs,* or mind-settings are used by criminal justice scholars and practitioners to evaluate what is going on. A paradigm or model in this context is a conceptual framework of goals and indicators to measure goal attainment with regard to the operations of the criminal justice system in its broadest dimensions. No suggestion is made here of the necessity for internal symmetry, carefully definied components or well-defined parameters, and boundaries; we are concerned with perceptual limitations about the meaning of facts due to a value bias built into a commonly used frame of reference.

Obviously, the policy evaluator will attempt to be rigorous in developing, within a carefully constructed framework of behavioral theory, quantified objectives related to policy goals and operationalized indicators of goal fulfillment. But the conception of goals and objectives usually begs a problem definition.

As an illustration, a goal to reduce recidivism may be pursued by community-based treatment centers and work-release and furlough programs. The evaluation of the program goal might, in simplified terms, compare recidivist rates among a stratified sample of offenders in such centers with a similar sample of offenders from traditional incarcerating institutions. Assuming the primary problem definition is the reduction of recidivism through modern correctional treatment, some "risk" of lawbreaking by the experimental sample of released prisoners must be tolerated. But the police problem definition is more apt to emerge from a day-to-day concern with increases in criminal behavior. Incarceration is 100 percent effective during the time of sentence, and the mind-set of the officer is not usually consonant with the short-term risk.[27] Moreover, the police perspective may have merit if the recidivist rate is only marginally reduced by community-based treatment, and serious offenses may increase. There is evidence that the community-based treatment's impact on recidivism is marginal.[28] On the other hand, the program budget analyst may indicate that community-based treatment is cheaper than traditional incarceration, whatever its impact on recidivism.[29]

Similar conflicts in value occur in drug problem evaluation. Drug squads measure their success by arrests and hard evidence against users and sellers, not necessarily by the offender's social recovery. Methadone clinics and Synanon-type centers consider the abandonment of illegal drug use and social adjustment their goal. But Alcoholics Anonymous might react with mixed emotions to indications of success from both police blotters and methadone clinics if a rapidly increasing pattern of alcoholism filled the social vacuum left by former illegal drug users.

The group that commissions an evaluation, be it police department, court, department of corrections, foundation, or government agency, will largely define the normative policy objectives and, consequently, the problem definition. Each group will inevitably "tunnel" perceptual reference for evaluation and explanation, as will actors in various subgroupings in the criminal justice system, in the academic community, and in the general public, each revealing its unique interests, values, and social roles.

Space does not permit a full catalog of models that have emerged from distinct mind-sets to evaluate criminal justice policy. Many civil libertarians and defense attorneys prefer due process models, which evaluate by drawing comparisons between court rules, as ideal conditions, and actual practice, although procedural barriers to fact-finding may result in less protection for potential victims through lower and slower conviction rates. The recent debate in New York State over corroborating testimony in rape cases is instructive here.[30] The same might be said for liberalizing bail[31] and *Miranda* warnings.[32]

[27] Substantially the same point is made in Martin A. Levin, "Crime and Punishment and Social Science," *The Public Interest* (1972), 27:102-103.

[28] Robert Martinson, "What Works?—Questions and Answers about Prison Reform," *The Public Interest* (1974), 35:47-48.

[29] Informatics, Incorporated, *Pennsylvania Community Treatment Services: An Evaluation and Proposed Evaluation Information Systems,* Pennsylvania Department of Justice, Bureau of Corrections, July 1972.

[30] Grace Lichtenstein, "Rape Squad," *The New York Times Magazine* (March 3, 1974), p. 11.

[31] J. Locke et al., *Compilation and Use of Criminal Court Data in Relation to Pre-Trial Release of Defendants: Pilot Study,* U.S. Department of Commerce, National Bureau of Standards, Technical Note 535 (August 1970), pp. 2-12.

[32] Seeburger and Wettick, Jr., "Miranda in Pittsburgh—A Stastical Study," pp. 11-12. Seeburger and Wettick provide evidence that the confession rate was reduced by *Miranda* and, by inference, conviction rates were reduced. Other studies have disputed the impact of *Miranda* on "coercive" practices to obtain confessions at the precinct level. See Richard J. Medalic, Leonard Zeitz, and Paul Alexander,

Closed system production flow models and utility curves tend to be favored by court administrators and trial judges with heavy dockets and by cost benefit-oriented planners because they emphasize administrative or economic efficiency as a value.[33] Of course, what is administrative utility from one point of view may be assembly-line justice from another. Professionally oriented police planners and administrators opt for models that measure police output in terms of clearance rates, response time, and criminalistic skills. Street-wise officers, while responding to administrative measures for promotion, informally evaluate performance in terms of social control, keeping the peace, preventing riot and disorder, maintaining morale, or simply keeping themselves out of trouble.[34] Finally, conflict-oriented social theorists frequently prefer the class conflict model, which emphasizes and measures inequities in the social structure, reflected in criminal justice, often with little concern for detection, apprehension, and deterrence.

THE INSOLUBLE PROBLEMS OF CRIME

I am not discounting the utility of any of the above perspectives for evaluating subgoal attainment. I am suggesting that such perspectives are at times insufficient for comprehensive planning and evaluation; subgoal problem definitions are sometimes too insular or inconsistent with other valued objectives of the system. That is, maximizing goal attainment in one problem area may be dysfunctional for goal attainment in another.

For example, the adversary system, prized by civil libertarians, contradicts administrative efficiency at many junctures; virogous law enforcement in high crime areas—using tactical squads and police dogs—may reduce burglary and armed robbery downtown, but at the cost of community relations and urban harmony. Utilizing "professional" standards for recruiting and training police officers, civil service testing, lateral entry, specialization, and educational attainment all may be contradictory to the goal of minority representation on the force in the short run.[35] In other areas, mention has been previously made of subgoals such as the continuance of low-visibility decision making by prosecutors or police

"Custodial Police Interrogation in Our Nation's Capital," *Michigan Law Review* (1968), 66:1347-1422.

[33]The literature is voluminous. For examples see Jacob Belkin and Alfred Blumstein, *Methodology for the Analysis of Total Criminal Justice Systems,* Carnegie Mellon University, Grant NI-026 (November 1970); Peter W. Greenwood et al., *Prosecution of Adult Felony Defendants in Los Angeles County: A Policy Perspective,* Rand Corporation (march 1973).

[34]Albert J. Reiss, Jr. and David J. Bordua, "Environment and Organization: A Perspective on the Police," in *The Police,* ed. David J. Bordua (New York: Wiley, 1967), pp. 25-55.

[35]See *Carter* v *Gallegher* 452 F2d 315 (1971); *Commonwealth* v *O'Neill* 348 F. Supp. 1084 (1972). The difficulty of reconciling professionalism, leadership, and representativeness in bureaucracy is discussed by Herbert Kaufman, "Administrative Decentralization and Political Power," *Public Administrative Review* (1969), 29:3-15.

in the administration of justice versus high-visibility administrative control permitted by rapid retrieval information systems and of improvements in rehabilitation techniques that may require higher social risks of criminal activity by the probationers. Finally, policy regarding which types of criminal behavior should be deterred, investigated, arrested, and prosecuted demand human and material resource allocation decisions. Investigating and prosecuting organized crime, narcotics, and forcible rape often requires the resource allocations necessary to deal with larceny, robbery, and motor vehicle violations. Unless resources are unlimited, a rare situation in criminal justice departments and agencies, a choice must be made between competing crime control objectives.

VICTIMIZATION AS A COMPREHENSIVE INDICATOR

One of the comprehensive goals of the criminal justice system most apt to be forgotten by the public and practitioners is protecting the citizen against being victimized. Ironically, protection of the victim is not a central concern in criminal justice. In a sense, police do provide a fundamental service in protecting life and property. But the protective measures that police invoke must be carried out within a large body of complex rules for police administration and criminal procedure and within an even more complex set of rules informed by the "street sense" of the patrolman.

Moreover, police do not act on behalf of individual complaints; they are concerned primarily with public order in an environment of danger,[36] perceived civilian hostility, shifting community values, and limited resources.[37] Police will use their discretion whenever possible to encourage private settlement of minor disputes when legal transgressions do not threaten public order. And the officer must be sensitive to private vengeance masquerading as public duty. For these and other reasons, Bordua and Reiss have characterized policing as a service without clients.[38]

Law enforcement and order maintenance are thus placed in a framework of law, a fact that results in confusion for policy analysis. The general parameters of criminal law actually refer to three moral-jurisprudential categories. The first reference is to a moral quality, using drugs, engaging in egregious sexual practices; adultery and stealing are considered social evils. However unfortunate it might be for social policy, "evil" behaviors, homosexuality, gambling, seeking pleasure, or hallucinating experience through drugs are often labeled as such by legislative proscription—sometimes even under circumstances where legislators

[36] Skolnick, *Justice without Trial*, pp. 45-67.

[37] See generally LaFave, *Arrest*.

[38] Reiss and Bordua, "Environment and Organization," *The Police* p. 30.

publicly acknowledge the impossibility of enforcement. The second category of criminal law meaning refers to legal culpability or *mens rea,* and conceptually it is the peculiar province of the attorney and judge. The standard of culpability is a separate, logical category that requires a demonstration, consistent with due process of both intent on the part of the defendant to perform a legally proscribed act and a commission of the act itself within the limitations of due process.

A third category of criminal law meaning can be deciphered from the perspective of the police officer and his concern for preventing trouble and maintaining orderliness and decorum. Public order concerns may prompt the police to move against behaviors that are not technically criminal but that, if ignored, may result, according to the perspective of the police officer, in administrative problems, disorder, or illegal behavior. Civil rights demonstrations in the South in the 1950s and organized attempts by antiwar groups to "shut down" the nation's capital in 1970 were well-publicized events that resulted in order maintenance conduct by the police. More common disruptive events are traffic snarls and accidents, loitering, drunkenness, and family disturbances.

None of these categories, of course, provide measures for victim suffering. To the extent that criminal justice policy analysis is to become comprehensive, it would do well to reduce its dependence on criminal law categories as reflected in arrests, reported crime, convictions, and riot control, and examine the impact policy has on reducing victimization. The Law Enforcement Assistance Administration has supported efforts for measuring stranger-to-stranger violence and burglary verified through survey data as a comprehensive indicator for its impact programs.[39] The measurement of crime by moral-jurisprudential victimization indicators currently in use would be significantly improved on by scaling victimization suffering in behavioral terms along the lines suggested by Sellin, Wolfgang, and Wilkins.[40] Both types of crime indicators would be complementary, one for measuring legal crime, the other for measuring suffering. Quantifying victimization in monetary instead of legal terms would raise considerably the power of analysis on the impact of crime control policies. Since victim costing would be unidimensional, the impact of alternative policies on a variety of crime types could be assessed, budget analysis would be enhanced, and costs of diversionary programs could be more readily reviewed. Perhaps most important, victim costing might provide essential illumination for that politically volatile question discussed elsewhere in this volume: what behaviors to criminalize or decriminalize.

We are not presently in a position to draw correlative relationships between

[39] Turner, "Victimization Surveying," pp. 1-3.

[40] Thorsten Sellin and Marvin E. Wolfgang, *The Measurement of Delinquency* (New York: Wiley, 1964); Leslie T. Wilkins, "New Thinking in Criminal statistics," *Journal of Criminal Law, Criminology and Police Science* (1965), 56:277-284.

victimization reduction and policy initiatives, although this is an important area for research. And many subgoals of criminal justice, due process protection, order maintenance, and the like cannot be evaluated by a suffering index. But the victim's suffering, as an output to measure the success of an anticrime policy, might be the key to comprehensive planning and evaluation in an area of public policy replete with contending problem definitions.

9

TECHNIQUES AND INDICATORS FOR CRIME POLICY ANALYSIS

It will be recalled that our interest is primarily in output and impact analysis. To analyze policy, first we need to identify policy *goals* or general pronouncements. These are often quite rhetorical, suggesting only in which direction the government intends to move. For example, making "the streets safe" is suggestive, yet snappy enough to gain political support. Unfortunately, what is snappy to the general public is likely to be murky to the policy analyst. Policy goals must be quantified as *objectives* if they are to be measured. For example, the detection and apprehension of criminal offenders is one objective that can be extracted from a vague concern for safe streets. *Indicators* refer to the units of measurement used to determine to what extent the objective has been reached (in our example, clearance rates—the ratio of crimes cleared by arrests or identification of the offender over crimes known to the police, and apprehension rates per population —those arrested by the police upon probable cause). Obviously, some indicators are more reliable than others. Department records on clearance rates, for example, are not usually reliable, since they may be doctored by reducing the number of crimes known to the police, thereby increasing the rate of clearance to make the department look more effective.

In addition, a choice of indicators requires theoretical knowledge about behavior and variables that affect behavior. Assume that the program to be assessed is a statewide innovation to upgrade prosecution. For the sake of simplicity let us assume that we are primarily concerned about improving conviction rates for violent offenders. The "test" samples (i.e., the prosecutor offices affected by the innovative program) are then compared to control samples over a period of time. We need to know a great deal about the likelihood of plea bargaining and its intensity, and about dismissal, *nolle prosequi,* and conviction rates that are the outcomes of interacting variables such as the number of prosecutors, the volume of cases, and the type of crimes being prosecuted, simply to construct our samples.

Both the choice of indicators and the interpretation of what results we get should be dependent on a clear understanding of how a prosecutor's office responds to salient variables.

TECHNIQUES OF CRIME POLICY ANALYSIS

The techniques of social science that can be employed in crime policy analysis are as numerous as the literature of social science itself. I would like to comment briefly on the techniques I will use in Chapters 9 to 14.

Several analysts have used budgetary expenditures in order to associate or correlate policy outputs to policy. Both the areas that government finances and the amounts it commits would seem to be reasonable indicators of their priorities. Moreover, comparing budgetary outlays with policy outputs (expenditures on a detective squad with increased crimes solved) permits us to compare alternative program expenditures. For example, we can compare units of men and women trained as both patrolmen and detectives with the traditional organizational divisions that separate the two functions. This would require assessing both patrolmen outputs and detective outputs in alternate programs by comparing budgetary outlays (costs) and crimes solved (benefits). Budgetary analysis and cost-benefit analysis are convenient techniques to employ for very large-scale programs. I will utilize such a technique when we examine alternative drug control programs in Chapter 12.

The limits of budgetary analysis, however, are twofold. First, line budgetary outlays have multiple purposes. One cannot assume that the formal objectives of an agency or department are its actual objectives. Second, it is very difficult to identify the linkage between budgetary outlays and policy outputs. For example, even if police budgets go up and crime rates go down, it is specious to conclude that higher budgets resulted in lower crime rates. Other intervening variables—median age, police policy not to arrest for certain offenses, chance variations, changes in reporting methods, and a dozen others—could be responsible. Budgetary analysis is advantageous precisely because it permits many activities to be examined in quantitative units (money), but it often leads to misleading conclusions that obscure multiple, intervening variables.

Systems analysis is another technique often employed effectively to aid in the analysis of crime policy. Generally, a system is composed of identifiable variables interacting with each other in measurable ways within a clearly specified boundary. The advantage of systems analysis is that many interdependent variables can be observed at the same time, often by programming the variables, parameters, and components in a computer. It is particularly useful to describe, evaluate, even predict the consequences of variables interacting in the flow criminal justice system, where the various legal and functional stages of the system can be quantified.

The system approach helps to organize masses of data and hundreds of interactions between variables and components in as clear a picture as possible. Some systems are merely descriptive, such as the description of the criminal justice system in Chapter 2. But with sophisticated data, predictions of systemwide responses to hypothetical inputs can be simulated. In Chapter 10 I will describe how simulation is employed in criminal justice planning.

The remainder of this chapter concerns the variety of indicators and conceptual frameworks with which the seriousness of crime is or might be measured in the United States. The discussion addresses the question of social science appropriateness in measurement and, also, the normative question: Are we experiencing a crisis of law and order? In many ways the two concerns are inseparable.

THE UNIFORM CRIME REPORT

Up to 1974, the only national measure we had for the seriousness of crime was the FBI Uniform Crime Report, the primary statistical model for police reporting at all levels of law enforcement. The UCR is calculated on the basis of offenses known to the police, as well as actual arrests made by the police. Offenses known and actual arrests are reported to the FBI by cooperating police departments throughout the United States; they are published quarterly in summary form and annually in analytical form by the bureau. The UCR is divided into Part I and Part II crimes; Part I crimes refer to the most serious "index" crimes. The index of serious crimes was developed by the FBI and the International Chiefs of Police Association in 1929[1] and includes the following offenses; homicide, forcible rape, robbery, assault, burglary, larceny, and auto theft. Approximately 92 percent of the national population is presently covered by the UCR.

Our analysis of crime statistics of the 1960s and 1970s leads to the conclusion that we did experience a sharp increase in both violent crime and property crime, particularly between 1963 and 1974, over rates prevalent in the 1950s. Our conclusions rest on the assumption that robbery, homicide, and auto theft are reasonably reliable indicators of increase in crime, since they are reported with more frequency and the events surrounding the crime tend to be more standardized in seriousness than with other types of offenses. As Table 9.1 demonstrates, all offenses sharply increased between 1963 and 1974. Annual rates of increase for robbery and auto theft between 1960 and 1963 were 0.015 percent and 0.06 percent, respectively, while homicide rates actually dropped on the average of 3 percent each year. However, beginning with 1964, a startling pattern of increases in serious crime occurred. Robbery increased at a rate of over 25 percent per year, auto theft rose at an equally alarming rate of 14 percent per year, and homicide increased by 11 percent per year. Both homicide and auto theft are especially

[1] National Commission on the Causes and Prevention of Violence, *Crimes of Violence: A Staff Report*, Vol. 11 (Washington, D.C.: U.S. Government Printing Office, December 1969), p. 13.

Table 9.1 Index of crime, United States, 1960-1974

Rate per 100,000 Inhabitants	Total Crime Index	Violent[a] Crime	Property[a] Crime	Murder and Non-negligent Man-slaughter	Forcible Rape	Robbery	Aggra-vated Assault	Burglary	Larceny-Theft	Motor Vehicle Theft
1960	1875.8	160.0	1715.8	5.1	9.5	60.0	85.4	505.6	1027.8	182.4
1961	1894.5	157.3	1737.2	4.7	9.4	58.1	85.0	515.7	1038.5	183.0
1962	2007.6	161.4	1846.2	4.6	9.4	59.5	87.9	532.0	1117.4	196.8
1963	3167.0	167.2	1999.8	4.6	9.3	61.6	91.7	572.9	1211.0	215.9
1964	2373.7	189.5	2184.2	4.9	11.2	68.0	105.4	630.9	1306.8	246.5
1965	2434.2	199.1	2235.1	5.1	12.1	71.5	110.4	658.7	1320.5	255.9
1966	2654.7	218.8	2435.9	5.6	13.2	80.6	119.4	716.6	1433.4	286.0
1967	2971.8	251.8	2720.0	6.2	13.9	102.5	129.2	821.5	1565.4	333.0
1968	3350.2	296.9	3053.3	6.9	15.8	131.5	142.7	926.6	1735.1	391.7
1969	3658.1	327.0	3331.1	7.3	18.4	148.0	153.3	978.2	1918.2	434.8
1970	3960.9	361.7	3599.1	7.8	18.6	171.7	163.6	1078.4	2065.5	455.3
1971	4140.0	394.0	3746.0	8.6	20.4	187.5	177.5	1156.4	2131.3	458.3
1972	3937.8	398.9	3538.9	8.9	22.4	180.3	187.3	1133.9	1980.4	424.6
1973	4129.7	415.3	3714.4	9.3	24.4	182.6	198.9	1215.1	2058.2	441.1
1974	4821.4	458.8	4362.6	9.7	26.1	208.8	214.2	1429.0	2473.0	460.6
Percent change 1960-1974[b]	+157.0	+186.8	+154.3	+90.2	+174.7	+248.0	+150.8	+182.6	+140.6	+152.5

[a]Violent crime is offenses of murder, forcible rape, robbery, and aggravated assault. Property crime is offenses of burglary, larceny-theft, and motor vehicle theft.

[b]Percent change and crime rates calculated prior to rounding number of offenses. Revised estimates and rates based on changes in reporting practices.

Source. FBI, *Uniform Crime Report,* 1974.

significant, since they are least apt to escape the attention of official police reports. Although criminologists and statisticians have long disputed the reliability of the UCR, such increases in the offense categories mentioned cannot fail to challenge the doubts of even the most cautious skeptic.[2]

However, having stated such a conclusion, we must also caution that the UCR does not permit us to conclude that out crime problem is of crisis proportions as compared with the past. Although the UCR does give a useful estimate of criminal offenses—particularly for offenses such as homicide and auto theft, and for police activity in general—*by itself* it remains an inadequate measure of criminal behavior in the United States for purposes of policy analysis. Indeed, the difficulties of measuring "crime" accurately are inherent in the difficulties of understanding the criminal justice system as a whole, so I wish to discuss the limits of the UCR at some length. This is not to provide a technical critique of criminal justice statistics or an exhaustive review of the UCR. Instead, it is to underscore the point that difficulties experienced in attempts to measure crime rates are similar to the difficulties of providing policy solutions to reduce them. The crux of the difficulty is that there presently exists little clarity as to what is meant by crime and by the problems of criminal justice.

DIFFICULTIES IN CRIME REPORTING

Several areas are identifiable as major stumbling blocks for accurate and meaningful reporting of crime, although by no means do they exhaust all the problems that could be raised about the UCR. To begin with, increases in UCR index crimes between 1963 and 1974 probably reflected more reporting than in the past. For example, in Pennsylvania during 1969, an estimated 972 police departments (mostly under five men) out of 1364 did not submit reports to the FBI. As of January 1, 1971, all police departments were required by statute to submit UCR information in Pennsylvania. As of 1973, many departments were still not reporting.

Moreover, police reporting is notoriously inaccurate according to police supervisors, especially where a rookie officer is involved. For example, an inexperienced patrolman on a "school beat" in Erie, Pennsylvania was reporting theft of lunch money as "armed robbery," since the 10-year-old youngster responsible was threatening other children with brass knuckles. The incident occurred 10 times and was duly recorded as 10 armed robberies. After the UCR report for this quarter was published, the aggregate rate was sufficiently alarming to provoke a lead editorial against armed robbery in the city.

Inaccurate reporting is not at all difficult to understand when one confronts the

[2]FBI, *Uniform Crime Report,* 1975, p. 55.

complex niceties of the penal law. After all, the criminal laws was written for jurisprudential (and, therefore, metaphysical) purposes to determine guilt or innocence, by attorneys who were interested in eliminating vagueness that could be exploited by prosecutors or defense counselors, with full appreciation that legal fictions were acceptable under special circumstances. For example, a fight between man and wife that results in the husband's being slapped by an irate spouse, although legally falling under the classification of aggravated assault, normally would not result in charges being filed by an officer or the filing of an indictment, unless under the unusual circumstances where the husband files a criminal complaint against his wife.

Examples abound of fluctuating arrest rates because of poor reporting or variables other than criminal activity. For years the Chicago Police Department reported seven and eight times as many robberies as did the New York City police. In 1949, the FBI stopped including New York figures because they did not consider them reliable. Of course, New York is much larger than Chicago and certainly had a similar robbery rate. But, for unknown reasons, they chose not to report criminal offenses that had taken place. In 1950 a central complaint system in New York replaced a precinct reporting system. The result was a four fold increase in the volume of robberies reported between 1949 and 1959.[5]

Police reporting is probably more accurate than in the past and technology has made the job somewhat more reviewable by permitting supervisors to exercise better administrative control over individual officer's reports. Ironically, as police officers are professionalized regarding investigation of crime and record keeping and have more resources at their disposal, they tend to tap a reserve of criminal activity that has not been reported in the past. That is, as the level of competence and resources of police officers goes up, the arrest rate and crime index are likely to increase proportionately. Curiously, this has led to situations where a local police chief has found himself in the bewildering position of being under attack by the media for "increases" in UCR index crimes in his jurisdiction—increases that have resulted from the men under his command doing a professional job.

Phillip Ennis' early study demonstrates the plausible extent of unreported crime reserves. Ennis' study was based on the National Opinion Research Center (NORC) survey conducted in the summer of 1965. By using sample survey methods, instead of police blotters or reports, Ennis discovered that rates for personal crimes and property offenses were higher than previous figures would indicate, except for auto theft and homicide (Table 9.2)

[5]National Commission, *Crimes of Violence,* Vol. II, p. 22.

Table 9.2 Unreported crime.

	NORC Estimated Rate per 100,000	1965 Uniform Crime Report Crimes Known to Police
Homicide	3.0	5.1
Forcible rape	42.5	11.6
Robbery	94.0	61.4
Aggravated assault	218.3	106.76
Burglary	949.1	296.6
Larceny ($50+)	606.5	267.4
Car theft	206.2	226.0

Source. Phillip H. Ennis, *Field Surveys II, Criminal Victimization in the United States:* A Report of a National Survey, National Opinion Research Center (Washington, D.C.: U.S. Government Printing Office, May 1967), p. 8.

Victimization surveying has undergone extensive refinement in methodology and retesting. Generally, however, contemporary evaluations of victimization rates in major cities have sustained the NORC survey regarding the extent of unreported crime in the United States. Most of this research has been financed by the Law Enforcement Assistance Administration (LEAA), which released its results in April 1974 for five major cities in the United States: Chicago, Detroit, Los Angeles, New York, and Philadelphia. (See Table 9.3)

The table reveals considerable underreporting by citizens to the police. For the five cities surveyed, only 30 percent of all crimes of theft (pocket picking, larceny, purse snatching), 36 percent of personal crimes (rape, robbery, assualt) , and 46 percent of household crimes (burglary, auto theft, household larceny) were reported. On the other hand, 77 percent of all commercial crimes (burglary, robbery) were reported. It should be noted that robbery often takes place on the street as well as in commercial establishments.

Research conducted by National Institute of LEAA has isolated and ranked numerous reasons for victims suffering in silence by not complaining to authorities, although the need for further research remains. The most commonly cited reasons given in LEAA's nationwide surveys (Table 9.4) for victims not reporting crime to the police were a belief that, because of lack of proof, nothing could be accomplished by reporting the incident, and a feeling that the incident was not sufficiently important to merit police attention.[6]

Why is there a much higher percentage of commercial crime reported? There are several reasons. First, commercial establishments in larger cities will report theft for insurance purposes as a matter of routine. In addition, robbery is a person-to-person crime always accompanied with either the threat of violence or

Table 9.3 Percent of victimizations reported to the police, by type of victimization and city, 1972

Type of victimization	Chicago	Detroit	Los Angeles	New York	Philadelphia
Personal	37	39	33	38	36
Crimes of violence	48	51	44	45	47
Rape and attempted rape	53	55	46	61	55
Robbery	52	60	48	47	50
Robbery and attempted robbery with injury	69	75	64	50	64
Serious assault	70	72	69	58	70
Minor assault	67	79	57	41	57
Robbery without injury	57	62	51	51	57
Attempted robbery without injury	27	39	27	33	27
Assault	44	42	42	41	44
Aggravated assault	52	53	52	57	51
With injury	72	68	57	73	59
Attempted assault with weapon	41	46	50	44	46
Simple assault	37	28	34	31	36
With injury	54	41	46	45	54
Attempted assault without weapon	31	25	30	27	31
Crimes of theft	30	31	28	33	28
Personal larceny with contact	41	48	37	37	39
Purse snatching	61	74	58	53	57

Table 9.3 Percent of victimizations reported to the police, by type of victimization and city, 1972 (continued)

Type of victimization	Chicago	Detroit	Los Angeles	New York	Philadelphia
Attempted purse snatching	19	(B)	(B)	22	(B)
Pocket picking	35	35	26	29	35
Personal larceny without contact	28	29	27	31	27
Household	48	50	44	49	46
Burglary	53	57	53	52	55
Forcible entry	74	75	75	71	78
Unlawful entry (without force)	40	44	45	52	44
Attempted forcible entry	35	35	30	25	31
Household larceny	26	25	25	24	22
Completed larceny	27	26	25	25	22
Attempted larceny	20	18	31	(B)	25
Auto theft	78	78	69	73	69
Completed theft	93	96	92	92	92
Attempted theft	35	26	26	26	32
Commercial	75	77	73	80	78
Burglary	71	76	71	79	75
Robbery	91	83	84	82	88
Completed robbery	97	90	95	89	96
Attempted robbery	81	61	50	64	66

Note: In general, small differences between any two figures in this table are not statistically significant because of sampling. B Percent not shown because estimated number of victimization in this category was too small to be statistically significant.

Source: U.S. Department of Justice, Law Enforcement Assistance Administration, *Crime in the Nation's Five Largest Cities, Advance Report,* Washington, D. C., April 1974.

Table 9.4 Reasons for not reporting crime

Reason	Personal	Household
Nothing could be done; lack of proof	34	37
Not important enough	28	31
Police would not want to be bothered	8	9
Too inconvenient	5	4
Private or personal matter	4	3
Afraid of reprisal	2	1
Reported to someone else	7	3
Other or not available	12	12

Source. U.S. Department of Justice National Crime Panel Survey of Chicago, Detroit, Los Angeles, New York, and Philadelphia.

its actual use. The victim is inevitably angry and frightened and will normally identify the offender and cooperate fully with the police in any investigation.

The National Crime Panel surveys also discovered that crimes of theft where no contact and no violence occurred were more likely to victimize affluent citizens and were more likely to be reported to the police, although not with the same regularity as offenses against commercial establishments.

Conversely, the victim of personal crime (i.e., offenses accompanied by violence) is likely to be a member of a minority group and have an annual income under $10,000. Moreover, households headed by members of minority races are more likely than white households to be burglarized and, except in New York City, they are also more apt to have their car stolen.

The fact that crimes predominately perpetrated on low-income groups are much less apt to be reported is probably attributable to the interaction of lower-class individuals and governmental authorities, including the police who, in most cases, represent the most visible symbol of government in the eyes of the poor. To what extent race and class are separate variables in nonreporting is not clear from the National Crime Panel surveys. However, it is a characteristic of lower-class behavior for individuals to lack assurance that they can control their envi-

[6]National Criminal Justice Information and Statistics Service, *Crime in the Nation's Five Largest Cities, Advanced Report,* U.S. Department of Justice, LEAA, Washington, D.C., April 1974, p. 2, table on pp. 3 and 5.

ronment by individually altering conditions or influencing government to do so.[7] The lower-class victim is also more skeptical of the ability of the police to prevent violence and theft by taking measures one way or another. Low expectations of law enforcement agencies correspond with low expectations of government effectiveness in general, particularly in terms of capacity to influence its actions.

The association of statistical crime increases with increases in police budgets has been insufficiently understood by both social scientists and the news media. In an interesting work in policy analysis for criminal justice, Cho[8] provides correlations between increased budgetary allocations for selected police operations (salary, increasing the numbers of sworn officers, increased patrol cars, scooters, and motorcycles, etc.) and *increases* in robbery, assault and auto theft based on the UCR index reports. Cho concludes "that raising the policy level (budgetary outlay) does not reduce the crime rate contrary to the simplistic expectations often manifested by the 'law and order' proponents." Cho's explanation for this apparently nonsensical convergence of higher crime rates and higher budgets for law enforcement is perfectly reasonable. It is that as crime rates go up, the citizenry will support higher budgets.[9] However, Cho misses the point that additional resource allocations to the police will, in all probability, result in more arrests and knowledge of offenses committed from a pool of hitherto unreported crime. In fairness, however, it should be added that the pool of unreported crime is not as deep for robbery, a crime accompanied by violence or its threat, as it is for crimes not involving violence or personal contact, such as larceny.

An additional reason for increases in crime reporting (and actual crime between 1964 and 1974) may be related to shifting age ratios in the population. UCR statistics themselves demonstrate that young people in the 15- to 18-year-old range are much more prone to commit serious crime than any other age group. For example, I previously commented on the fact that persons arrested in Pennsylvania under the age of 25 from 1960 up to 1975 accounted for over 50 percent of all violent crimes and at least 82 percent of all property crime. According to the U. S. census report for 1970, the median age of all Americans dropped from 30.2 years in 1950 to an estimated 28.1 years in 1970. Although obviously there are many variables affecting increases in crime, the dip in the median age between 1960 and 1970 roughly corresponds to a dramatic increase in crime during that

[7] Lester W. Milbrath, *Political Participation* (Chicago: Rand McNally, 1966), pp. 77-78.

[8] Yong Hyo Cho, *Public Policies and Urban Crime* (Cambridge: Ballinger, 1974), tables on pp. 168-170.

[9] Ibid., p. 169.

period. Each year since 1961 approximately 1 million youngsters more reached the age of 15 years than did the year before. The result may have been a predictable increase in crime.

Crime propensity is particularly acute for blacks whose median age, 4.5 years lower than that of whites to begin with in 1950, has dropped even faster than the white decrease between 1950 and 1970. There are several reasons for this. Black birth rates during that period were about one third higher than whites, increasing the size of the crime-prone age group.[10] On the other hand, part, but not all, of the lower median age can be explained by a lower life expectancy of blacks.[11]

The arrest rate of blacks for violent crimes is much higher than that of whites, but to what extent this is a consequence of age, as suggested here, or of socio-economic status, region, or racial discrimination is not clear. Race prejudice is strong among policemen, particularly in high-crime, black areas. Vitriolic and dehumanizing language is frequently used by officers to describe blacks, but there is some evidence that police caricatures of lower-class blacks reflect a combative hardening of the officer who must deal under dangerous circumstances with what he considers "the criminal element."[12] In nonblack high-crime areas, ethnic slurs about the population are common, too. It is also true that the incidence of violent crime is correlated with lower-class behavior and southern culture. It is the legacy of American history that the American black disproportionately falls into both categories. Still, some scholars have argued that black crime may be attributable to a subculture of violence that, to some extent, operates independently of class and region. Others have provided evidence that black-white crime differentials are attributable primarily to class and regional origin.[13] Whichever is correct, it is very difficult to isolate race discrimination as a factor in the decision to arrest. It is clear, however, that both black and white crime rates must be understood historically according to shifting age ratios as well as economic status (Table 9.5).

[10] If the rural background of the mother is held constant, however, the black birthrate is comparable with that of whites. See Pascal K. Whelpton, Arthur A. Campbell, and John E. Patterson, *Fertility and Family Planning in the United States* (Princeton, N.J.: Princeton University Press, 1966), pp. 342-348.

[11] U. S. Census, 1970.

[12] Donald J. Black and Albert J. Reiss, Jr., *Field Survey III: Studies in Law Enforcement in Major Metropolitan Areas,* Vol. II, Section II (Washington, D.C.: U.S. Government Printing Office, 1967), Table 25 at p. 135.

[13] Wolfgang and others found black boys three times more likely to be chronic offenders than whites from their tenth to their eighteenth birthdays when low socio-economic status was held constant, and

Table 9.5 median age of population (United States)

	Black	White	All
1950	26.2	30.7	30.2
1960	23.5	30.3	29.5
1970	22.4	28.9	28.1

Source. Statistical Abstract of the U.S., 1972, p. 24.

American history has demonstrated a rough correlation between immigration and migration movements and increases in criminal behavior in the inner city where immigrants are most apt to settle. Precisely what the causal links between immigration and criminal behavior are not altogether clear. Jewish and Japanese immigration did not result in significantly higher crime rates; Italian and Irish immigration did. Apparently family structure and cultural variables were salient factors affecting crime. The immigrants were not necessarily the perpetrators of the increased number of crimes, but often were the victims. Much more quantitative historical analysis must be done in this area, and any comments I make must be considered exploratory.

However, we have experienced for the last 35 years or so a massive migration of rural, southern blacks and whites into urban areas. In 1940, for example, 72 percent of American blacks lived in the South. In 1960 that percentage was 54 percent. By 1970 approximately 75 percent of all American blacks, most of whom had rural roots, had moved to urban areas. Considering the lack of jobs for

they attributed this difference partially to a subculture of violence. Marvin E. Wolfgang, Robert M. Figlio, and Thorsten Sellin, *Delinquency in a Birth Cohort* (Chicago: University of Chicago Press, 1972), p. 91. The subculture thesis is supported by Savitz's finding that native-born blacks in Philadelphia were more apt to be arrested for delinquency than migrating blacks. Leonard Savitz, "Delinquency and Migration," in *The Sociology of Crime and Delinquency,* pp, ed. Marvin E. Wolfgang, Leonard Savitz, and Norman Johnston (New York: Wiley, 1970), pp. 473-480.

Conversely, Green's Ypsilanti study concluded that black-white crime rate differences were accountable due to socio-economic and nativity variables, the latter referring to offenders migrating from the south. Green found no evidence, one way or another, of race discrimination in the decision to arrest. Edward Green, "Race, Social Status, and Criminal Arrest," *American Sociological Review* (1970), 35:476-490. However, Goldman's examination of juvenile arrests tends to support the thesis that cultural variables in separate communities play a prominent part in the decision to arrest juveniles. Nathan Goldman, *Differential Selection of Juvenile Offenders for Court Appearance* (New York: National Research and Information Center of the National Council on Crime and Deliquency, 1963), pp. 85-92.

unskilled labor attendant with a modern, technological economy and the complexity of social and economic life today, and racial bigotry, it is likely that southern migrants have experienced even more severe cultural conflict and discontinuity than that experienced by most previous immigrant groups. Although southern rural migration to urban areas has apparently abated somewhat in the 1970s, there is some evidence that Mexican immigration and migration to urban areas, mostly illegal, has greatly expanded in the past decade.

Data are very difficult to come by in this area, and the relationship between crime rates and immigration cycles remains largely conjectural. However, the historical perspective is by and large ignored in the UCR graphs from which depictions of crime customarily stretch over no more than a generation of ten years. Comprehensive crime data were not collected until after 1933, but studies of individual cities were made prior to that time, and they show that crime characteristically has not been steadily increasing but has had rhythmic cycles. In all probability the most serious crime rate in our history was not in modern times, but occurred between 1860 and 1870. Studies in Boston, Chicago, New York, and other cities have shown that the rates were higher in the World War I years and in the 1920s than they were in the 1940s.[14]

Although reliable data for most crimes committed prior to 1933 do not exist, we do have comprehensive data for homicides since 1900. One can readily see from observing Figure 9.1 the cyclical characteristic of homicide in American history. There is no question about the sharp increase in homicide since 1964.

As previously suggested, there is significant distortion when statistical analysis ignores qualitative distinctions in criminal offenses. In this respect the "seriousness" category of the FBI index of serious crimes must be questioned. It will be recalled that murder, burglary, robbery, larceny, auto theft, and forcible rape are identified by the FBI as the seven index crimes to measure crime in the United states. Burglary and larceny are relatively easy to index, but thus are not nearly as serious as "child beating" by parents and intrafamily assault. It has been estimated that child beatings take more lives in the United States each year than all childhood diseases combined, whereas intrafamily violence is much more common than street confrontations, but much less apt to be reported by family members. Additionally, child abuse and intrafamily violence are not usually counted among index crimes.

When we equate each larceny and burglary offense with each incident of violence, a qualitative distortion occurs if we assume that human safety takes

[14] Graham, "A Contemporary History of American Crime," in *The History of Violence in America*, pp. 489-491.

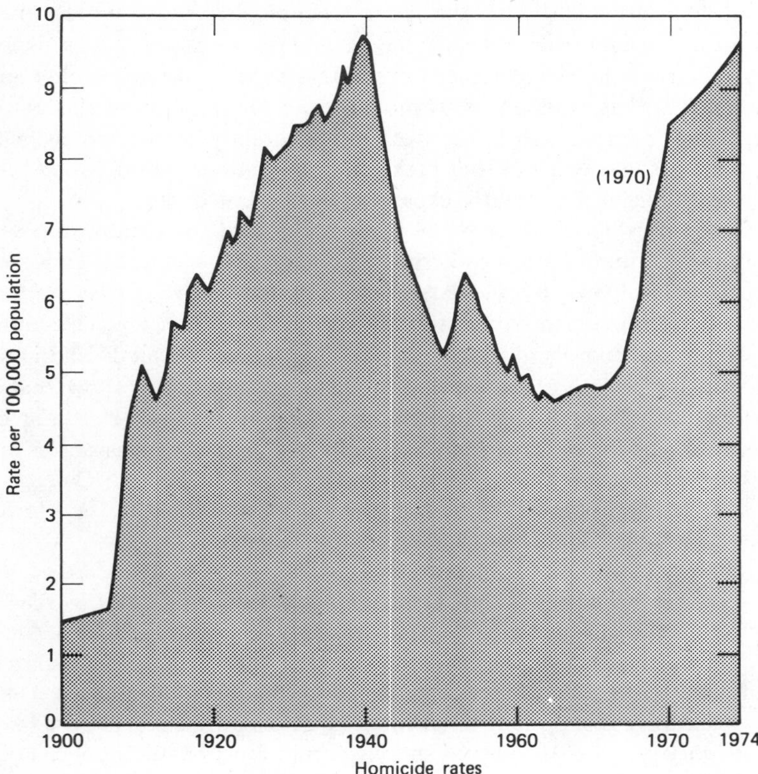

Figure 9.1 Homicide rates, 1900-1974. (Sources. *FBI,* Uniform Crime Reports, *1960-1974;* History of Violence in America, *p. 491.*)

precedence over loss of property. By equating the much more numerous incidences of property crime with crimes of violence, the FBI figures make the crime problem in the United States appear qualitatively more serious than it actually is. This distortion can be seen clearly in Figure 9.2.

Moreover, property crime is not weighted according to the value of the property. There are in the criminal justice system an overwhelming number of larceny cases processed each year, but the routine case that finds its way into the index crime totals usually amounts to no more than several hundred dollars maximum. According to the Pennsylvania Crime Commission, the numbers racket alone in Pennsylvania nets over $250 million each year, and gambling is not an index

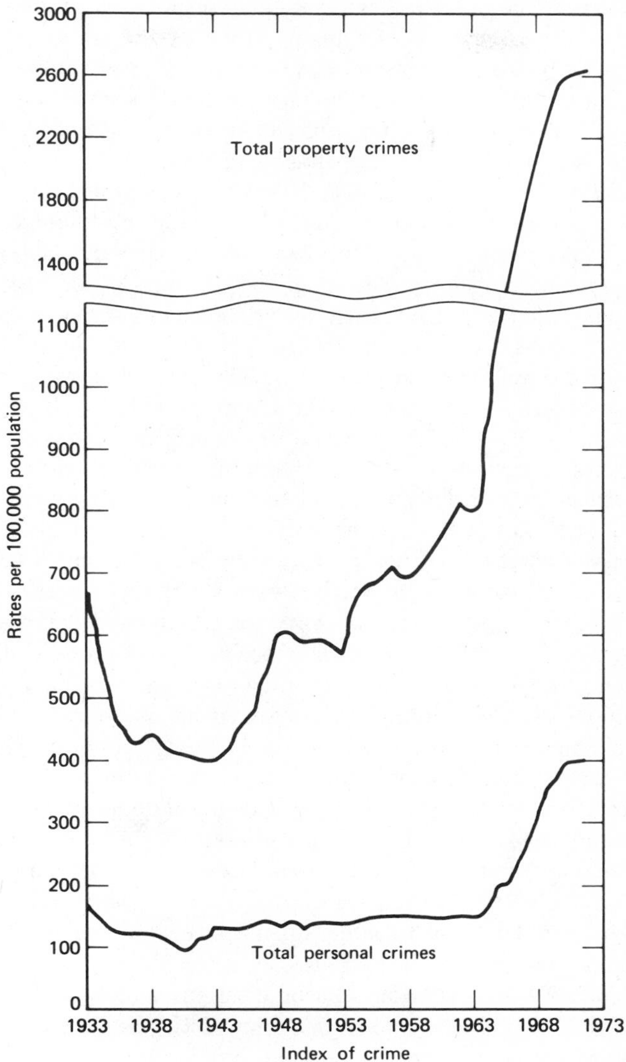

Figure 9.2 Index of crime, 1933-1973. (Source. *FBI,* Uniform Crime Reports, *1933-1973.*)

crime.[15] Of course, large-scale illegal gambling operations cannot operate without a plethora of serious crimes, ranging from loan sharking, extortion, and bribery of public officials to evasion of income tax. None of these crimes are in the index of serious crimes, partially because the FBI has traditionally been more interested in "subversive activities" instead of organized crime, and partially because such offenses are extremely difficult to detect.

Former director of the FBI J. Edgar Hoover was identified for many years as insisting that communist activities and general subversive movements in the Unites States take priority for federal law enforcement and investigation over organized crime. It is estimated that up to one third of all FBI agents were assigned to surveillance and investigation of subversive activities at the time of the Kefauver Hearings on Organized Crime in the U. S. Senate during 1955. Hoover simply did not believe organized crime to be as serious a problem as the Communist Party. In fairness, it should be added that public apathy and tolerance of organized crime activities provided little encouragement for public officials to conduct aggressive campaigns against gambling, sharking, and the like. It has proved much easier to rally public indignation against the representatives of foreign ideologies, particularly in the 1950s.

The dramatic increase in crime portrayed by the UCR index (Figure 9.2) is largely a function of equating property crimes, which have increased more than 700 percent since 1933, with crimes of violence, which have increased 48 percent over the same period. A 700-percent increase in violent crime would approach being deserving of the term "crisis" in anyone's scale of values. A 48-percent increase over 24 years is still serious, but somewhat more manageable.

Similarly, income tax evasion, price fixing among corporate giants such as occurred in 1963 between electrical corporations amounting to $7 million in extra profits, organized theft from trucking lines and international airports—all of these offenses, although few in number, result in losses to the public that dwarf the typical larceny loss. However, it is the small larceny that makes up nearly all the index crime total for theft. Moreover, the distortion built into indexing crimes of property by offense instead of by value stolen has become even more pronounced as a consequence of inflation in the 1970s. What would have amounted to petty larceny (under $50) in 1962 would become serious larceny several years later according to the FBI standards for index crimes. Bicycle theft, a common form of petty theft years ago, became larceny, an index crime, by virtue of an over-

[15] Projections made from records seized by the Intelligence Division of the Internal Revenue Service reveal that the volume of business conducted by major numbers banks in Pennsylvania totals over $240 million per year. The total volume of *all* banks in the state would greatly exceed this figure. Pennsylvania Crime Commission, *Report on Organized Crime*, Pennsylvania Department of Justice, 1970, p. 26, footnote on p. 119.

heated economy. Finally, in 1973 all larcenies were included as index offenses by the FBI, ending the influence of the inflation variable on crime, but sharply increasing the crime rate by definition.

The basic problem of measurement for property crime is that crime statistics are based on units of illegality, a jurisprudential, moral quality, instead of on economic units of value. The former is necessary to determine guilt or innocence, but the latter measurement is infinitely more useful for policy analysis, for indicating how serious our crime problem is and to what extent our policy has addressed them.

10

MODELING A VICTIM-ORIENTED CRIME POLICY

Any measurement is an intended ordering of objects within a frame of reference engendered by some conceptual imagery.
Paul F. Lazarsfeld[1]

What one measures implicitly begs the significance of the phenomenon that is measured. The conceptual imagery of our analysis of crime policy clearly is value laden in the direction of reducing victim suffering as a comprehensive goal. However, for those who reject this *value* premise, a victim-oriented index provides many advantages for measuring both crime and the impact of crime policy on crime, regardless of any normative reluctance to assert a reduction of victim suffering as a comprehensive goal. Indeed, there are so many advantages to measuring the seriousness of crime by victimization perspectives that one wonders why, prior to the mid-1960s, there were no substantial efforts by scholars in this country or elsewhere to produce valid estimates of the amount of victim crime by interview surveys[2] or seriousness of crime by weighting psychological anguish, property loss, and physical harm to the victim.[3]

[1] Paul F. Lazarsfeld, "Notes on the History of Quantification," in *Quantification,* ed. Harry Woolf (Indianapolis: Bobbs-Merrill, 1961), p. 160.

[2] G. Turner and Richard W. Dodge, "Surveys of Personal and Organizational Victimization," paper presented at Symposium on Studies of Public Experience, Knowledge and Opinion of Crime and Justice, Washington, D.C., March 16-18, 1972, p. 1. See also National Advisory Commission on Criminal Justice, "Victimization Surveying—Its History, Uses and Limitations," in *Criminal Justice System,* Washington, D.C., 1973, Appendix A, pp. 199-206.

[3] Sellin and Wolfgang's *The Measurement of Delinquency* was the first serious effort to scale crime seriousness.

State-financed victim compensation schemes have considerable merit, although they have had more than their share of administrative problems. At any rate, I am concerned in this textbook with crime policy to *prevent* victim suffering, not with victim compensation policy.

In customary police court reporting, criminal definitions are applied to a large number of logically unrelated but frequently confused categories. Three of the most frequently confused categories are (1) criminal events, (2) legal decisions regarding criminal events, and (3) individual offenders.[4] It is essential to discriminate among these categories if we are to assess the seriousness of crime for public policy.

A fundamental advantage to victim surveying is its capacity to generate data on the frequency of criminal activity through the lens of the victim instead of through the records of officialdom. Neither the records at the station house or central file nor those in the National Crime Information Center can provide as accurate an account, as I have earlier discussed, as victim surveys. The police are concerned with keeping the peace, arresting offenders, and protecting the integrity of their organization. Consequently, their data are arranged for professional supervision of officers in the field and accumulation of criminal records for purposes of reporting police activities. But police reporting is not designed to measure the seriousness of a criminal event through the eyes of the victim or according to the vantage point of commonly accepted social interpretations of an event.

An earthy example within the experience of us all can illustrate the point. A male and female are apprehended conspiring to encourage a young girl to remove her undergarments. Obviously this is a pathological sex crime. When we are informed that the young conspirators are 6 and 7 years old, respectively, and the delinquent whose morals they were corrupting was also of tender years, the *event* becomes a universal prepuberty child game (at least in Western cultures where small children wear clothes) known to all of us as "You show me and I'll show you." Similarly, youngsters stealing apples from a barn or professional thieves climbing through a window in a residence to break open a safe represent obviously different degrees of seriousness, although each event is classified as a burglary, a felony. The young boys would not be treated as "typical criminals"; the wisened thugs would be so treated. Consequently, quite different "events" are likely to be classified as the same crime by the police, although they are treated differently; and the opposite is possible as well. Similar criminal events may be treated

My focus on a crime policy to prevent victim suffering should not be confused with the idea of compensating individuals after they have been victimized. Victim compensation can work in two ways. The offender can be required to make restitution, or the state may pay for loss of property and injury. A sentence requiring restitution is as old as the criminal law. The problem, of course, is that many offenders are poor and are unable to make restitution.

[4] Wilkins, "New Thinking in Criminal Statistics," p. 57.

differently by the police, especially when racial or class bias is present, when value structures differ from community to community, and when organizational or social control exigencies demand differential treatment for perfectly rational purposes. In the latter situation, smoking marihuana at a college party that is raided will result in an arrest, while smoking pot at a mass rock concert will most likely be ignored, top priority for law enforcement resources at the concert being given to crowd control and public health.[5]

Moreover, court reporting is as far removed from an accurate measurement of victim suffering as it is distant from a valid measurement of the crime problem as defined by police reporting. Indeed, court records of legal decisions and procedure pay little attention to the suffering of victims at all, even when they are witnesses.[6] instead, court statistics reflect essentially metaphysical and procedural concerns. Even when there is no finding of legal guilt, plea negotiations are sometimes confessional in tone. Juvenile judges almost always use juvenile hearings as a forum for announcing moral obligations along with legal implications, and the adult court has long been considered a morality play of dramatic dimensions in literature and drama. Informal sanctions at a hearing or sentencing often flow even when they are not part of statutory punishments.[7] Even when a finding of legal culpability is made, it is not logically related to the victim's suffering, but to the rules of evidence, the availability of witnesses, the reasonable doubt standard, the resources of the prosecutor's office, procedural requirements of the appellate courts, and a plethora of other variables that go beyond both the police officer's standard of probable cause and the victim's sense of wrong.

Victim surveying gives a more accurate gauge of "criminal events" than the legal categories of the Uniform Crime Report. Police reporting, based on arrests and crimes known to the police, will include multiple offenders who are charged with the same crime, and offenders reported as "known to the police" may be innocent of the charge or nonexistent. The emphasis of police reporting is toward the offender whom the police are charged to apprehend, not the victim. In fact, recording a single burglar as the perpetrator of a large number of unsolved burglaries is common—it sends clearance rates soaring. But conviction on, or a sentence of restitution for, large numbers of burglaries is not common, reflecting to some extent disingenuousness in the police who may attempt to improve their clearance rates by attributing unsolved burglaries to an offender who will normally plea bargain the additional charges away, at any rate.

[5]For examples of how misleading and arbitrary official classification can be see Edwin Lemert, "Juvenile Justice—Quest of Reality," *Transaction* (June-July 1967), pp. 30-40; Sellin and Wolfgang, *The Measurement of Delinquency*, pp. 71-86.

[6]Michael Ash, "Court Delay, Crime Control and Neglect of the Interests of Witnesses," in *Reducing Court Delay,* U.S. Department of Justice (Washington, D.C.: U.S. Government Printing Office, 1973), pp. 1-44.

[7]Maureen Mileski, "Court Encounters," p. 501.

On the other hand, current surveying by the National Crime Panel measures crime by the total number of victims, including those who are victimized more than twice, by the criminal events, including the combinations such as robbery-assault, and by describing crimes contextually (stranger-to-stranger crimes, street crimes, business crimes, etc.), and by incidence of crime (the total number of events).[8] These measurements of incidence give the panel a statistical walkway for purposes of cross checking the UCRs, while event and victim statistics permit more sophisticated analysis of the seriousness of crime.

The logical distinctions between behavioral categories for crime statistics—events, legal decisions, and offenders—partially explain the statistical discrepancy between actual criminal incidents, multiple crimes within a criminal event, police-reported crime, indictments, convictions, sentences, and numbers of offenders.[9] As previously suggested, one arrest may "clear" 50 burglaries and send clearance rates soaring. Confusing the categories results in intermingling the proverbial apple-and-orange type groupings. This is precisely what the Uniform Crime Report has done. Ironically, police officers are sometimes prone to point to the lack of prosecution for these crimes as definitive proof of the leniency of the criminal courts. What was needed was an index of crime, convertible to the standard UCR index, while at the same time being sufficiently descriptive of the actual event of a victimization in terms of personal intimidation, property loss, and physical injury. It was recognized that the instrument for collecting the data should not depend on police activity. During the 1960s the federal government and a few universities developed the complex methodology for victim surveying. After 1968 this development grew very fast, encouraged by the National Institute of the Law Enforcement Assistance Administration, and the first of a series of the National Crime Panel surveys was published in November 1974.[10] Continued victim surveying of this nature promises to provide a reliable index to measure criminal events. Although it has its limitations for crime policy analysis (limitations that will be discussed later), its event categories of crime are not tied to legal definitions, and its data, free from dependence on police reporting, are closer to a major participant in the event—the victim.

A second advantage of victim surveys is that they generally avoid the dark area of crime—that proportion of criminal activity (around 50 percent) that goes unreported. As noted in Chapter 2, the total number of crimes recorded as "known to the police" is a function of more than actual criminal behavior. Police

[8]Turner and Dodge, "Surveys of Personal and Organizational Victimization," pp. 20-21. These are, of course, logically distinct categories and are identified as such.

[9]See Uniform Crime Report, 1973, pp. 28-30.

[10]National Criminal Justice Information and Statistics Service, *Criminal Victimization in the United States, January-June 1973,* National Crime Panel Survey Report, U.S. Department of Justice, LEAA, Vol. 1 (November 1974).

patrol practices determine which types of crimes will be uncovered and police discretion frequently will screen out many types of offense from a report. State police have mentioned to us that drunk driving cases, a felony in Pennsylvania, necessitating arrest, preliminary arraignment, hearings, and possibly trial, will normally be ticketed and reported as reckless driving, a summary offence, so that the officer may avoid 8 hours on the job, at night, and another 8 hours in court the very next day. And nonreporting manipulations, either to improve "clearance rates" or to improve "crime rates" by not reporting crimes at all, are apparently common practices among police departments. Even when citizens file a formal complaint, police may, after investigation, find the complaint "unfounded." Scattered statistics of unfounded crime totals for rape (25 percent), robbery (13 percent), and gun assaults (19 percent) of urban police departments reported by Skogan suggest that the reduction of UCR totals because of "unfounding" may be considerable.[11]

In spite of the victim surveys' capacity to explore the "dark areas" of unreported crime, victim-reported data probably continue to underestimate the total considerably for particular offenses. Assault and rape are such crimes. According to the National Crime Panel, the number of rapes and attempted rapes that were reported to the police amounted to between 35 and 51 percent of those reported to interviewers for the National Crime Panel. For aggravated and simple assault only 30 to 49 percent of the total reported to interviewers were reported to the police.[12] Yet, in a study to *test* the validity of the survey methodology, only 66 percent of all rape victims and 48 percent of all assault victims *who had* reported such crimes to the police mentioned the event to the survey interviewers. Clearly, the trauma of rape places strong pressures on the victim not to recall for herself or anyone else that brutal moment. Similarly, assault may be psychologically less traumatic although equally brutal but, like rape, it frequently occurs between family members, relatives, and erstwhile friends. Both the psychological dynamics and the continuing social dynamics probably continue to make measurement of assault and rape crimes a tenuous enterprise.[13]

[11] Wesley G. Skogan, "Measurement Problems in Official and Survey Crime Rates," *Journal of Criminal Justice* (1975), 3:22.

[12] National Crime Panel, *Crime in Eight American Cities, Advanced Report,* U.S. Department of Justice, LEAA, National Criminal Justice Information and Statistics Service, July 1974, Table 8 on p. 38.

[13] National Institute of Law Enforcement and Criminal Justice, *San Jose Methods Test of Known Crime Victims: Statistics Technical Report No. 1,* LEAA, Washington, D.C., June 1972, Table C on p. 6; National Criminal Justice Information and Statistics Service, "Crimes and Victims: A Report on the Dayton-San Jose Pilot Survey of Victimization," U.S. Department of Justice, LEAA, June 1974, p. 12. I believe that the National Crime Panel underestimates the difficulty of assessing the number of assaults between relatives. They identify assaults in which the offender was a relative as constituting only 5 percent of total assault incidents. One might conjecture that the total assault rate between relatives is much larger but is not reported to "outsiders," whether interviewer or police

In addition, police reports have an informal but fortuitous dimension not contained in victimization surveys in that they may not include inconsequential behaviors that are formally crimes but can be dealt with informally by the officer. Schoolboy brawling and petty larceny—petty shoplifting by small children or stealing trinkets from a home—are obvious examples. More than half of the unreported crimes in the Dayton and San Jose victimization surveys, which were pilot studies to test the feasibility and reliability of victim survey methodology, were larcenies under $50. Serious crimes represented only 5 percent of the crimes unreported to interviewers.[14] Citizens interviewed who did not report incidents of crime to which they had been subjected, a full 35 percent in Dayton and 42 percent in San Jose, gave "not important enough" and "no material loss or physical harm suffered" as their justification.[15] For this and other reasons, it seems clear that multiple indicators, including both UCR reporting and victimization surveying, are important for assessing the problems of crime.

Beyond its usefulness for assessing unreported crime, victimization surveying permits study of the victim himself. It has been argued that[16] victims in some situations encourage crime and have a vital role in potential prevention. Examples are legion: vacationing residents who fail to cancel their newspapers or mail while they are away; intoxicated down-and-outers sleeping it off in a city park or street; the young girl who is unaccompanied late at night on a remote highway or dimly lit city street; and the defaulting banker, swindled in a desperate attempt to keep the institution's head above water.[17] As we learn more of the victim's role in the criminal event, we may be in a position to prevent crime, not simply by deterrence or incarcerating offenders, but by encouraging potential victims to alter their behavior. For instance, the U.S. Chamber of Commerce has attempted to make their membership more aware of the penetration of organized crime and prevent crime-potential situations from arising by pointing to access points for organized crime into legitimate business.[18] Although it is doubtful how such exhortations can dry up the business market for organized crime without reexamining the eagerness of the "victim" to borrow from a loan shark, gamble, or use narcotics, we may still heed the point of C. Ray Jeffery and design the urban environment

officer. See "Crimes and victims," p. 14. Skogan also questions the underreporting of rape and interfamily violence in victim surveys. Skogan, "Measurement Problems in Official and Survey Crime Rates," p. 24.

[14] "Crimes and Victims," p. 24.

[15] Ibid., Table 12 on p. 24.

[16] An early work on the role of the victim in crime was Hans von Hentig, *The Criminal and His Victim* (New Haven,: Conn. Yale University Press, 1948), especially pp. 419-433.

[17] Pennsylvania Crime Commission, *Report on Organized Crime,* pp. 54-55.

[18] U.S. Chamber of Commerce, *Deskbook on Organized Crime,* Washington, D.C., 1969.

with a mind to crime prevention.[19] After warning buzzers were mandated for automobile keys left in the ignition in 1972, auto theft went down 17 percent—a good illustration of the potential efficacy of environmental design for crime policy. Still, hardening targets is a responsibility primarily for potential victims, as our illustrations suggest. There are limits beyond which public policy cannot go to design a crime-resistant environment.

LIMITS TO VICTIM SURVEYING

Not all types of crime can be successfully measured by present victimization surveys. I hardly need mention the illogic of measuring victim rates for victimless crime. And the methodology of the National Crime Panel cannot distinguish petty burglaries from serious burglaries in terms of dollar amounts stolen, although the data are designed to distinguish between forcible and nonforcible entry, income of the victimized household, commercial versus noncommercial establishments, and large commercial operations from small operations.

In addition, there are many crimes of which the victim is not aware. Fraud and embezzlement are good examples. In other situations the victim is all too aware of his own illegal or at least questionable and sometimes embarrassing collusion in the commission of the crime: the accountant who is being blackmailed to extort from a bank; the restaurant owner who pays off the police for protection or for overlooking the extended hours of an after-curfew bar; the confidence man's victim who feels foolish and guilty over his greed for first buying and then attempting to defraud someone else by selling, a "jewelry franchise" in a pyramid fraud; the indebted businessman who participates in illegal conspiracy such as a staged burglary or arson for insurance monies;[20] and the "John" who is fleeced by a prostitute or her male accomplice. All of thse victims are understandably reluctant to admit their shortcomings to an interviewer.[21] At present most victimology studies have concentrated on criminal events with victims who understand what happened to them and how it happened and who are willing to report what they know.

There are also many technical and practical difficulties with victimization surveying, not the least of which is cost. For the average citizen, being victimized is somewhat rare statistically. For this reason, survey designs based on probability require a sample large enough to contain a sufficient number of observations (victimizations) for reliable measurement. Highly trained and expensive survey teams must conduct personal interviews each time a sample is drawn, and each

[19] C. Ray Jeffrey, *Crime Prevention through Environmental Design* (Beverly Hills,: calif.: Sage Publications, 1971), pp. 214-224.

[20] Pennsylvania Crime Commission, *Report on Organized Crime,* pp. 53-54.

[21] "Crimes and Victims," p. 34.

interview costs the project $5 to $12. Moreover, interviewed heads of households do not provide nearly as accurate a response as self-respondents.[22] Savings can be had if the number of days for recall is lengthened; the longer the recall, the smaller the sample size that is needed to generate data at a given level of reliability. However, the accuracy[23] of the data *decreases* as the recall period *increases,* so economies are secured at the price of accuracy.[24]

VICTIMIZATION SURVEYING AS A PERSPECTIVE FOR PUBLIC POLICY

In spite of its limits a victim approach to crime policy represents a refreshing and direct alternative to the traditional law enforcement and adjudication approach. The legal categories and descriptions so fundamental to law enforcement and criminal litigation are not designed for policy analysis. Instead, such categories serve legal-moral purposes, such as the determination of the degree of guilt or innocence of a defendant. The legal conception of guilt *mens rea* is not acceptable as a behavioral concept, since it contains jurisprudential values and subjective judgments that cannot be tested empirically. Sentencing, for example, requires a moral judgment, by jury or judge, that often reduces the statutory punishment for an offense. A first-offender "drunk driver" will normally receive a suspended sentence in Pennsylvania, a state that mandates a sentence for the offense. The punishment is mitigated due to the conventional wisdom that many "respectable citizens" are liable to be arrested for drunken driving at least once, and the mandatory sentence in that state is unduly harsh. It is assumed that apprehension is more a matter of contingency instead of inveterate recklessness. Yet empirical relationships between the disposition of drunk drivers and highway victims are rarely explored prior to sentencing practices. The penalty for drunken driving represents the moral indignation of the legislature toward drunken driving in general and the assertion of that indignation by the sentencing judge in a specific case. Judgment does not normally wait for statistical analysis of the deterrent effect of the law.

Western jurisprudence has developed highly complicated techniques to assess culpability surrounding an event in which the law was contravened. Unfortunately, the same traditions of individualism and emphasis on moral culpability instead of on social defense rendered the concept of criminal events and victim

[22] Ibid., pp. 34, 36 (Table 11).

[23] Note that accurate data are not the same as reliable data. Accuracy refers to the quality of data; reliability refers to the probability that a sample reflects the true proportion of the universe being measured

[24] "Crimes and Victims," p. 34. See also National Institute of Law Enforcement and Criminal Justice, "San Jose Methods Test of Known Crime Victims," pp. 7-8.

and his suffering irrelevant to the criminal process, except as the victim's plight helped to define the depth of guilt.

As far as policy formation for public defense, there are even more compelling reasons for having statistics on events and victims as supplements to statistics on "crimes" or arrests. Of primary importance is the capacity of victimization events to be "scaled." Instead of treating "aggravated assault" as equal to "auto theft," as the Uniform Crime Report does, we can, with some difficulty, develop monetary values for all crimes according to the suffering of the victim. By this means the costs of social policy for public protection (e.g., police investigation and court costs) can be compared and evaluated with social costs (death, personal injury, loss of property), all the consequences of crime in the absence of a crime protection policy. Victimization surveys are useful at the local, state, and federal levels for policy makers who are concerned with allocating scarce resources where they provide the highest potential for reduced suffering.[25] Surveys that generate data in terms of monetary units would be particularly useful.

At present criminal statistics are grouped in the Uniform Crime Report as if every legally proscribed behavior was the equal of the other. Thus, in the crime totals for cities in the UCR, homicide is lumped with burglary, and thefts involving five figures are treated as comparable to petty larcenies of less than $50. Obviously, this grouping represents a serious flaw to the policy analyst who attempts to interpret crime seriousness and suggest alternative crime policy. The pattern of burglary offenses in Mercer County, Pennsylvania,[26] explains why. Here a handful of serious burglary offenses in terms of value lost by the proprietor dwarfs the amounts of more numerous but less serious burglaries. Clearly, an apprehension or prevention policy geared to burglaries where large amounts are stolen or where personal injury is likely is more rational than a policy designed to prevent all "burglary crimes." In Mercer County, for example, local and state police clearance rates for burglaries above $1000 were over 80 percent, although their clearance rate for all burglaries was approximately 25 percent. But the 80-percent figure is more meaningful if monetary data are used in place of offense data. A careful look at the quantitative difference in burglaries explains why. All burglaries in Mercer above $1000 averaged over $11,000 and were committed by out-of-county residents. All burglaries under 1000 average under $400 and were committed by local residents, most often juveniles. The serious burglaries appeared to be professional in nature and involved highly marketable goods such as firearms, appliances, televisions, stereos, and new furniture, and they were primarily directed against commercial establishments. On the other hand, the petty burglaries involved residences and storage structures, and many items taken

[25]Turner and Dodge, "Surveys of Personal and Organizational Victimization," pp. 4-5.

[26]Unpublished data analyzed by me. I would like to thank Mr. Robert Lechner of the Pennsylvania State Police for his assistance in compiling the data.

by local residents were of little value, stolen more because they were accessible than because they were profitable.

Similar cost differentials exist for police enforcement policy, for court adjudication and, considering police and courts, for prevention.[27] Various crimes do not cost the same to defend against (in the sense of protecting victims after the act has been perpetrated) by arresting, investigating, prosecuting, adjudicating, and institutionalizing. Law enforcement as well as adjudication and corrections are flexible costs for which crime type is a salient variable.

CRIME MEASUREMENT FOR RATIONAL CRIME CONTROL

There are two dimensions in assessing the seriousness of crime that can more accurately be measured by victimization data scaled in seriousness by monetary units for purposes of policy analysis. The first dimension is that of the seriousness of actual criminal behavior from the perspective of the victim. Victimization surveying is a more reliable indicator of the seriousness of actual criminal behavior than arrests or crimes known to the police. The second dimension, consonant with victim surveying, is that of social costs associated with the actual *events* of a crime—the actual money stolen or physical harm done—irrespective of the *legal* definition of the crime. Each of these dimensions needs to be considered at lenght; although each holds promise for more rational crime control, each has pitfalls and limitations for both the researcher and policy formulator.

Perhaps the first scholars to point out the difficulty of depending on legally defined criminal events as a basis for criminal justice administrative statistics were Thorsten Sellin and Marvin Wolfgang. In their volume, *The Measurement of Delinquency,*[28] Sellin and Wolfgang proposed eliminating crimes other than bodily injury and property theft or damage for indexing purposes. Sellin and Wolfgang indexed criminal "events," not criminal law violations. For example, under robbery there were 20 combinations, each of which included the presence or absence of (1) the amount stolen (much or little); (2) the method of intimidation (gun, instrument, verbal, physical); (3) the method of inflicting harm (gun, instrument, physical); and (4) the degree of harm (hospitalization or minor). In all, 141 different specified events emerged from the various combinations of offenses to be analyzed. After extensive testing with representative samples, these categories were scaled and narrowed to evaluate the degree of seriousness in a criminal event, isolating event components with valid numerical weights from 1 to 26. When the weights were added together, each event was given a score that represented its delinquent value. The Sellin-Wolfgang scale for the indexing of

[27] See Table 9.7 on p. 328.

[28] Sellin and Wolfgang, *The Measurement of Delinquency.*

delinquency based on median scores of regressions from representative evaluators is showing (Table 10.1).

Table 10.1 Sellin-Wolfgang index

Criminal Events	Seriousness Weight
I. Victims of bodily harm	
(a) Receiving minor injuries	1
(b) Treated and discharged	4
(c) Hospitalized	7
(d) Killed	26
II. Victims of forcible sex intercourse	10
(a) Victims intimidated by weapon	2
III. Intimidation (except II above)	
(a) Physical or verbal only	2
(b) By weapon	4
IV. Premises forcibly entered	1
V. Motor vehicles stolen	2
VI. Value of property stolen, damaged, or destroyed (in dollars)	
(a) Under 10	1
(b) 10-250	2
(c) 251-2000	3
(d) 2001-9000	4
(e) 9001-30,000	5
(f) 30,001-80,000	6
(g) Over 80,000	7

Source. Thorsten Sellin and Marvin E. Wolfgang, *The Measurement of Delinquency* (New York: John Wiley, 1966), p. 402. Reprinted by permission of the publisher.

The Sellin-Wolfgang index avoids many problems of traditional statistical measurements for crime. For example, as previously mentioned, the UCR method counts as one offense the crime, which may include several offenses, thus providing only a partial enumeration of the specific criminal offenses known to the police. Second, by equating all offenses that carry the same legal label, differences in the degree of seriousness within any given category are conceded.

It must be noted that the Sellin-Wolfgang is not to be mistaken for a random sample or survey. The items used in constructing the index were chosen by logical judgment, statistical analysis, and a scaling procedure that were designed to produce a crime index that is functional within the cultural norms of our society as a whole.

A major criticism of such a subjective scale is that communal values may be variable. Sellin and Wolfgang have assumed away the conjecture that regional variations in the United States would significantly alter the proposed index. In their own words, "We suspect that the effort to maximize efficiency and minimize components for weighting has proposed an index . . . applicable to a wide band of general cultural variants, but only further research can determine the correctness of this assumption."[29]

The advantage of this scale becomes clearer as we look at planning and evaluation simulation models designed to measure the differential costs of new programs as well as the standard operations of the criminal justice system. The model used as an example, Jussim, was developed by Professor Alfred Blumstein and has been utilized by the Allegheny County (Pittsburgh) Regional Planning Council since 1971. Variations of similar simulation models may be found in other urban areas as well.[30] Jussim permits analysis of the components of the criminal justice system as they interact and accounts for the systemic costs of each interaction. Thus, policy innovations can be simulated for planning and evaluation purposes. For example, a magistrate policy of setting extraordinarily high bail at preliminary arraignment may *increase* the number of defendants detained and increase costs and pressures on the detention center; a defense counsel, reacting to mandatory sentences for narcotic crimes, may insist on jury trial, having nothing to lose for his client, thereby increasing both costs to the system and delay in the courts. Conversely, a pretrial probation program may decrease detainees and trials and generally reduce utilization of resources in the courts, although it may increase the need for resources in the probation office. The relative costs at given stages in the system are calculated as new values (increased numbers of detainees) or new parameters (e.g., increased numbers of prosecutors and judges) are entered into the system.

[29] Ibid., p. 332. An assessment of the Sellin-Wolfgang index through duplication was made by Akman, Normandeau, and Turner. The study supported the ratios of score values of the Sellin-Wolfgang study, although not necessarily the absolute numbers. See D. D. Akman, A. Normandeau, and S. Turner, "The Measurement of Delinquency in Canada," *Journal of Criminal Law, Criminology and Police Science* (1967), 58:241-243. However, using cross-cultural and particularly cross-sexual comparison of community value judgments, Hsu found the weighting of the crime components was not universally applicable. For example, Chinese women considered rape more serious than murder. Marlene Hsu, "Cultural and Sexual Differences on the Judgment of Criminal Offenses: A Replication Study of the Measurement of Delinquency," *Journal of Criminal Law and Criminology* (1973), 64:348-353.

[30] Jacqueline Cohen et al., "Implementation of the Jussim Model in a Criminal Justice Planning Agency," pp. 117-131; Jacob Belkin et al., "Jussim, an Interactive Computer Program and Its Uses in Criminal Justice Planning," unpublished paper, International Symposium on CJS Information, *Proceedings,* Project Search, October 1972, pp. 470, 477.

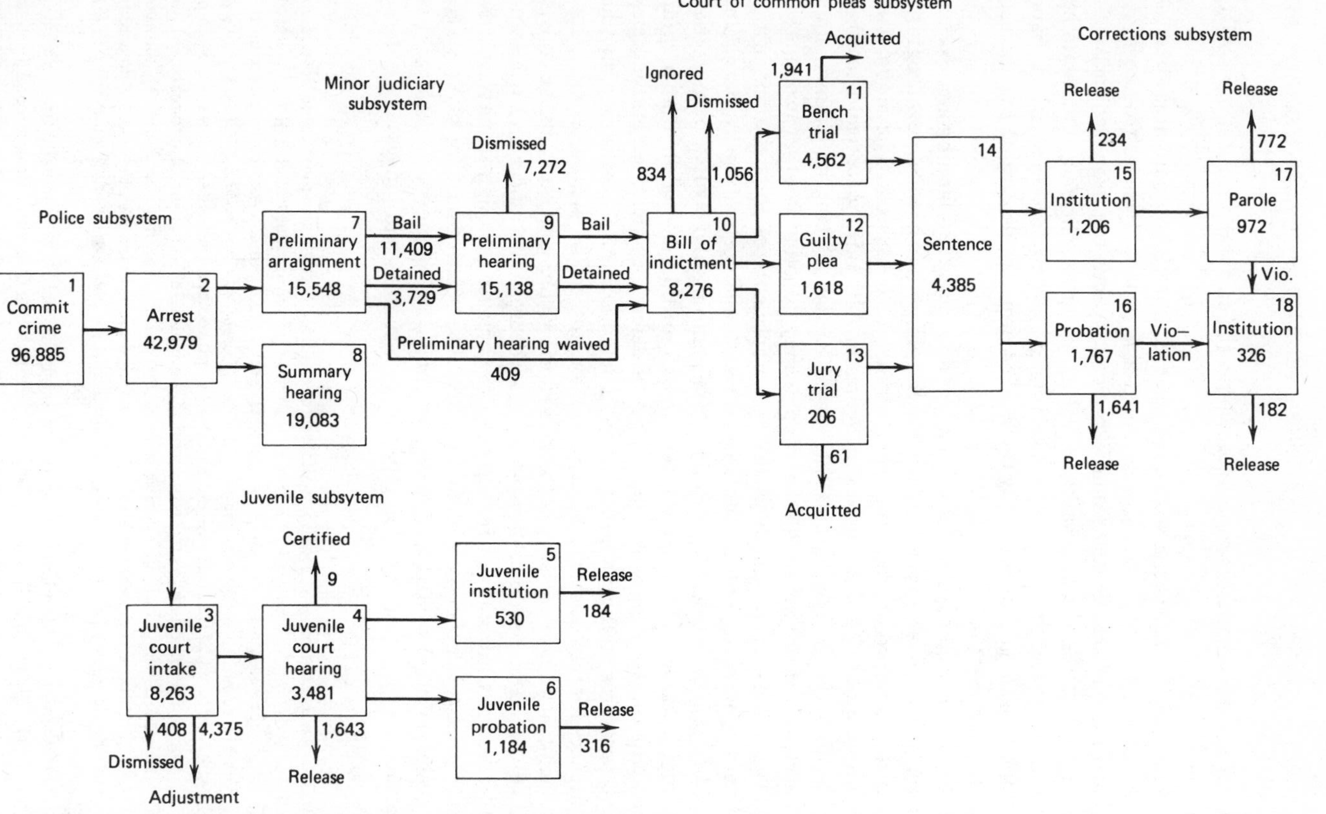

Figure 10.1 Flow diagram of the Allegheny County Criminal Justice System. (Source. *Jacqueline Cohen, Kenneth Fields, Michel Lettre, Richard Stafford, and Claire Walker, "Implementation of the Jussim Model in a Criminal Justice Planning Agency,"* Journal of Research in Crime and Delinquency *(1973), 10:120.*)

The simulated system is illustrated by the following modified flow diagram (Figure 10.1). The flow diagram specifies processing stages (stages are numbered 1 to 18 in the right corner). The connecting paths indicate both the direction of the flow path and the ratio of output from each stage. For example, Allegheny County data for this diagram indicate that of the 15,548 defendants at preliminary arraignment, 16.8 percent (or 2616) are released on nominal bond or their own recognizance (R.O.R.); 58.5 percent (or 9095) are released on a cash or surety bond; and 24.7 percent (or 3837) are held in detention until a preliminary hearing.

Using variable hourly costs and workloads of probation officers, judges, police officers, detectives, prosecutors, and correctional officers and adding fixed costs (upkeep, maintenance, etc.), it is possible to calculate, per crime type, the cost of proposed or current enforcement prosecution policy. The costs for each function at each stage that is simulated in the system per crime type, or groupings of crime type, can also be calculated in monetary units. As long as crime seriousness is measured by nominal crime categories (i.e., legal definitions) instead of by ratio indices, comparing seriousness of a crime problem with probable cost factors of social defense policy to respond to the problem is a very awkward affair. Using monetary units for both seriousness and social defense program costs would provide a convenient ratio to measure the maximization of social defense budgets in reducing the suffering of victims for a given type of crime. For example, assuming that armed robberies will be deterred by a joint police-court program to assure more certain apprehension and speedier trial,[31] the costs of the counter-armed robbery program may be simulated to assist intelligent planning. Indeed, the enhancement of rational planning governed the design of Jussim. But simulations of this kind also represent a powerful tool for critically assessing the total effort for social control over comparative crimes. As I have previously argued, some criminal offenses consume greater resources than others as they are responded to by various stages in the system and in the aggregate. (Jussim does not deal with crime *prevention* costs, only with processing costs.) The defferential costs per crime type in Allegheny County are to be found in Table 10.2.

As Table 10.2 demonstrates, the crucial cost factor is in courts and corrections which, for the average adult arrest, consumes almost 90 percent of all resources.

Of course, merely adding resources to various stages of the criminal justice system will not necessarily reduce a given crime type. Homicide is a good example of criminal activity unresponsive to specialized program innovations and continuity in the manner with which each case is processed. Homicide is also very expensive to process; evidence is painstakingly collected, defense attorneys are very active in introducing motions, and a lengthy trial is virtually certain. It

[31] Obviously, such an assumption cannot be absorbed uncritically. For a critical appraisal of deterrence, see Chapter 10.

Table 10.2 Average subsystem costs for each Unit of input, Allegheny County, Pennsylvania.

	Police	Courts	Corrections	Juveniles[b]	Total System
Average Cost per Report[a]					
Murder and non Neg. manslaughter	$319	$1936	$2527	$ 0	$4782
Robbery	45	91	277	191	604
Aggravated assault	24	49	82	94	249
Burglary	24	34	97	52	207
Larceny	32	14	19	19	84
Average Cost per Arrest					
Murder and non Neg. manslaughter	$350	$2120	$2767	$ 0	$5237
Robbery	183	374	1132	780	2469
Aggravated assault	109	223	370	426	1128
Burglary	167	239	679	368	1453
Larceny	277	117	167	160	721
Simple assault	11	76	29	185	301
Stolen property	53	129	94	162	438
Narcotics	67	171	379	192	809
Gambling	84	59	76	3	222
Runaway	8	0	0	844	852
Truancy	9	0	0	9218	9227
Ungovernable	7	0	0	22811	22818

[a]Average cost per report refers to the total crime types shown that police reported, divided by subsystem costs. The amounts are much smaller than they are under average cost per arrest, since arrests were not made in many cases. For example, only one out of eight reported larcenies was cleared. Consequently, costs for larceny are eight times as great under average cost per arrest.
[b]Court and correctional costs are grouped together under the juvenile column.
Source: Allegheny Regional Planning Office, Pennsylvania Governor's Justice Commission.

makes no sense to add to the expense of traditional homicide procedures and expensive programs to reduce homicide if it is generally outside of the control of law enforcement to reduce. This is not to suggest that homicide rates would not be higher if we had done nothing at all. But few murders involve the precalculation of professional murders;[32] the deterrent value of police and court processing, while having value as a diffused sanction, is probably secondary to the influence of subcultures of violence[33] or mere social contingencies, such as the availability of cheap handguns.

For those crimes that *are* responsive we can measure the costs of social defense policy of police, courts, and corrections against the costs of victimization. Racket squad efforts in hours and expenses of personnel can be totaled and divided by the number of arrests that result in convictions. Foot patrol or patrol-detective programs can be designed to combat strong-armed robbery and larceny; narcotic squads charged with apprehending drug traffickers can be assessed in the same manner.

So far, this approach to planning is consistent with "crime specific planning," a mode of planning promoted by the Law Enforcement Assistance Administration Bureau of Planning between 1970 and 1974. That posture has been fairly criticized on grounds that there are vast differences in degrees of seriousness between robbery of lunch money in a schoolyard and robbery in a liquor store on Saturday night for substantial sums of money. Crime specific planning does not take cognizance of these differences, but tends to discourage reporting of minor crimes or to encourage apprehension of nickel-and-dime offenders to build up a glowing record of success.

But this bias can be controlled partially by introducing the concept of victim-serious scales per crime type. Using the Sellin-Wolfgang scale of seriousness (see Table 10.1), we can roughly convert the Uniform Crime Report Index offenses (robbery, forcible rape, homicide, larceny, aggravated assault, auto theft, and burglary) to the scale of seriousness. Allowances could be made, based on local policy, for "minor" robberies, larcenies, assaults, and burglaries, whose events reveal only technical interactions or special circumstances. Objections will be raised that the Sellin-Wolfgang indicators are not compatible with the UCR indicators. But recent research has questioned the necessity of utilizing the Sellin-Wolfgang "seriousness" index in preference to the familiar, and usually available, UCR index.[34] Using scores developed by Heller and McEwen[35] for 9728 reported crimes in St. Louis between April 4, 1971 and May 20, 1971, Blumstein

[32]The classic study of homicide is Marvin E. Wolfgang, *Patterns in Criminal Homicide* (Philadelphia: University of Pennsylvania Press, 1958).

[33]Marvin E. Wolfgang and Franco Ferracuti, *The Sub-culture of Violence: Toward an Integrated Theory in Criminology* (London: Tavistock Publications, 1967), pp. 276-284.

[34]Alfred Blumstein, "Seriousness Weights in an Index of Crime," *American Sociological Review* (1974), 39:854-864.

[35]Nelson B. Heller and J. Thomas McEwen, "Applications of Crime Seriousness Information in Police Departments," *Journal of Criminal Justice* (1973), 1:241-253.

applied the "seriousness" scores to the FBI *index* for national crime statistics. Applied to aggregate crime totals for the nation, the level of seriousness along a linear time regression, using the Sellin-Wolfgang index, was almost identical ($r = 0.9994$) to the regression slope resulting from the weighted FBI index. Blumstein concluded that the difference between a weighted UCR index and the Selling-Wolfgang index appeared to be a matter of scale values, not measures of seriousness, at least in the aggregate.

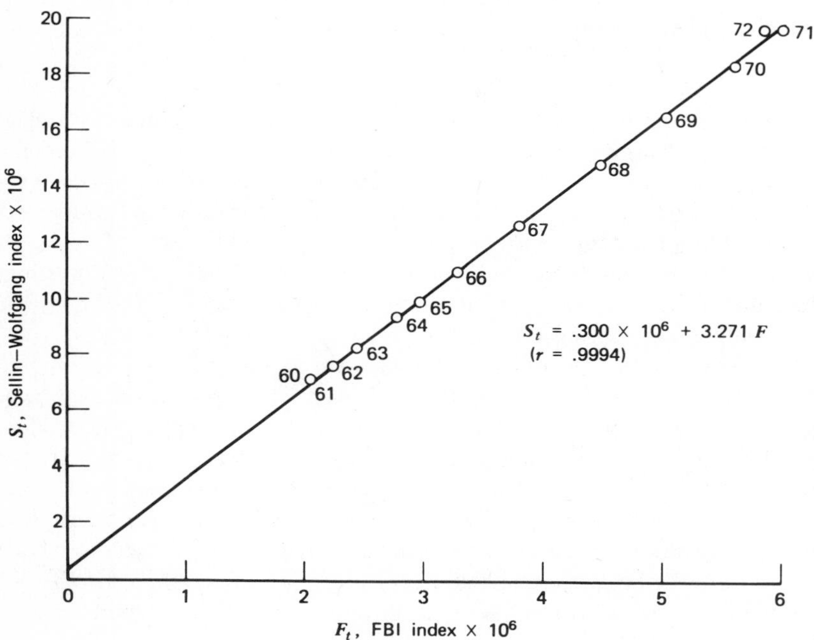

Figure 10.2 Sellin-Wolfgang and FBI crime indexes, 1960-1972.

The possibility of transposing the Sellin-Wolfgang index to the already established FBI index has importance for policy analysis. It will be recalled that the Sellin-Wolfgang index scored property loss, physical loss, and trauma. For example, the auto theft of \$1000 would be scored 2 for the theft and 3 for the property loss, a total of 5.[36] Blumstein's computations demonstrate that the average

[36] Sellin and Wolfgang, *The Measurement of Delinquency,* Table 69 on pp. 288-289.

seriousness scores for FBI index crimes, developed by Heller and McEwen, can be used with almost identical results, *even though* only the most serious charge is reported by the police for multiple crimes by the same offender (Figure 10.2). Thus, the fact that the FBI index does not account for serious weights according to criminal events, but relies on the legal definitions and categorization of the police officer who discovers the crime, does not seem to affect the usefulness of a scaled UCR for indexing an aggregate scoring of crime seriousness nationwide. Apparently, this is because each index crime over a long period of time increases or decreases proportionately to the other crimes. The mix reflects a secular trend (Table 10.3).[37]

Table 10.3 Correlation matrix among residuals of reported index crimes, corrected for linear time trends, 1960-1972

	Homicide	**Forcible Rape**	**Robbery**	**Aggravated Assault**	**Burglary**	**Larceny**	**Auto Theft**
Homicide	1.000	0.927	0.909	0.976	0.891	0.845	0.441
Forcible rape		1.000	0.794	0.956	0.734	0.765	0.336
Robbery			1.000	0.861	0.979	0.978	0.685
Aggravated assault				1.000	0.836	0.809	0.355
Burglary					1.000	0.944	0.734
Larceny						1.000	0.716
Auto theft							1.000

Source. Alfred Blumstein, "Seriousness Weights in an Index of Crime," *American Sociological Review* (1974), 39:858. Copyright © the American Sociological Association.

However, the Sellin-Wolfgang insistence that crime be scaled according to seriousness remains very relevant for a crime policy apart from projecting national trends. It is particularly important to use weighted values for separate crimes when the "mix" of crime veers sharply from past combinations. Heller and McEwen did *scale* crime according to seriousness, instead of categorizing raw numbers of observations of crimes in the UCR, where murder is the equal, in the aggregate crime totals, of burglary or larceny. And Wolfgang and Sellin also provide a power function for money[38] that permits transforming the interval

[37] Blumstein, "Seriousness Weights in an Index of Crime," Table 5 on p. 857.

[38] Sellin and Wolfgang, *The Measurement of Delinquency,* pp. 284-285.

values for crimes involving nonmonetary suffering (rape, homicide, aggravated assault) to metric or dollar values.

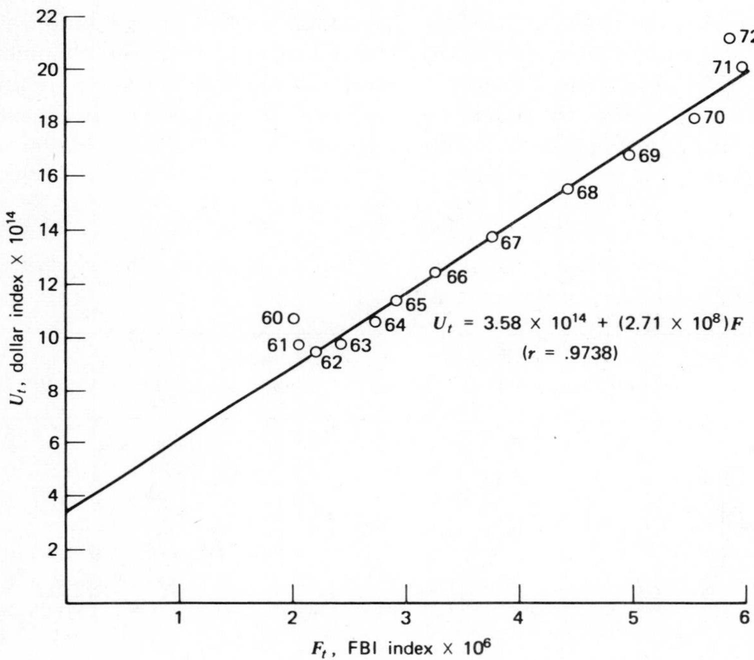

Figure 10.3 Dollar index versus FBI index, 1960-1972. (Source. *Alfred Blumstein, "Seriousness Weights in an Index of Crime,"* American Sociological Review *(1974), 39:860. Copyright © the American Sociological Association.*)

Blumstein[39] illustrates how monetary values "fit" the scale of values developed by Heller and McEwen. Figure 10.3 shows that the correlation remains high ($r = 0.9738$), but that there is more dispersion from the FBI index (Figure 10.4) than in comparisons to the original Sellin-Wolfgang index (Figure 10.2). However, the dispersion in 1960 to 1961 and 1971 to 1972 is largely a function of

[39] Blumstein, "Seriousness Weights in an Index of Crime," p. 859.

homicide rates increasing (between 1960 and 1961) and then decreasing (between 1971 and 1972). Other crimes remained proportionate to the total number. That is, the proportion of larcenies, burglaries, robberies, rapes, auto thefts, and aggravated assaults remained stable. At the same time, homicide accounts for a high degree of seriousness on the Sellin-Wolfgang scale in terms of dollars. Consequently, the observations for 1960 to 1961 and 1971 to 1972 deviate slightly from the almost perfect linear correlation of the previous figures. Moreover, Blumstein argues that the close correlations between the two indexes are not dependent on the mix of the St. Louis data,[40] but are apparently the result of the constancy of the increase (or decrease) in crime. A sharp drop or increase for one or two years of one crime type, particularly homicide and, marginally, aggravated assault and rape, would produce lower correlations between the two indexes.

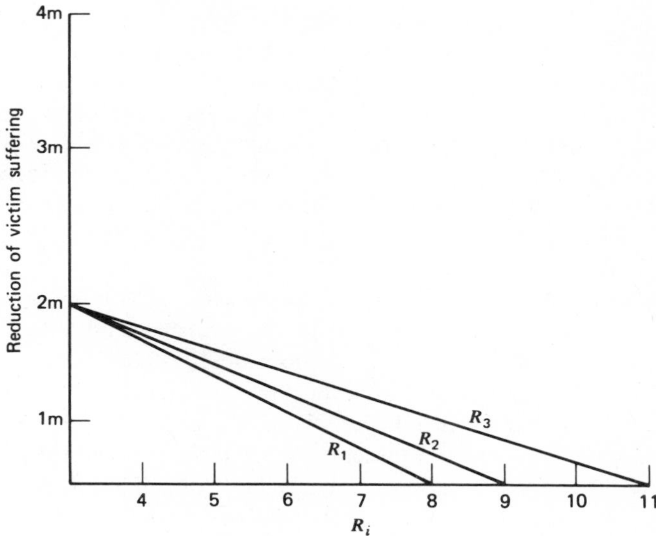

Figure 10.4 Saturation patrols (hypothetical data).

Of course, all indicator "slopes" and curves in a graph are likely to be highly correlated when the phenomenon is examined in the same direction and in the

[40] Ibid., pp. 862-863.

same proportion regarding its components. There is an additional problem in validating a "monetary score" for traumatic crimes such as rape, assault, and murder. But the UCR index can be used with greater accuracy for local and national policy analysis if we attach monetary values. A scale of seriousness, transferable to monetary units, is a powerful index for criminal justice policy regarding deterrence and prevention. The fact that the UCR index can be treated in monetary terms permits quantitative comparison of alternative crime control policies with measurable reductions of victim suffering. Moreover, applying suffering scales to existing UCR data provides one answer to the standard criticism that the Sellin-Wolfgang victim scale is too complex, too expensive, and requires duplication of crime data collection.

Additionally, victim surveying remains a crucial check on the accuracy of UCR reporting, particularly on the "dark area" of unreported crime. Both victim surveying and UCR reports might enhance each other if we could assume that the gap between police reports and victim reports is a constant, and if we could allow for this discrepancy by proportionately increasing the average victim cost for each UCR offense. Thus, if the average burglary loss is equivalent to $500 and only 50 percent of all burglaries are reported, adjustment might be made by adjusting up the total losses for burglary. In doing so, we would need to arrrive at victim losses for unreported crimes, which are likely to be considerably lower than those reported. But there appears to be no basic reason why a monetary scale cannot be applied to victimization categories and, thus, include the "dark area" of criminal offenses.

The problem of qualitative variance within a given UCR crime type has been addressed at the prosecutor level for the district attorney's office in the District of Columbia by Joan Jacoby.[41] Jacoby has been closely associated with the design of a prosecutor management information system, developed by the Office of Crime Analysis of the District of Columbia. Designed to alert the prosecutor to backlogging of serious cases, Prosecutor's Management Information System (PROMIS) utilizes an adaptation of the Sellin-Wolfgang seriousness scale,[42] modified by the Gottfredson base expectation scale[43] and, if desired by local prosecutors, further modified by the prosecutor's own priorities for serious versus nonserious cases. Prosecutorial policy for evaluating incoming cases was quantified along three categories to determine the priority of applied resources: (1) the seriousness of the offense in terms of personal injury and property loss or damage,

[41] Joan E. Jacoby, "Case Evaluation: Quantifying Prosecutorial Policy," *Judicature* (1975), 58:-486-493.

[42] Office of Crime Analysis, District of Columbia, Systems Overview and Report Formats for PROMIS (Prosecutor's Management Information System), May 1971; Office of Crime Analysis, District of Columbia Government, Final Report, Project TRACE, January 1972.

[43] Don M. Gottfredson and Kelley B. Ballard, "Differences in Parole Decisions Associated with Decision Makers," *Journal of Research in Crime and Delinquency* (1966), 3:112-119.

(2) the seriousness of the defendant's past record, and (3) an assessment (by an assistant prosecutor) of the evidentiary strength of the case. In the latter category, subjectivity raises a fundamental problem of arbitrary discretion. However, a quantified evidentiary "screen" for the Bronx district attorney's office in New York City does show promise. The offense evaluation developed for that office in 1973 has predicted the prosecutor's judgment on evidentiary strength 60 percent of the time.[44]

The advantages of utilizing seriousness scales are clear. The overworked prosecutor's office can cull serious cases from nonserious cases without ignoring the actual events surrounding the criminal act. The selection criterion is based not on legal categories in a police complaint or indictment, but on victim suffering and evidentiary strength. Standardizing each case in the screening process thus permits the release of prosecutors to pursue serious cases on an individual basis. In the case of the Bronx project, all major offenses were handled by a Major Offense Bureau. Although noncomparative statistics must be considered with a jaundiced eye, the results of the Bronx project are impressive. In its first year of operation the Major Offense Bureau diverted 454 defendants and secured convictions 97 percent of the time. At the same time, the median time from arrest to final disposition was 74 days, a remarkably short period for any urban court, particularly in New York City.[45]

There are several policy-oriented, conceptual problems that must temper optimism regarding the use of both scaling and verifying victimization. First, personal loss and social costs for certain types of crime are not easily measured. We have previously noted rape, murder, and robbery; calculating the social costs of victimless crime is particularly difficult. Of course, if harm is understood from the perspective of the victim, the conceptual problem is less severe. Procurers and users of drugs, prostitutes and their clients, and gamblers are not understood according to the perspective of suffering as are the victims of a mugging. Procurers of drugs, prostitutes, and gambling games do not suffer as do the victims of burglary. But the rationale behind vice law is that society, individual character and, especially, the integrity of the family, may suffer. Both informed and uninformed opinion will divide on the impact of victimless crime on our social institutions and the ancillary influence of vice (e.g., illegal gambling operations' influence on government corruption) may be intelligently documented. But few social scientists are sufficiently intrepid to measure the general social consequences of vice on institutions such as the American family.

Objections to a victim-oriented conception of crime policy have a deeper dimension, however, that goes to the root of a politics of crime and the intractability of its problems. Crime is defined by law, and statutes reflect the taboos of a

[44] Jacoby, "Case Evaluation: Quantifying Prosecutorial Policy," p. 491.
[45] Ibid., p. 493.

culture. Frequently, it makes little difference that the forbidden behaviors are regularly indulged in, or that one social class proscribes for another less powerful class. Even when prestigious commissions accumulate evidence that no one suffers from a victimless crime to a degree that can be ameliorated by invoking a criminal sanction, recommendations based on decriminalization for reasons of social harmlessness are met, *a priori,* with a studied rejection. Such was the attitude of the White House toward the recommendations from both the *Report of the Commission on Obscenity and Pornography,*[46] commissioned by President Johnson and received by President Nixon, and the *Report of the National Commission on Marihuana and Drug Abuse.*[47] (Indeed, former Attorney General John Mitchell rejected any recommendation to "legalize marihuana" even prior to the final report of the National Commission on Marihuana, whose members were appointed by President Nixon.)

Some behaviors are considered inherently deviant by the political culture and are banned, at least symbolically, by the criminal law.[48] A challenge to those proscriptions, well reasoned or not, will cut deeply into entrenched values. After all, criminal law regarding vice reflects the social values of the dominant culture; it is not an analysis for social defense against victimization suffering. Arguments that police are wasting valuable time and resources closing down sex shops, arresting prostitutes, and pinching numbers runners fall on deaf ears. Protests that vice corrupts police and courts and leads to violation of civil liberties and hostility from cultural minority groups are to little avail. Crime has to be understood, in part, as a threat to the social order and its values as they are politically defined, and not simply as a threat to individuals who are potential victims. This is not to say that the social order does not, or should not, change regarding tolerance or other forms of control for our social ills or peccadillos. It is to suggest that crime policy will respond only after the political culture permits it to do so.

Control of vice is an especially delicate political problem because threats to the social order and its values denote a belief system not easily measured, but very susceptible to conflict and polarizing politics. One needs only to mention topics such as abortion, drugs, pornography, prostitution, adultery, homosexuality, and gambling—all victimless crimes for which suffering on the part of the adult victim must be considered nonexistent, since the crime is consensual. However, vital social values that the community insists its members accept in outward practice and at least give lip service to *are* at stake—the care of children, including the unborn as well as the underaged dependent against what cultural norms deem threats to their well-being (abortion, drugs, and pornography); and the integrity

[46] *The Report of the Commission on Obscenity and Pornography* (New York: Bantam Books, 1970).
[47] The Official Report of the National Commission on Marihuana and Drug Abuse, *Marihuana, A Signal of Misunderstanding* (New York: New American Library, 1972).
[48] Becker, *Outsiders,* p. 3.

of the the family unit, as opposed to individual sexual opportunity, gambling, prostitution. In addition, our culture continues to place a high value on avoiding artificially induced suspensions of consciousness or drug-induced pleasures—outside of acceptable sources such as alcohol. No social scientist can predict the consequences of serious challenges to these values, although some immediate consequences of continuing to treat the behaviors that run counter to these values as criminal offenses can be indicated.

Without discounting the limitations, both technical and economic, of conducting victim surveying and scaling criminal offenses in monetary units of suffering, conceiving of the seriousness of crime in this manner at least has the virtue of focusing on the forgotten component of the criminal justice system—the victim. As Chapter 8 argued, crime policy analysis has not achieved anything approaching agreement as to what goals should be pursued in crime policy. Perceptual differences as to crime problem definitions have made crime control planning characterized more by bargaining between interest groups for LEAA, State Planning Agency funding, or local budgetary allocations than any deliberate plan. As a comprehensive indicator for successful policy implementation, victimization may provide a base for a rational policy for social defense. Such a policy might be developed, if the following assumptions hold true, along the lines described below.

Given the following conditions:

1. Unidimensional objectives that can be cost accounted.
2. Comparative costs for alternative social defense policy.
3. Comparative reductions in victimization costs for alternate social defense programs.
4. Costs of victimization.

n = number of crimes
$i \ldots 30$ = type of crimes
$V_i \ldots 30$ = variable cost of crimes to victim per crime type (seriousness of crime)
R_i = resources for social defense program per crime type
Seriousness = V_{ni}
Cost of social defense = R_i

The idea is to find optimization points of reducing victim suffering considering the limited resources that criminal justice agencies have at their disposal.

Social benefit = $i \ldots 30$
$V_{ni} - R_i$
$i = 1$

Of course, the relationship between R and V is not so simple. A criminal justice program may have *no* effect on V, such as saturation patrols (Figure 10.4), or it may have little effect unless substantial sums are invested, such as strike forces against organized crime (Figure 10.5). More likely, it will have an immediate effect, with diminishing returns as resource allocations are increased (Figure 10.6). The latter assumes, as this textbook assumes, that any reduction of crime resulting from public policy will not be dramatic, although significant reductions can be made to an optimum level of resources invested.

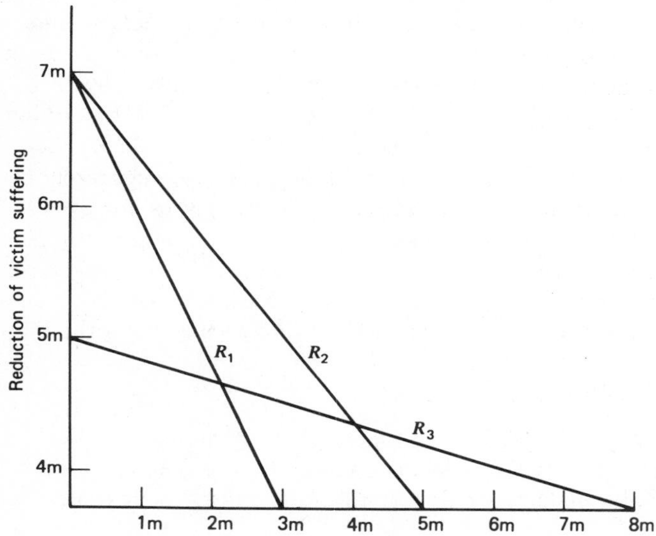

Figure 10.5 Strike forces against organized crime (hypothetical data).

A victim perspective, then, can provide a comprehensive, quantifiable indicator to measure the success of a policy for social defense against crime. It shifts the balkanized focus of interested groups from subsystem objectives—apprehension and clearance, crowd control, due process, recidivism, and treatment—back to the fundamental purpose, in my view, of protecting the citizen. As a conceptual framework, victimology encourages assessments of reduced victim suffering resulting from the public investment of resources in alternative programs and policies.

Realistic proposals on which criminal justice institutions could act, given the present political climate, to reduce the propensity for individuals to commit street crime will be discussed next.

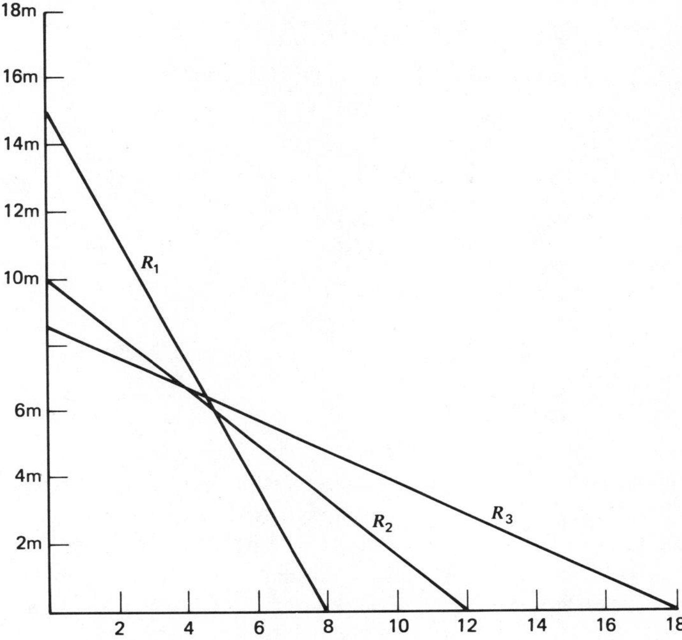

Figure 10.6 Armed robbery (hypothetical data).

11

POLITICAL REALISM AND CRIME REFORM: DETERRING AND PREVENTING CRIME

It should be clear by now that two themes recur throughout this textbook: the inherent limitations in traditional criminal justice policy in sharply reducing crime, and the lack of consensus in the body politic regarding solutions for our crime problems. The lack of consensus regarding solutions is fed, in turn, by perceptual differences within the political system, producing cleavages over how we define priority crime problems. For the most part these cleavages cannot be reconciled in a crime policy; they reflect broader-based differences throughout the political system. But some significant refocusing of perspectives can be made that may lead to realistic, although limited, crime policies. This book has argued that a victim-based perspective provides not only a technical, but a conceptual advantage for a crime policy, and comprehensive planning.

I reiterate that a victim-oriented crime policy is not designed to repress civil liberties, to disregard treatment or offenders, to discount the importance of social reforms in income distribution, discriminatory practices, health delivery systems, and employment, or to minimize the volatile issue of vice and personal morality. All of these subjects have played prominent, historic roles in whatever crime policy we have had, and nearly all remain to some degree politicized issues.

Law enforcement agencies cannot resolve these issues. Criminal justice agencies can assist the poor when they are desperate, or in need of referral, as they often are. Police remove drunks from the street and prevent prostitutes from soliciting in public places. Police arrest drug users, homosexuals, and other officially labeled "deviants" in public places. These are examples of the regulation and control of public behavior, and the police are capable of doing it reasonably well. Arrest may even reduce these practices somewhat by raising the costs and risks involved. But an antivice crime policy based on *prohibition* simply does not provide a viable solution to the problems of poverty and vice outside the boundaries of minimal social control. Such a task is beyond the resources of the criminal justice system.

Moreover, the evidence that I find most convincing is that the criminal justice system errs in attempting to eliminate victimless crime by traditional policing and prosecution methods. Hard-line crime control policies in the area of victimless crime, those that stress *prohibition,* probably produce *more* victim suffering, not less, and tend to be criminogenic. That is, antigambling, antiprostitution, and antidrug crime policies tend to generate more crime in terms of victim suffering than they eliminate. Yet public pressures are strong, if mercurial, to continue such policies, and that cold, political fact must be taken under advisement by policy makers, too.

The same may be said about police and court responsibilities for "social justice." Beyond regulating public behavior and providing emergency services, criminal justice agencies and departments are not capable of doing very much more about social problems than they have already done. Police, courts, and corrections cannot redistribute income, provide additional health services to the poor, or lower unemployment. They can be required to cleanse racism and sexism from their ranks, but they cannot be expected to provide the vanguard for ending discrimination.

WHAT CAN BE DONE

In summary, a realistic crime policy must limit itself to goals that are feasible both politically and behaviorally instead of those that appear necessary or desirable. Reform here means doing less. On the other hand, action can be taken in other directions. Specifically, three problems are widely recognized, and they are susceptible to vigorous social intervention. The first problem is that of deterring or isolating repeatedly serious offenders by altering current sentencing policy. The second and third problems are closely related: reducing delay time between arrest and final disposition and substituting a more equitable and effective bonding system for our current dependence on the bail bondsman. All of these problems confront continuing philosophical, legal, and empirical issues over due process versus preventative detention, alacrity in justice versus assembly-line justice, and rehabilitation versus punishment. Among these issues, the latter remains the most likely to invoke heated and partisan objection to implementing some of the suggestions outlined here. Partially, the disagreement stems from ideological differences in the various perspectives of criminological thought. I would like to discuss three common perspectives and suggest their limitations and advantages for raising policy questions, particularly in the area of deterrence.

THREE PERSPECTIVES IN CRIMINOLOGY

The perspective of positivist criminology was common for at least the first half of the twentieth century. Central to the positivist approach was the assumption that individuals violate the law because of psychological, physiological, or social factors in their heredity or social backgrounds or in their present personality. A standard behavioral approach to identify these factors was to compare samples of "known" criminals with noncriminals.[1] Causes of crime were centered on the actions of the criminal in his environment, and not on the treatment, processing, or interpreting by others of his activities.

In reaction to the alleged aridity and class bias of positivism, the transactional school of sociology led to a perspective on criminal behavior that is presently termed "labeling theory." According to labeling theory, almost everyone commits crimes, including respectable, middle-class juveniles and adults, but only a few are labeled "criminals," most commonly the poor and minority groups who lack the political power and status to be the labelers. As Thomas Szasz puts it, "in the animal world, it is kill or be killed; in the human kingdom, it is label or be labelled."[2] Although all scholars do not share anywhere near a theoretical consensus on criminal behavior, labeling theorists point out that the degree of deviancy, including criminal behavior, is a function of how deviants are processed, socially controlled, and perceived in institutional settings. Deviant *careers* are, as the phrase implies, developed over a period of time as the deviant interacts with official institutions—schools, police departments, juvenile and adult courts —and especially total institutions—mental hospitals, prisons. In turn, the deviant learns to adapt to the manner in which he is treated to avoid unpleasant sanction. For example, a juvenile's status will go up in the eyes of his peers as he is processed by the juvenile courts, and the "labeled" juvenile delinquent will continue to act out his role. Prisoners in group therapy sessions will learn "how to confirm" their "leader's" psychological diagnosis and act it out, to survive the prison routine, even get an early parole.

To be sure, positivist criminology has, as charged, a built-in bias for justifying one class dominating another. It ignores the power of stigma and interactive manipulation in the shaping of human personality, and its assumption of a pathological or individual-centered criminology minimizes "normal" crime behavior and the normal deterrent effect of law enforcement and the desirability of criminal law reform. In its place, positivist criminology substitutes the redeeming features of rehabilitation, education, and therapy.

But labeling theory also has its limitations. After all, stigmatizing behavior is inherent in most sanctions applied as a deterrent to unwanted behavior. It is

[1]David Matza, *Delinquency and Drift,* (New York: Wiley, 1964), pp. 1-30.

[2]Thomas Szasz, *The Second Sin* (Garden City, N.Y.: Anchor Press, 1973), p. 20.

impossible to have a criminal law that does not stigmatize, because systems of justice are *supposed* to stigmatize objectionable behavior. Moreover, it is very doubtful if rape, armed robbery, extortion, and professional burglary are products largely of a "labeling process." While official sanctions, a criminal record, for example, may and do place limits on legitimate opportunities, it is also plausible to argue that *lack of sanctions* encourages illicit pleasure or profit—beating someone up for fun or robbing a gas station. Moreover, labeling theory is short on empirical support.

Still, it is argued that the criminal sanction is differentially applied, that we are nearly all violators of the law, but those with status and social skills are not easily caught and, consequently, escape stigma and labeling. In a frequently referenced article James Wallerstein and Clement Wyle in 1947 surveyed 1020 men and 678 women in the New York metropolitan area, asking whether or not they had committed any of 49 listed offenses. Written replies revealed that 99 percent had committed one or more; 64 percent of the men and 29 percent the women admitted to commiting felonies. The authors concluded that "unlawful behavior, far from being an abnormal social or psychological manifestation, is in truth a very common phenomenon."[3] But serious crimes of the kind we have just mentioned, when placed in context, are not common, but are heavily concentrated in violent subcultures. I have already commented on the limits of deterrent criminal penalties to discourage crimes of passion, such as interfamily violence and lovers' quarrels. But some violent crime is being deterred by sanctions. It is tragic when such sanctions fall on individuals who compose violent subcultures, because these are the members of the society who suffer most from political powerlessness and economic deprivation. It will not do to suggest that deterrent policy is not effective simply because it stigmatizes or is directed toward those who are disadvantaged. Instead, we can direct our efforts at both social reform *and* crime control.

Both positivist criminology, because it is focused on root social cause, and labeling criminology, because it implies that crime is relative to the perspective of officials doing the labeling, tend to downplay or even attack the role of deterrence in crime policy. As a consequence, positivist criminology has difficulty explaining differences in crime rates from one period or geographical region to the next. And labeling theorists tend to suggest that differential crime rates are basically questions of definition instead of class and culture variables and the relative absence of effective deterrents.

An older criminological perspective, that of classical criminology, is being "rediscovered" by some modern criminologists. Classical theory was developed in the eighteenth-century intellectual atmosphere of the Enlightenment and was

[3]James S. Wallerstein and Clement J. Wyle, "Our Law Abiding Law-Breakers," *National Probation* (1947), 25:107.

essentially a liberal reaction against the unquestioning acceptance of aristocratic tradition and authority. Best represented by the writings of Cesare Beccaria, classical criminology opposed the use of law to enforce moral virtues unrelated to broader social needs, emphasized the natural rights of individuals against arbitrary claims of the state, and insisted that the law be comprehensible to the individual and be considered part of the social contract.

Punishment was considered necessary by Beccaria, but it was to be employed only when the rights of others were impaired by an offender's behavior. Moreover, the punishment was only to be severe enough to ensure that the penalty outweighed the advantage derived from the crime. Beccaria believed that punishment should be swift and certain, but it should not be used either to rehabilitate or "set an example," since all individuals were to be treated equally under the law.

A growing utilitarian perspective in criminology has its intellectual roots in the classical school. The utilitarian approach avoids many of the preceding problems encountered by the positivist and labeling approaches, although it has difficulties of its own, as we will see. Modern utilitarian criminology focuses on infractions in the law, particularly when the propensity to commit crimes can be calculated according to quantified deterrents and rewards. The emphasis of utilitarian theory in criminology today is on more or less rational choice. This is not to reject ignorance or passion as influencing, even dominating preference, as critics have maintained, because rational choice refers to the perspective of the potential perpetrator. A young burglar who "likes" a cheap trinket in a five-and-ten store may "risk" his liberty for very small gain, an irrational act for the more sophisticated, but not to a boy who does not know a trinket from the real thing. For him, the theft is a calculated act and a deterrent policy will be effective to the extent that it enters into his calculation.

Where utilitarian theory is weakest is in its simplistic assumptions regarding official definitions of crime, apart from its social context, and about the multiple factors most important in actual decision-making calculations. After all, obeying the law is largely a function of habit and socialization, even legitimatization of the law itself. The wholesale violation of marihuana laws by youngsters today is more appropriately explained as a lack of legitimacy in the law than by any cost-benefit formula. Utilitarian models that identify "cost" and "risk" factors against "gain" are, if relied on alone, likely to simplify motivation in a framework of propensities and disinclinations, to the neglect of broader social and political analysis. Such a framework is particularly inappropriate when criminal definitions represent (1) class definitions such as gambling or drug laws, or (2) race or sex discrimination, such as differential arrest and prosecution. Pareto curves are convenient ways to express pieces of reality in operationalized, symbolic terms, but we should guard against conceiving of robberies and larcenies as simply commercial transactions by illegal businessmen.

There is a politics of crime that can easily be diguised by stereotyped, criminal conceptualizations. Crime definitions frequently represent class bias, race or sex discrimination, or political intolerance. The history of gambling and drug laws, the differential prosecution in the South of rape involving black assailants, but not white assaillants on blacks, or different arrest patterns for prostitutes but not their male accomplices, and the criminal penalties for illegal assembly and strike breaking contempt convictions are all facile examples. Taken alone, utilitarian crime modeling for these conceptualizations will surely lack critical power.

Murder, juvenile crime, and rape are also clear examples of complex social relationships. Most homicides are products of social contingency—chance interaction and passion. And juvenile crime is equally difficult to model consistent with utilitarian assumptions. Albert Cohen developed a full-blown theory of delinquent subcultures based on the fact that youngsters will purposely flout middle-class values, including the law, and take stoic delight in being arrested but not "deterred." In this instance the social setting of a successful, dominant middle and working class is that of lower-class children "caught up in a game in which others are typically the winners and they are the losers and also rans."[4] Their response is to repudiate the game as a reaction formation. Utilitarian modeling would have to control many variables to described incentives and disincentives in Cohen's "boys."

PUNISHMENT AND RESPONSIBILITY

H. L. A. Hart has argued that Anglo-American law still retains two contradictory concepts of punishment.[5] The first position is that punishment should be directed for acts according to strict liability. In this instance it is not necessary for conviction to show that the accused either intentionally committed the proscribed act or could have avoided doing it by reasonable care. Selling uninspected meat or selling liquor to a minor fall under this category.

Strict liability is justified in two ways. First, it is argued that certain punishment for offenders who were careless or thoughtless may have a utilitarian effect on others. Second, it is extremely difficult to prove intent in many cases, the butcher and bartender illustrations being cases in point. Without strict liability, it is argued, we could not prevent spoiled meat from being marketed or prevent alcohol from being sold to minors.

To others the concept of strict liability is odious. They would inquire as to the state of mind of the alleged offender, arguing that punishment is not rational unless it is directed toward those who have voluntarily broken the law. The sophist objection of Protagoras sounds contemporary:

[4]Albert K. Cohen, *Deviance and Control* (Englewood Cliffs, N.J.: Prentice-Hall, 1966), p. 66.
[5]H. L. A. Hart, *Punishment and Responsibility* (London: Oxford University Press, 1967), p. 20.

If you will think, Socrates, of what punishment can do for the evildoer, you will see at once that in the opinion of mankind, virtue may be acquired. No one punishes the evildoer under the notion, or for the reason that he has done wrong-only the unreasonable fury of a beast is so vindictive. But he who desires to inflict rational punishment does not punish for the sake of a past wrong which cannot be undone: he has regard to the future and is desirous that the man who is punished, and he who sees him punished, may be deterred from doing wrong again. He punishes for the sake of prevention, thereby clearly implying that virtue is capable of being taught.[6]

Although Protagoras accepts the utilitarian principle of punishment as a deterrent on the wrongdoer and his fellow citizen, he adds the positivist concept of rehabilitation to the purposes of punishment, revealing that "virtue" is a kind of habit created by "teaching," which is a kind of punishment, in this instance at least. The contemporary American mind remains as confused as Protagoras.

On the one hand, we still adhere to the Austinian doctrine of strict liability—that acts that are legally proscribed must be punished. On the other hand, like Protagoras, we want to punish only those "minds" and "wills" that voluntarily commit the proscribed act. Virtue can be taught through compulsion to those who are likely to be receptive. Those who are either stupid or incorrigible (Protagoras referred to them as "lacking in capacity") we commit either to institutions for the mentally defective or to penal institutions for long sentences. Interestingly, Protagoras would have them exiled or put to death; until recently, no society could afford to imprison anyone in an institution for extended periods of time.

The point is this. It is very questionable whether punishment can instruct those convicted for crimes to lead an acceptable life within the boundaries of the law, although the certainty of punishment may generally or individually deter repetition of a crime. But consistent, measured, and undelayed punishment of shoplifters and scoff-law offenders holding parking tickets may be a very effective deterrent. Punishment need not teach an offender how to behave. Instead, it teaches what to expect, in general, if one is caught.

In the literature of criminology and in popular literature, punishment assumes a number of contradictory meanings. Two general types of definitions should suffice to illustrate. The general public, some newspapers, and a number of judges I have observed maintain a religious notion of responsibility, one that Protagoras rejected. This position maintains that individuals must be rewarded or be made to suffer for their choices. Indeed, penitentiary once meant doing penitance for one's sins. The punitive disposition becomes an end in itself and is perfectly consistent with Martin Luther's admonition to temporal Princes to utilize their

[6] *Protagoras,* Gregory Vlastos, ed. (New York: Bobbs-Merrill, 1956), p. 22.

"Christian rods for the chastisement of sin."[7] Any notion of rehabilitation such as Protagoras implied, or concern for secular positivist deterrence such as Austin suggests, is secondary to the principal object of casting blame and opprobrium on the guilty party. Fortunately, this harsh position is infrequently found among most contemporary authorities in the judicial process, but it is not to be underestimated, particularly when the crime is one that shocks the community's sense of propriety.

A more widely held concept of responsibility is modeled on the causal relationships of physical properties and on the behavioral sciences. At the outset, let me say that few contemporary behavioral scholars would accept an ethical concept of responsibility that is derived from behavioral models or theories. But practitioners whose orientation has been from the social sciences, welfare personnel, probation personnel, forensic psychiatrists—those who must make professional judgments in litigation where responsibility is at issue—sometimes conceive of responsibility in terms of the model outlined here. Moreover, the particular public laws that give these vocations responsibilities in the courts also tend to reflect the model. According to this perspective, responsibility is diminished in proportion to the intensity of psychological or social factors that lie behind the criminal act. It is significant that judges frequently anticipate this kind of an orientation toward responsibility from social workers, probation staff, and psychiatric testimony and treat such personnel recommendations as pleas for mercy as much as expert analysis of human behavior.[8]

If this short discussion of individual criminal responsibility is not agreeable, it is at least familiar. What is not always familiar is the concept of responsibility appropriate for a crime policy. Punishing sin may save souls, but it will probably do little to reduce the UCR index. And the sanguine expectations of rehabilitationists are dropping precipitously as research demonstrates the difficulty in still another area of resocializing people.[9] By no means need we give up on trying alternative modes of treatment. Nor should we discontinue probation and parole as gradations of punishment for less serious crime. But treatment does not seem to be the most effective instrument of crime control. Instead, the metaphysical arguments over responsibility that lie behind the popularized "behavioral" approach to crime and punishment appear more relevant to the question of *mens rea* in court than to a crime policy.

[7] Martin Luther, "Address to the German Nobility," in *Western Political Heritage,* ed. William Elliott and Neil McDonald (Englewood Cliffs, N.J.: Prentice-Hall, 1958), p. 396.

[8] This was pointed out by David Matza in *Delinquency and Drift,* p. 124. My own observations in family courts support this view.

[9] Robert Martinson, "What Works—Questions and Answers about Prison Programs," pp. 22-54; Leslie Wilkins, *Evaluation of Penal Measures* (New York: Random House, 1969), Chapter 6. Wilkins sees little success in rehabilitation but suggests that more resources be placed into evaluations of treatment measures.

THE SERIOUS OFFENDER

Concerning the most violent and serious offenders, utilitarian approaches appear more useful for crime policy than analyses of social injustice, the "root causes of crime," or labeling theory. This is particularly so if we add the utility function of isolation from society by incarceration to the general and specific deterrent functions.

A study in Philadelphia by Wolfgang, Figlio, and Sellin, sharply at odds with the Wallerstein and Wyle conclusions cited earlier, is instructive. Examining the history of a birth cohort of all males born in 1945 who resided in Philadelphia between the ages of 10 and 18 years, and in most cases between birth and 18 years the researchers discovered that 3475, or 35 percent, of the boys out of 9946 were delinquent. Delinquency was considered to mean at least one police contact. Of the 7043 white boys studied, 2017, or 30 percent, were delinquent. Of the 2902 nonwhites, 1458, or 50 percent, were delinquent. But the most powerful findings relate to the "chronic offenders," those who committed five or more offenses before their eighteenth birthday. Only 627 boys were so classified, 6.3 percent of the birth cohort. This small percentage was responsible for 5305 delinquencies, or a stunning 52 percent of all the delinquencies of the entire birth cohort.

Moreover, the chronic offender was responsible for the bulk of the serious and violent crime. The offenses committed by the chronic offender constituted 53 percent of the 815 personal attacks (homicide, rape, aggravated and simple assault), 62 percent of the 1397 property offenses, and 71 percent of the 193 robberies. Seventy percent of violent offenses were committed by black youngsters from a chronic group; 45 percent of violent offenses were committed by white youngsters from a chronic group.[10]

Other literature tends to confirm the thesis that serious criminal offenses are concentrated in a small percentage of the population. Belkin, Blumstein, and Glass found that over 87 percent of all offenders arrested in Allegheny County will have been previously arrested.[11]

According to the Careers in Crime study of the FBI, out of 68,914 offenders arrested during 1971, 68 percent were repeat offenders and 47 percent had committed three or more serious offenses.[12] This is a very conservative figure, since others may have committed offenses and not been caught, or may have been incarcerated and not able to recidivate. Moreover, in a follow-up study of offenders released during 1965, 63 percent had been arrested. Of those persons who were acquitted or whose cases had been dismissed in 1965, 85 percent were arrested

[10] Wolfgang, Figlio, and Sellin, *Delinquency in a Birth Cohort.*

[11] Jacob Belkin, Alfred Blumstein, and William Glass, "Recidivism as a Feedback Process: An Analytical Model and Empirical Validation," *Journal of Criminal Justice* (1973), 1:7-26.

[12] FBI. *Uniform Crime Report,* 1971, pp. 36-37.

for new offenses. Those who received fine and probation or a suspended sentence had 37 percent and 56 percent recidivist rates, respectively.[13] Obviously, these figures are related to variables other than the deterrent value of a sentence. For example, crime type is associated with the kind of disposition. But 85 percent is a very high figure.

It is well established that a prior record is an excellent predictor of future criminal behavior. However, in the allocation of resources, prosecutors appear much more sensitive to the strength of evidence in a case and, to a lesser extent, to the seriousness of the offense, than to the criminal history of the defendant. Preliminary evidence supporting this view is provided by Forst and Brosi in a study of the District of Columbia district attorney's office. Using the number of days for which the prosecutor's office carried a case as an indicator of prosecutor resource allocation, they found that in applying their resources the office made no distinctions between those most recently and frequently arrested and those with fewer arrests.[14]

Table 11.1 1972 Convictions for index crimes

Index Offense	Conviction	Acquittal or Dismissal	Conviction by Reduced Charge
Homicide	45	33	23[a]
Forcible rape	36	47	17
Robbery	46	na	na
Aggravated assault	39	44	17
Burglary	49	na	na
Larceny	69	na	na

[a]Represents highest rate of charge reduction for entire table.
Source. FBI Uniform Crime Reports, 1973, p. 35.

Why the prosecutors did not weigh criminal history in their resource allocation is not known. The information was readily available through a court information system designed especially for the office. Perhaps it is because lawyers are trained to win, and prosecutors are also conscious of serious crimes that put them in the

[13]FBI, *Uniform Crime Report,* 1970, pp. 38-39.

[14]Brian E. Forst and Kathleen B. Brosi, "A Theoretical and Empirical Analysis of the Prosecutor," unpublished paper, The Institute For Law and Social Research, Washington, D.C., February 26, 1976, pp. 12-16.

public eye. But lawyers may be less attuned to the policy implications of recidivist defendants who are not vigorously prosecuted. Or, as the authors recognize, perhaps "days carried" is a faulty index of prosecutor resources, or the District of Columbia is not reflective of national practice, or police are more apt to arrest on less evidence those with criminal records than those without serious records. Whatever the reasons, repeat offenders do seem to make out well.

There is an additional disturbing fact regarding conviction rates. Generally, the more serious the crime, the less the probability of conviction on the original charge. This tendency is probably the result of plea bargaining as serious crimes appear statistically as a guilty plea for a lesser crime (Table 11.1).

Table 11.1 could be criticized for obscuring the fact that innocent people are acquitted and that forcible rape and homicide are difficult to obtain convictions on—hence the sizable reduction in charge percentage. Both criticisms would be valid, the latter particularly. But few knowledgeable observers of the criminal courts would assume that more than 5 or 10 percent of the defendants charged are actually innocent.

Moreover, between 1960 and 1970, there has been a decided drop in the commitment rate and the length of sentence imposed by courts. For example, in 1960 the chance of being sent to a prison after committing a violent crime (murder, rape, robbery, assault) was about 1 out of 10. In 1970 the figure was under 3 percent. During the same time span the average time spent in prison for those who committed a violent crime in New York State dropped from 0.35 years to 0.06 years.[15] At the same time, the probability of a resident, in New York City at least, being victimized by a violent crime more than doubled.[16] It is true that no causal relationship can be empirically drawn between either lower conviction rates or shorter sentences. Nor can New York City's precipitous rise in violent crime during this period be considered typical of other cities. It was not. But the relationship is certainly suggestive of a utilitarian hypothesis: victim suffering will go up as the relative costs of engaging in crime are minimized and the rewards of criminal activity, monetary or otherwise, remain constant.

Moreover, sentencing does not seem to reflect in any consistent manner the past record of serious offenders. What is potentially a national scandal, but is received by the public with a great yawn, is the disposition of organized crime offenders.[17] The Careers in Crime program of the FBI compared La Cosa Nostra (LCN) offenders with average federal offenders. Whereas LCN offenders had a criminal career of 20 years and 7 months, the ordinary probation offender had

[15] Shlomo Shinnar and Reuel Shinnar, "The Effects of the Criminal Justice System on the Control of Crime: A Quantitative Approach," *Law and Society Review* (1975), 9:584.

[16] Ibid., p. 582, Table 1.

[17] The President's Commission on Law Enforcement and Administration of Justice, *Task Force Report: Organized Crime* (Washington, D.C.: U.S. Government Printing Office, 1967), pp. 19-20.

9 years and 3 months. Just under 60 percent of the LCN offenders had records of at least two prior felony convictions; only 22 percent of the average offenders had a felony conviction. Seventeen percent of the charges against LCN offenders were for violent crimes, whereas the corresponding figure for average offenders was only 4 percent.

LCN offender charges were dismissed or they were acquitted at trial twice as frequently (69.7 percent) as average offenders (34.8 percent). The same lenient pattern continues in the sentencing of racketeers convicted of income tax evasion. Income tax evasion is frequently the most convenient charge to prove, given limited investigating resources, even though more serious crimes have been committed by the racketeer. An additional study showed that only 3 percent of the racketeers convicted of income tax evasion between 1952 and 1954 received prison terms, a considerably lower percentage than income tax evaders in legitimate professional and business life.[18]

The Pennsylvania Crime Commission, which investigates organized crime, relates a typical case of judicial and political corruption in Philadelphia.

> *In 1968 Illgas approached Sgt. Christopher DeCree of the Philadelphia Police Department's Chief Inspector's Squad through another police officer. DeCree was offered a substantial sum by the intermediary if he would agree to protect Illgas' numbers writers, runners, and office workers from arrest. He reported the incident to his superiors, and both Illgas and the intermediary police officer were indicted on charges of attempted bribery. Illgas was convicted and given a sentence of 11 ½ to 23 months.*
>
> *Shortly after imposition of sentence, Illgas complained of a previous back injury —an injury which he had failed to mention during his presentence investigation. His sentence was subsequently reduced to 6 to 23 months. Illgas' attorneys then filed an appeal to try to overturn the conviction; although this was done in 1968, the case has not yet been heard by the Superior Court. The court reporter who transcribed the notes at Illgas' original trial mysteriously left Philadelphia for Tennessee, and cannot be located; nor can the notes of testimony be retrieved. The entire case may have to be retried, and authorities are skeptical about winning it again.*[19]

The Pennsylvania Commission documents overwhelming corruption in the 1950s and 1960s throughout the state, from judicial magistrate offices, to the President Judge's chamber in Philadelphia, and to the Governor's office in the 1940s and early 1950s.[20] Government intervention in behalf of racketeers during this time included character witnesses by U.S. congressmen and senior county

[18] Pennsylvania Crime Commission, *Report on Organized Crime,* 1970, p. 98.
[19] Ibid., p. 75. On corruption in Pennsylvania, see also John Gardiner, *The Politics of Corruption.*
[20] Pennsylvania Crime Commission, *Report on Organized Crime,* 1970, pp. 65-72.

judges, unprecedented reduced sentences, and six timely gubernatorial pardons for larceny, bombing, robbery, operating a lottery, and murder.

Even without corruption and organized crime, serious offenders in urban courts are more apt to have their cases dismissed and are more apt to receive prison sentences than they are for the same offense in suburban or rural areas.[21] Particularly significant is the *minimal* impact of a serious prior record on sentencing for crimes such as burglary and robbery. For example, in Los Angeles in 1970 only 37 percent of those convicted of robbery, who had already served a prison term, were returned to prison.[22] Similar patterns of placing those previously convicted of a felony on probation are recorded in Pittsburgh[23] and the State of Wisconsin.[24]

EMPIRICAL RESEARCH IN DETERRENCE

Does punishment deter crime? Given the multiple number of variables that are related to crime—unemployment, income, urban settings and the like—it has been difficult to control for these variables while isolating the punishment variable. Moreover, for most of this century, very little empirical research on the utility of punishment was conducted. As suggested earlier, the topic was distasteful and ideologically unacceptable to many criminologists. Recently empirical work has been done, although findings are very tentative, and policy implications must be taken with caution. We are primarily interested in the empirical findings that concern themselves with the general deterrent capacity of the criminal law as it is applied by arrest, adjudication, and sentencing.

The methodological problems of deterrent research are complex.[25] To begin

[21] See James Q. Wilson, *Thinking about Crime* (New York: Basic Books, 1975), Chapter 8; Greenwood, *Prosecution of Felony Defendants in Los Angeles County,* Table 72 on p. 107.

[22] Greenwood et al., *Prosecution of Adult Felony Defendants in Los Angeles County, pp. 109—110, Tables 74 and 75.*

[23] Martin A. Levin, "Urban Politics and Policy Outcomes: The Criminal Courts," in *Criminal Justice,* ed. George F. Cole (No. Scituate, Mass.: Duxbury Press, 1972), p. 335.

[24] Dean V. Babst and John W. Mannering, "Probation versus Imprisonment for Similar Types of Offenders," *Journal of Research in Crime and Delinquency* (1965), 2:61.

[25] An outstanding review of the literature on which rely heavily for my contentions can be found in Johannes Andenaes, "Criminology: General Prevention Revisted; Research and Policy Implications," *The Journal of Criminal Law, Criminology and Political Science* (1975), 66:338-365. For a review of the economic literature see Gordon Tulloch, "Does Punishment Deter Crime?" *The Public Interest* (1974), 36:103-111; and Charles R. Tittle, "Punishment and Deterrence of Deviance" in *The Economics of Crime and Punishment,* ed. Simon Rottenberg (Washington, D.C.: American Enterprise Institute for Public Policy, 1973), pp. 85-102. The questions of certainty and severity are addressed by William C. Bailey, J. David Martin, and Louis N. Gray, "Crime and Deterrence: A Correlational Analysis," *Journal of Research in Crime and Delinquency* (1974), 11:124-143; George Antunes and A. Lee Hunt, "The Impact of Certainty and Severity of Punishment on Levels of Crime in American States," *The Journal of Criminal Law and Criminology* (1973), 64:486-493.

with, isolation or, to use the jargon of social scientists, the "incapacitative" function, must be distinguished from the general deterrent function of imprisonment.

Scholars sharply disagree over the probable impact of isolation on crime rates. The disagreement is not surprising, since it is extremely difficult to separate the impact of isolation from the deterrent or rehabilitative functions of incarceration. It is equally difficult to determine recidivism rates for specific crimes. If police records are used, they have limited usefulness, since clearance rates are very low. Most offenders are simply not caught. If court records are used, the charge at conviction will not necessarily reflect the actual offense, since the original charge may have been altered by plea bargaining or evidentiary problems. Yet identifying the universe of offenders and their specific offenses is crucial to identifying the impact of incarceration.

Nevertheless, early findings are interesting. Greenburg concluded that the physical restraint of the present prison population was responsible for approximately an 8-percent reduction of index crime. A critic of increased incarceration, Greenburg points out that if the present average sentence length of 2 years were increased to 3 years, the 9 percent figure would increase to a modest 12 percent.[26]

Shinnar and Shinnar are most sanguine about the isolation function's capacity to reduce crime. Mugging provides an example. According to Shinnar and Shinnar, the chance of a mugger being arrested is about 12 percent per crime. His chance of being imprisoned after arrest is about 10 percent per offense, and there is only a 0.012 percent chance of imprisonment for every mugging. These percentages are roughly confirmed by other research. For larceny, burglary, and auto theft, Tittle found the likelihood of imprisonment to be 3.6 percent, 3.4 percent, and 1.5 percent, respectively. Shinnar and Shinnar conclude that if we imprison every *convicted* mugger and robber for 5 years, we would reduce muggings by a factor of five.[27] At the same time, if we increase conviction rates and clearance rates, we would greatly reduce crime incidents even without increasing prison sentences.

However, methodological problems in researching these areas are severe. Neither Greenburg nor Shinnar and Shinnar had access to jail data. They had to rely on prison data. Moreover, even prison data are suspect, since many correctional departments list as "prisoners" those who are out on educational furlough, in community-based treatment centers, or work release. Conclusions in the area of incapacitation must be considered tentative.

[26] David F. Greenburg, "The Incapacitative Effect of Imprisonment: Some Estimates," *Law and Society Review* (1975), 9:572.

[27] Shinnar and Shinnar, "The Effects of the Criminal Justice System on the Control of Crime," pp. 604-605; Charles R. Tittle, "Crime Rates and Legal Sanctions," *Social Problems* (1969), 16:409.

Along with incapacitation are questions over the effect of *certainty, severity,* and *alacrity* in punishment. Here, the methodological questions are equally perplexing. Much of the certainty of punishment research refers to the risk of being imprisoned. But being punished may involve a fine, probation, or a short stay in a local jail. Some states make wide use of probation; others rely on prison terms. Considering these vagaries, it is difficult to operationalize punishment. Moreover, the problem of unreported crime makes it impossible to determine an exact universe of crimes committed. Finally, we also have in deterrent research a similar problem to that found in budgetary cost-benefit analysis. If the crime rate *decreases* at the same time a deterrent policy is implemented, the decrease might be falsely attributed to the policy. In fact, the deterrent policy itself might have been a response to a temporary rising crime rate that returns to a "normal" rate by chance.

In spite of these limitations and many others that I have not mentioned, we can provide some cautious conclusions regarding the effect of incapacitation and deterrence on serious crime. Although the evidence is mixed, the preponderance of the literature suggests the following. The certainty of punishment will tend to reduce the amount of crime, although we are not sure by how much. The severity of punishment also has a deterrent effect, although probably its effect is curvilinear. That is, long sentences will have a diminished impact on deterring crime. Considering the expense of prison, its effect on humanistic values, the deterrent effect of long sentences will be in most instances marginal, although the isolation impact on serious crime may be somewhat more than marginal.

Of particular interest to the policy analyst, however, is the fact that punishment must be perceived in advance if it is to deter effectively. Earlier I spoke of the low visibility of crime problems in the general public. Certainly, most people have little idea of the actual penalties levied for criminal acts.[28] But the portions of the population most interested, those most likely to violate the law, are better informed. In one study, some 76 percent of the population in adult correctional institutions in California gave correct answers to questions regarding the punishment for robbery with bodily injury and 65 percent of college students accurately identified the penalty for marihuana.[29] Thus, there is considerable evidence that the deterrent effect of criminal penalties is dependent on publicity and effective law enforcement. If publicity accompanies a deterrent policy, the crime rate may go down. However, if the publicity exaggerates the risk of apprehension and conviction, the evidence is that its deterrent effect will soon wear off.[30]

[28] Social Psychology Research Associates, *Public Knowledge of Criminal Penalties: A Research Report* (San Francisco: Social Psychology Research Associates, 1968), p. 20.

[29] Andenaes, "Criminology," p. 335.

[30] Donald T. Campbell and H. Lawrence Ross, "The Connecticut Crackdown on Speeding: Time Series Data in Quazi-Experimental Analysis," *Law and Society Review* (1969), 3:33-53; H. Lawrence

Merely discussing an isolating function is odious for most individuals interested in prison reform. Angry voices often charge "warehousing" and urge that existing prisons be torn down, that budget requests for new institutions be voted down. Prisons are seen as schools for crime, as dumping grounds for the poor, the black, and the ignorant, and as harbingers of cruelty.

There is irony, even tragedy, in the absence of realistic discussion. First, no distinction is made by such rhetoric between prisons that are humane and those that allow unrestrained homosexual rape, murder, and lesser brutalities. It is assumed, first, that all prisons and jails are brutal and, second, that a moratorium on constructing new ones will put an end to brutalityand usher in an age of rehabilitation. The consequences of such opposition to any construction is that many existing institutions will continue to have overcrowded and outmoded facilities and inadequate protection of inmates from other inmates.

The tragedy of much prison reform is that it often confuses three separate goals: providing *rehabilitation,* something we do not know how to do, although we certainly ought to keep trying; eliminating *physical coercion,* something that society, with considerable wisdom, will not permit; and improving *conditions* in the prisons. It well may be that some prisons can be torn down and fewer people forcibly restrained. It is certainly true that too many prisoners are daily exposed to degrading and vicious environments. But improving the conditions under which men and women are restrained need not wait for the resolution of who should be restrained, how we should go about rehabilitating offenders, or how we should answer metaphysical and behavioral questions about punishment. There is no reason why we cannot, as ends in themselves, encourage friendships, provide for family and conjugal visitations, offer vocational training and educational opportunities, end overcrowding, and protect the inmates from physical harm. Granted, the higher the degree of security at a prison, the more difficult humanitarian reform will be. But some degree of prison reform can realistically be achieved if the issues of rehabilitation, physical constraint, and brutality are separated.

I have suggested that the deterrent result of the certainty of punishment is greater than the severity of punishment for most offenses.[31] We now turn to an additional problem affecting the certainty of punishment in the offender's psyche —court delay.

Ross, "Law, Science and Accidents: The British Road Safety Act of 1967," *Journal of Legal Studies* (1973), 2:1.

[31] Antunes and Hunt, "The Impact of Certainty and Severity of Punishment," pp. 486-493; see also Bailey, Martin, and Gray, "Crime and Deterrence," pp. 124-143.

DELAY AND THE COURTS

Urban court delay is universally deplored and almost universally continues for a variety of reasons, discussed in Chapter 4. Median elapsed time of felony cases from indictment to disposition ranges from 285 days in Washington in 1968 to 101 days in San Diego according to the Indicator's Program of the Urban Institute,[32] and with singular exceptions there is little evidence, overall, that delay periods in urban courts will be reduced in the near future.

Court delay causes immeasurable amounts of frustration for witnesses, many of them angry victims called back for interminable hearings, lineups, and scheduled trials that seem never to take place.[33] Most never do. For the defendant without bond, delay can also mean an extended period of incarceration without a finding of guilt. For the police, delay can mean hours of wasted time by witnesses and patrolmen waiting for hearings, grand juries, and trials. Worse, delay can result in increasing the probability that the officer will rearrest the same offender out on bail who he arrested earlier.

What can be done to reduce court delay? Answering that question has already consumed millions of dollars of systems research management consulting, design of countless management information systems, promotion of a new, highly paid and highly trained profession, court administration, and the reorganization of criminal courts through the United States. Court delay problems differ greatly from jurisdiction to jurisdiction, and it is presumptuous to propose general reforms without a generous number of qualifiers. One court that I have studied suffers most from anachronistic scheduling. Many other urban districts are understaffed with public defenders, prosecutors, and judges, while the flow of case volume into urban courts, both criminal and civil, increases its pressure. Certainly, reducing criminal activity or decriminalizing much of our effort to control vice and maintain the peace is our first line of defense against excessive delay. Indeed, many of the pretrial diversionary projects that have been enthusiastically urged and implemented throughout the United States in the last several years, often as a partial solution to court overcrowding, may be a consequence of the overcriminalization of our laws in the first place.

Structural changes also can be made. Some jurisdictions have eliminated grand juries, relying on the preliminary hearing for "probable cause" testimony to determine whether a defendant should be charged, A prosecutor's affidavit after the constitutionally guaranteed preliminary hearing is held provides a much more efficient charging procedure and does not diminish the protection afforded the

[32] Pasqual A. Don Vito, "An Experiment in the Use of Court Statistics," *Judicature* (1972), 56, Table on p. 57.

[33] Ash, "Court Delay, Crime Control and Neglect of the Interests of Witnesses," pp. 1-34.

accused. Unlike grand juries, a preliminary hearing is an adversarial process with the defense counsel present.

Grand juries are almost universally a rubber stamp for the prosecution anyways, and much delay and inconvenience for those required to serve on grand juries as well as a considerable expense to the state could be eliminated by its demise. Special investigating grand juries that still perform a vital function should be retained, to be convened by a trial judge or by state agencies, such as the attorneys-general offices responsible for investigating organized crime.

Considerable delay is also the result of increased procedural safeguards both prior to trial and, to a lesser extent, at appeal. Most jurisdictions today have a plethora of motions that a defense attorney can make to quash (dismiss) a charge, an indictment, evidence, or a warrant. Such may be the price of civil liberty. It certainly is one of the costs of enforcing victimless crime, relying as it does on public stealth in search and seizure, wiretapping, and undercover work. Much delay is the consequence of multiple hearings on collateral suits. In fact, collateral suits are an additional reason for continuances. If many of these issues could be addressed at the same time in the same court, a great deal of time and energy could be preserved. Specialized courts trained in the sometimes esoteric law that raises these questions might speed the course of justice along. Moreover, *all* cases do not need excessive time to prepare motions to quash; set periods in which such motions can be made, while still allowing for the exceptional case, would facilitate case volume flow.

Other streamlining recommendations are more difficult, not because they are technologically difficult but because they affect important interests of the legal profession. Certainly the wide-spread abuse of granting continuances at hearings, arraignments, and trials to facilitate a private attorney collecting a fee or to permit the continuity of a profitable civil practice can be brought under control. Perhaps this will require a "criminal law bar" without outside commitments and, in the case of public defenders, without the need to pressure clients for their fee prior to court appearance. Indeed, private attorneys do tend to request more continuances[34] are associated with longer delay times than are public defenders.[35]

Ending the abuse of continuance procedures will certainly require judges who will insist on rigorous demonstrations of need before continuances are permitted. To do so judges need more than the will to transcend the personal interests and professional life-style of their brethren who appear before them at bar. The president judge or supervising, administrative judge needs information—offend-

[34] Leslie G. Foschio, "Empirical Research and the Problem of Court Delay," *Reducing Court Delay,* p. 43.

[35] In the Commonwealth of Pennsylvania, cases represented by privately retained attorneys experience longer average delays than those of public defenders. Data supplied by the Office of Criminal Justice Statistics, Pennsylvania Department of Justice, 1975.

er-based, current, easily retrieved, and meaningfully organized—to follow individual case delay, to identify obstructed queueing at bottleneck stages in the system, to recognize attorneys who receive inordinate numbers of continuances, and to plan for rational court calendaring at busy times of the month. The modern urban court with a heavy volume of cases cannot operate justly without professional court administration, systems analysis, and a management information system.

Perhaps statutory discharge rules such as the new federal rule of a 60-day limit to disposing of a case may provide the catalyst to manage court dockets and scheduling efficiently. But exceptions are frequently written into such statutes to waive the rule—an exceptional problem locating a witness, a late report, an illness. And the exceptions turn into routine continuances. For example, California requires that criminal cases be brought to trial or disposition, or be dismissed within 60 days of filing, unless the defendant consents to a delay. But the time lapse for pleas of guilty after arraignment for Los Angeles, San Diego, and San Francisco were 93 days, 87 days, and 114 days, respectively.[36] Obviously, many defendants consented to a delay. Mandatory limits on bringing cases to trial, combined with proper court management and supervision by concerned personnel in criminal justice exercising their discretion to promote a policy of reducing delay, remain the most fruitful approach.

BAIL BOND

Issues concerning bail bond are so interwoven with delay and recidivism by defendants awaiting trial that it is useful to discuss them jointly. Bail bond has two functions: one explicitly spelled out in criminal procedures and constitutional law, to guarantee, by threat of forfeiture of a sizable amount of money or property (in English and Colonial procedures it could be the liberty of a fellow watch-and-ward society member), the appearance of the suspect for trial.

The other function is often implicit, although not consistent with the law, in the decisions of magistrates and judges. High bond is regularly used to prevent the release of "dangerous" defendants, regardless of their propensity to appear for trial. The defendant who seeks vengeance on a complaining citizen, the suspect who is also suspected of wanting to destroy evidence, and the violence-prone offender are often denied a realistic bail to prevent the defendant from committing additional crimes. In some crimes bail is not permitted by statute and the defendant must rely on *habeas corpus.* Attaching a policeman, homicide, and prison breach are typical examples.

There can be no institution in criminal justice where fewer positive remarks can be made than the traditional bail bond system. Typically, the system works in the

[36]Don Vito, "An Experiment in the Use of Court Statistics," Table on p. 57.

following manner. A defendant is preliminarily arraigned before a magistrate, bail-commissioner, clerk, judge, or J.P. and charged with a crime. If it is a serious crime (requiring arrest instead of a summons) the judge can provide nominal bail of $1, in some states, permit R.O.R. (release on one's own recognizance), release the defendant in the charge of parents or family, or set money bail. If the defendant does not have independent sources of cash or surety, the judge may provide a list of bondsmen from which the defendant may "hire" the money he needs, to borrow Calvin Coolidge's term, but at a usurious interest rate, usually 5 to 10 percent, depending on the principal. The premium the defendant pays is *not* refundable, even if he is acquitted or charges are dismissed. In return, the bondsman guarantees the court that he will produce the defendant or forfeit the entire bond.

As presently structured, the bondsman system is patently discriminatory against the poor, particularly if they are innocent. Those of means provide bail from their own resources. Those without are granted bond if the bondsman considers them a good business risk. Moreover, those not bonded are more likely to be convicted than those who are released prior to trial. Bondsmen have argued in the past that they provide an essential service in encouraging liberal release, insuring appearance at court by reminding defendants of scheduled appearances and the consequences of not appearing. Recent research questions this service, as defaulting seems as high under the bondsman as it is under percentage deposit bail systems where there is no need for bondsmen.[37]

Finally, the fluid and complementary relationship between bondsmen and the lower-level clerks, sergeants (for station house bail), J.P.s, and magistrates who set and administer bail bond produces a routine chemistry readymade for corruption and mischief. Unscrupulous bondsmen not uncommonly enter into collusive agreements with lower-level judges to set unnecessarily high bail or to increase the bondsman's bail premiums. For his part, the magistrate may receive a kickback or collect an illegal fee from bondsmen. At the same time, the magistrate returns the favor, granting to a favored few bonding firms a monopoly in illegally soliciting customers at local lockups or detention facilities, boosting the profits of co conspirators, and encouraging firms to charge interest rates higher than permitted by law. Bondsmen who enjoy this corner on the market know that a defendant has no option but to pay an exorbitant ransom instead of remaining in jail.[38] The success of such collusion and illegal rates and fines depends on the low visibility of bonding agents, the absence of review of records by an outside agency or administrative judge, and the ignorance of defendants. The present bail bond system is frequently characterized by all three criteria.

[37] John E. Conklin and Dermot Meagher "The Percentage Deposit Bail System: An Alternative to the Professional Bondsman," *Journal of Criminal Justice* (1973), 1:300, Table on p. 311.
[38] For example, see Pennsylvania Crime Commission, *1971-1972*

Bail bond corruption does not end at the magistrate level; it is too lucrative. For example, in Chester, Pennsylvania in 1968 all police captains had been instructed by the mayor to call only two favored firms to provide bail for defendants—unless a defendant requested another bondsman by name. A third bond firm, owned by a black citizen and therefore able to capture some of the market of black defendants in spite of the mayor's favoritism, wanted a cut of the market. In 1969, the mayor found it necessary to orchestrate personally a division of the bail bond market in Chester between the competing firms, although the latecomer was eventually told it was an established bondsman firms's "turn to dominate the business in Chester." His firm was newer and he "would have to wait his turn."[39]

Several alternative approaches to bail bond have been proposed or implemented. Nominal bond, or R.O.R., requires only that several dollars be put up by the defendant. Less serious defendants are thus spared the costs of high bond. But magistrates have been found reluctant to utilize nominal bond in many cases, particularly if there is no screening device to select good risks from bad ones. Moreover, nominal bond does not solve the problem of effectively reviewing the bonding decision's criteria for granting or providing bail.[40]

An early reform for more serious defendants was pioneered by the Vera Institute's Manhattan Bail Project, which begain in 1961.[41] The program provides a careful screening service employing explicit criteria to estimate the potential of each defendant's not appearing for trial. It also attempts to predict whether or not a defendant will commit additional crimes after being screened and released on his own recognizance. Criteria used range from employment, local residence, and family stability to the existence of a prior criminal record.

Views regarding the ability of screening instruments to predict either failure to appear (FTA) rates or rearrest rates differ considerably. Freed and Wald indicate that bail projects such as the Vera Foundation have released vast numbers of inmates and suffered few defaulters and virtually no commissions of crimes by those on bail prior to trial.[42]

Recent empirical examination of Vera-type bail screening is equally enthusiastic about the program's success, although the data do not lend themselves to enthusiasm. In an interesting project that attempts to validate the Vera criteria of predictability, Gottfredson concludes, "The vast majority of defendants were

[39] *Report,* Pennsylvania Department of Justice, pp. 65-84. *Ibid.,* p. 70.

[40] Conklin and Meagher, "The Percentage Deposit Bail System," p. 300.

[41] Vera Institute of Justice, *Fair Treatment for the Indigent: The Manhattan Bail Project, Programs in Criminal Justice Reform, Ten-Year Report, 1961-1971,* Vera Institute of Justice, Inc., 1972.

[42] D. Freed and P. Wald, *Bail in the United States: 1964,* U.S. Department of Justice, Washington, D.C.

successes while on pre-trial release"[43] according to a sample tested for FTA. but in the first of his two samples, 50 percent failed to show up for trial unprompted and, in the other 25 percent, six were FTA. Even after bench warrants were issued for their rearrest or other notification was given, the percentages were 85 percent and 73 percent, respectively.[44]

Such percentages are not surprising to those experienced with the life-style of most individuals who are processed as defendants. Their time span is very brief: they are forgetful and official notices of hearings or trial, even bench warrants, are confusing to them. Without personal reminders and warnings from a court detective, clerk, attorney, or other official, many are likely to disregard official notices, fail to prepare for babysitters, or caution their employer that they will be absent.

Most FTAs do not attempt to evade trial. Considering the advantages of having defendants continuing to hold their family together, to work, and to be able to compensate their victims and prepare their case, and the equal advantage to the state of not having detention facilities inundated with unbonded defendants, a 15-percent FTA rate is manageable. But the FTA percentages are not low and there are indications that continued careful screening is vital to prevent absconding and recidivism from 15 to 25 percent that may attempt to evade.

An additional bail bond alternative is widely proposed that appears to permit even larger numbers of bailees than at present. Variously labeled a "cash bail program,"[45] or a "percentage deposit bail system,"[46] the method of release generally operates as follows: After a defendant is arrested and brought to a bail commissioner or judge in a court of first instance, the defendant is permitted on bailable offenses to post 10 percent of his bail in cash with the guarantee that 90 percent of his collateral will be returned when his case is finally disposed. The 10-percent cash bond roughly corresponds to the premium that the bail bondsman would normally retain as his fee for posting the larger amount.

There are a number of benefits said to flow from cash bail. Since the 10-percent figure is easily redeemable, the money can be borrowed from a bank or family

[43] Michael R. Gottfredson, "An Empirical Analysis of Pre-Trial Release Decisions," *journal of Criminal Justice* (1974), 2:293.

[44] Gottfredson's samples included a control sample of felons given R.O.R. in California and an experimental sample of felons who normally would have been screened out of an R.O.R. program but, by special arrangement, were left in. Excluded from experimental group, however, were all homicide, robbery, forcible rape, and assualt cases. It is a fair assumption that such offenders would be *most* likely to be FTAs and commit additional offenses while on bail, which raises serious questions about even the 73-percent figure. Ibid., pp. 287-304.

[45] Information on cash bail program proposals in Pittsburgh and Philadelphia was derived from personal communication between myself and the Allegheny Regional Office of the Pennsylvania Governor's Justice Commission.

[46] Conklin and Meagher, "The Percentage Deposit Bail System," pp. 299-315.

and few indigent defendants need to languish in jail because a bondsman considered them a poor business risk. Greater numbers of defendants may return to court with the incentive of having 90 percent of their collateral returned. Corruption will be minimized as dependence on the bondsman declines. Moreover, there is empirical eivdence that cash bail systems do make it easier for defendants to obtain bail without altering FTA rates.[47]

The cash bail alternative might be coupled with a statutory requirement that 10-percent cash bail is available to *everyone,* unless the state can demonstrate the need for higher bail or the denial of bail based on prior record or past performance. At the same time, screening of the more questionable defendants should continue, along with statutory denial of bail for selected offenses. The screening process and the statute presumption in favor of the defendant would serve two functions—providing a record that permits the state to supervise bonding decisions as to their reasonableness and providing a screen for dangerous or absconding defendants. Obviously, a bail system will not do if it promotes recidivism.

The latter point is brought home forcefully in a study by the National Bureau of Standards of pretrial release of defendants in Washington, D.C.[48] In a carefully designed pilot study of 8712 defendants who entered the criminal justice system during four sample weeks in 1968, they found 11 percent of those released charged with misdemeanors or felonies were subsequently rearrested. Of those charged with violent crimes and released, 17 percent were rearrested; of those charged with dangerous crimes and released, 25 percent were rearrested. Seven percent of those initially charged with a felony were charged with the commission of another felony.

Most instructive, however, was the relationship the study illustrated between days on release (as a result of court delay) and recidivism. Excepting a few days before trial, when rearrest rates dropped, the longer the wait for trial, the higher the recidivism rate, particularly if the delay is longer than 240 days, and if the offender is charged with a violent or dangerous crime.[49] Such a pattern is consistent with the "present-oriented" behavioral characteristic that many scholars associate with lower-class life-styles.

Bail bond reform and delay reduction represent a rare amalgam of civil liberty and deterrent objectives; speedy trials would go a long way to mitigate the injustice of the serious offender who, because of his crime or his indigency, or both, must await trial over an extended period. It would also reduce the anguish for some who await trial over extended periods of time. Finally, to the extent that street crime is a lower-class phenomenon, alacrity in justice followed by a short

[47] Ibid., pp. 306, 311.

[48] J. Locke et al., *Compilation and Use of Criminal Court Data in Relation to Pre-Trial Release of Defendants.*

[49] Ibid., pp. 160-163.

sentence will provide a better deterrent than protracted proceedings after which the defendant only vaguely remembers what he has done.

In summary, we must take a fresh look at crime policy regarding the serious, repeating offender and at deterrent and isolation policy. As a matter of policy, judges and prosecutors can reduce victim suffering by identifying the serious offender early in the court process and prosecuting him without delay. This is not a call for repression. Serious offenders represent only a small minority of defendants. But making a special effort to prosecute and sentence the serious offender based on his criminal record as well as his current offense is a realistic, feasible policy alternative. Such a policy initiative represents an area where local officials can do more to reduce victimization. Chapter 11 and 12 represent a change of pace and point to several areas where the system would do well of it did considerably less.

12

DRUGS DELINQUENCY, AND DISEASE: PRELIMINARY THOUGHTS

There is no area of criminal justice where data are more disputed, conceptual clarity more diluted, polemic more common, and stereotype more influential than drug policy. The very term "drug" connotes a mixture of scientific wonder and weakness of character. Indeed, American "drug use" is a function of the development of modern chemistry, pharmacology, and medicine, and sedating substances with technical labels like meprobamate and chloralhydrate that appear more ominous than their equivalent West African tribal sedatives—palm wine, the much more dangerous and potent cane juice rum, or powerful stimulants such as cola nuts. Yet one hears that only today does West Africa have a "drug problem" growing within its cities; the drugs involved are cocaine, marihuana, and heroin—the more primitive and traditonal substances are being forgotten.

Legal definitions of "dangerous drugs" have historically been dependent on both the limits of scientific knowledge regarding the physiological effects of a drug, particularly if it was habit-forming, and the social or political acceptability of a stimulant or depressant. Many substances that appear to be reasonably safe and nonaddictive—marihuana is a leading example—have been labelled as narcotics or dangerous drugs almost entirely as a by-product of *other* political events. Vigorous administration of the Harrison Act of 1914, culminating in marihuana being treated in law as a dangerous narcotic, was a spin-off of police policy during Prohibition and later, to use the broad brush of conjecture, a reaction against youthful challenges to sexual mores, racism, and war in Southeast Asia.

In 1933, use of the drug "alcohol," physiologically dangerous and addictive, was officially removed from the criminal code after a disastrous 14 years of trying to enforce small-town and prairie morality on large and influential segments of American society. Today, more than 9 million Americans are considered alcoholics. An additional stimulant, nicotine, certainly represents a public health hazard, but also represents a legal drug used by 50 million Americans today,[1] although sale of cigarettes was once outlawed in 14 states.

Concentrating on the esoteric psychological properties of drugs instead of the social and political context of users of "drugs" permits government officials and social elites to avoid invidious comparisons of *their* drugs with those that are illegal. Such ostrichlike postures also lead to reductionist constructs about the nature of "drug users"—that is, those who use illicit drugs, as opposed to the generally legal drugs of social and political elites.

Stereotypes about marihuana users are a product of such constructs. As with all stereotypes, some commonly held perceptions of marihuana users are correct: among the behaviors statistically associated with marihuana use are radical politics, visits to psychiatrists, and sexual freedom.[2] But the National Commission on Marihuana and Drug Abuse also found that young people who experiment with marihuana are fundamentally the same people, socially and psychologically, who will drink alcohol and smoke cigarettes (see Table 12.1). Similar conclusions were reached about adult smokers and nonsmokers. Laws proscribing sale of tobacco and alcohol, both much more widely used by youngsters aged 12 to 17 than marihuana,[3] are either ignored or enforced sporadically.

Table 12.1 National survey of high school students

	Currently Smoke Cigarettes (%)	**Currently Drink Alcohol (%)**
Tried marihuana	50	27
Nonmarihuana smokers	3	2

Source. Data taken from The Official Report of the National Commission on Marihuana and Drug Abuse, p. 51.

Stereotyped reductionist constructs[4] are found not only among marihuana smokers, but among heroin users as well. The "junkie" is a popular and strangely ambivalent archetype of degradation and heroism in the cinema and literature—

[1] *Marihuana,* p. 187.
[2] Ibid., p. 51.
[3] Ibid., pp. 172-173.
[4] James A. Inciardi, "Drugs, Drug Taking and Drug Seeking: Notations on the Dynamics of Myth, Change, and Reality," in *Drugs and the Criminal Justice System,* ed. James A. Inciardi and Carl D. Chambers (Beverly Hills, Calif.: Saga Publications, 1974), pp. 203-218, especially pp. 207-209.

The Man with the Golden Arm, Valley of the Dolls, and *Superfly.* Typically, he is black, poor, delinquent, and smoking pot as prelude to heroin. Once he becomes an addict he steals and commits desperate violent acts to satisfy uncontrollable craving for the drug. Early death from an overdose or a long term in prison are the most likely prospects at the end of the road, although a few are "saved" from the horrors of self-destruction.

Even the modern heroin addicts, for whom stereotypes are closer to reality than for other kinds of drug usage, are likely to be poly-drug users, particularly if they are young. Alcohol, LSD, sedatives, marihuana, and amphetamines are all used by many heroin addicts today.[5] Yet the modern public would have difficulty identifying Samuel Taylor Coleridge or Edgar Allen Poe as "junkies"—to say nothing of the local physician[6] or the young of the middle class—and they are all too ready to assume that *their* son or daughter, although fortified by religious and family admonishments, may fall prey to the wiles of a pusher. Closer to reality is the potential of a friend or friends exerting peer group pressures. It is the peer group that represents alternative avenues to status for modern youths in industrial economies who cannot yet, or perhaps ever, be absorbed into the world of work and adult success patterns. Drug use reflects a drug culture of intimate friends, not individual enterprise and solitary dissolution. The profitability of drug sales depends more on the fact that the enterprise is illegal with no regulation or tax to pay on profits than on the craft of a seductive salesman-pusher.

Finally, the stereotype of illegal drugs is that they are more dangerous than those that are legal. It may be true that heroin is chemically more dangerous than alcohol or tobacco, particularly because of its capacity to produce psychological dependency. It is probably less true that many softer drugs are more dangerous than what is now legally available. But the inherent danger in drugs is largely dependent on the context within which they are used.[7]

Overdosing heroin is a good example. Certainly heroin addicts have a higher death rate than the general population, but the high rate is largely due to the lack of professional supervision and regulation in its use. Street heroin is almost always diluted or cut with sugar, flour, or more dangerous substances. State narcotic officers told us that, on several occasions, dry Clorox was used to cut heroin, almost certainly resulting in illness or death to the user. Even when heroin is cut

[5] Ibid., pp. 209-218.

[6] Charles Winick, "Physician Narcotic Addicts," *Social Problems* (1961), 9:174-186, Herbert C. Modlin and Alberto Montes, "Narcotic Addiction in Physicians," *American Journal of Psychiatry* (1964), 1:358-365; Michael J. Pescor, "Physician Drug Addicts," in *Narcotic Addiction,* ed. John A. O'Donnell and John C. Ball (New York: Harper and Row, 1966), pp. 164-167.

[7] We are indebted to the research of Erich Goode for background material on overdosing. See Erich Goode, "The Criminology of Drugs and Drug Use," in *Current Perspectives on Criminal Behavior,* ed. Abraham Blumberg (New York: Alfred A. Knopf, 1974), pp. 168-170.

with harmless substances, its percentage of "good" stuff will vary from none at all on occasions when the user is swindled to 20 percent or more. Consequently, a user accustomed to relatively low percentages of heroin, perhaps 3 percent, who purchases a 20 percent package may overdose his individual system.

Heroin is a toxic drug; its use can result in coma and death.[8] But no one knows how many of the "deaths by overdose" reporting each year are actually by overdoses. Autopsies are rarely performed, yet it is likely that the majority of these deaths are caused by complications apart from the drug. Nutritional deficiencies common among alcoholics are also common among heroin addicts. Pneumonia is another characteristic pathology for alcoholics and addicts. Tetanus and hepatitis are associated with unsterile needles[9] and are contracted by drug users other than heroin addicts, who inject their drugs. Individuals lacking in experience with hypodermic needles may also inject bubbles in their veins or miss a vein and directly enter an artery. Both errors may result in death. In contrast, there is some evidence that those who are under expert supervision enjoy good diets, receive professional injections, and have standardized dosages also enjoy good health.[10]

The point of this brief discourse on the social context of "harmful drug" labelling and criminalization is to emphasize that harm to drug users may result not only from the drug itself, but also from the manner in which we attempt to control dangerous drugs. Additionally, the definition of the drug problem that conditions the manner in which we control drugs will reflect differential moral aspirations and group perceptions of the behavior, perhaps quite apart from their social harm.

Second, a confusing plethora of conclusions may be found in an afternoon of library research regarding how many addicts and drug users there are in the United States, what the street prices of drugs are, what number of crimes can be directly attributed to drugs, how harmful some drugs are, and what kinds of "personality" attributes are associated with drug use. The dissonance in statistical output is particularly bewildering because answers to these questions challenge or support political positions on very volatile issues. If heroin is criminogenic, or leads to robberies, burglaries, and the like, law enforcement has a responsibility to protect the public first and "treat" the addict second. If it is not criminogenic, the problem becomes a question for private and public health and for family welfare. Of course, questions of health and welfare are also addressed by police powers, even in the age of *laissez-faire.*

[8]Milton Helpern and Yong-Myun Rho, "Deaths from Narcotics in New York City," *International Journal of the Addictions* (1967), 2:53-84; Donald B. Louria, "Medical Complications Associated with Heroin Use," *International Journal of the Addictions* (1967), 2:241-251.

[9]Harris Isabell, "Medical Aspects of Opiate Addiction," in *Narcotic Addiction,* pp. 62-63.

[10]Winick, "Physician Narcotic Addicts," pp. 174-186.

Sharp dichotomies cannot be maintained between public health and law enforcement. Public health officials can quarantine certain diseases; malaria victims arriving from other countries are forcibly hospitalized in the United States before they infect anopheles mosquitoes in the United States. But there is a difference in emphasis in how to handle public health problems as opposed to crime problems. Here the logical distinction between public health and private health and public order is important. If a behavior is classified as a public health problem the function of the treatment may be to control the spread of the disease—as in smallpox quarantine. But the function of the treatment may be to exercise social control over potential disruption of a family or community tranquility. In the case of a police officer arresting an alcoholic, the distinction is quite clear—public order is the primary concern, although the health of the drunk may be temporarily restored through detoxification and proper diet in a hospital.

Treating drug addicts or treating almost any user of dangerous illicit drugs raises the murky question of whether the treatment's objective represents public health, private health, or public control. The question of whether or not professional treatment represents social engineering for public health or private health thereapy is found in the answer to the question: For whom does the therapist work? Those who treat drunks and addicts who have been arrested do not "work" for the drunk or addict. They are paid by and are responsive to the interests of the state. Nor is their object to prevent contagion. Drug use is not contagious in a pathological sense, although the term may popularly refer to peer group pressure.

With these qualifications, and others that I will add later, it remains useful to divide the problem of drug use into three problem categories: *moral problems, personal and public health problems,* and *crime problems.* Once again, both between and within these categories, we discover that disagreement as to the crime problem definition is fundamental to sharp political cleavages between advocates of one kind of drug policy and advocates of opposite policy persuasions. The first two categories will be dealt with presently. In Chapter 12 we come to grips with alternative crime policies to control the use of drugs.

DRUGS AND MORALITY

Anyone who has been asked to speak or provide consultant services regarding victimless crime has seldom missed the opportunity to respond to a question of the gender: Are you in favor of legalizing marihuana (or abortion, or homosexuality, or gambling)? Often the interrogator poses the query in a manner that makes clear that one's response will indicate for whose team one is playing, the sinners or the home team. The illustration points to one of the serious impediments to a rational drug policy. As a political-legal culture, we tend to see social problem definitions in terms of the criminal law. However, opposing criminalization of gambling as a form of social control does not mean favoring gambling either as a valued behavior or as socially beneficial. There are many alternatives to criminal law for minimizing the undesired consequences of gambling—taxing income, requiring gambling licenses, prohibiting individuals with criminal records from receiving licenses, restricting wagering to particular areas, and providing state monopolies of gambling operations. Each of these is a plausible regulatory method that does not prohibit the behavior, but limits and shapes its impact on society, resorting to criminal law only in extreme cases. The control of income tax evasion is of good illustration. Moreover, many other social institutions have an influence on behavior far greater than the influence of the criminal law. Among these are religious institutions, schools, families, places of employment, and peer groups. In addition, socio-economic status, ethnic and subcultural practices, and regional differences may subvert the objectives of criminal law.

Of course, the body politic may and often does draw merely symbolic attention to particularly powerful norms by condemning certain behaviors in the criminal law, even when such prohibitions cannot be enforced. Adultery is a prime example. At other times there is more than symbolism to laws that are difficult to enforce.

To some extent, increased sanctions on drug usage in the 1950s and 1960s reflected frustration in law enforcement agencies because of their inability to enforce criminal statutes regarding behavior between consenting individuals. Drug prohibitions, like statutes penalizing sexual conduct or gambling, are heavily endowed with moralistic overtones. The attempt of legislators to deal with moral behavior with which they disagree, and which may very well be immoral, but which they are powerless to control simply through criminal statutes alone, has led to dysfunctional efforts at enforcement. The stronger the efforts to control the behavior, the more widespread the behavior.

I have emphasized the importance of recognizing that criminal law itself is partially a product of the political culture, not an *a priori* set of statutes dealing with universal criminal types. The moralistic content of American criminal law, pointed out earlier by Max Lerner, is a reflection of political power. Deference to the moral standards of those in power is written into the criminal statutes. Or, the converse may be stated. The norms and values of those groups out of power are not protected by the law when they offend the sense of propriety of the majority.

Oliver Wendell Holmes put it succinctly: "I once heard that the German population would rise if you added two cents to the price of a glass of beer. A statute in such a case would be empty words, not because it was wrong, but because it could not be enforced."[11] Holmes was opposed to excessive intervention that disregarded long-established patterns of behavior commonly accepted

[11] Holmes, "The Path of the Law," *The Holmes Reader,* p. 43.

in the community, whether such intervention represented judicial formalism or a legislative moralism that could not be enforced in the community.[12]

Another perspective on drug use, in a curious way closely related in the public and *private* mind to questions of morals, draws attention to the *public health* implications, stressing the physiological dangers of drugs. Here again we must separate public health from private health. There is nothing "catching" about drugs, although peer pressure may entice those who abstain into experimental and then regular use. The "public" component in the problem has to do with criminogenic consequences, threats to the integrity of the family, or an incapacity on the part of a drug-taking individual to hold a job and stay off public assistance. To define "public" more broadly would require a philosophy of state paternalism toward individual problems of living beyond their social consequences.

At this point we encounter the objection of John Stuart Mill.

> *. . . The sole end for which mankind are warranted, individually or collectively, in interfering with the liberty of action of any of their number, is self protection . . . the only purpose for which power can be rightfully exercised over any member of a civilized community, against his will, is to prevent harm to others. His own good, either physical or moral, is not a sufficient warrant.*[13]

To a considerable extent saving unfortunates from drug abuse is not consistent with minimizing the social effects of drug abuse, as we shall see. Yet Mill's objection, so often given and so rarely examined with rigor, is philosophically simplistic. There are few individual behaviors of consequence that do not have potential for harm to others, and drug use is not always one of them. For example, serious addiction can drive a family into welfare, prevent the head of household from holding a job, and result in death, all potential public expenses.

On the other hand, findings that particular drugs can, if heavily indulged in, cause serious physiological damage need not inexorably lead us to the conclusion that any use of the drug will be dangerous. Producing brain damage in rats subjected to the equivalent of 60 marihuana cigarettes per day for 10 years does not lead to a conclusion that normal use is dangerous. Moreover, criminalizing deviant and morally objectionable behaviors may have consequences which are unforeseen. As in Greek tragedy, the very attempt to prevent deviancy and immorality makes two tragedies inevitable. The first tragedy has to do with liberties, both in terms of philosophy and due process.

Mill was concerned with personal liberty or "individual spontaneity free from external control."[14] The general theme of his argument was not directed to the

[12] Holmes, *The Common Law,* pp. 31-32.

[13] John Stuart Mill, *On Liberty* (New York: Appleton-Century-Croft, 1947), p. 9.

[14] Ibid., p. 11. Mill added this important qualification: " . . . this doctrine is meant to apply only to human beings in the maturity of their faculties. We are not speaking of children, or of young persons below the age which the law may fix as that of manhood or womanhood."

social consequences of morality legislation, except for general references to the dangers of conformity. But current research in criminology has developed the social side of Mill's theme through the concept of "secondary deviance" or "labeling theory."

Secondary deviance refers to the phenomenon of individuals for whom "contingency"[15] or momentary opportunity[16] leads to a deviant label or status applied to what otherwise is capriciously aberrant behavior. Ironically, the very institutional arrangements for those formally labeled "deviant" increase the likelihood of deviant behavior as an established behavior pattern. Those who argue from labeling theory use the concept of a "career" to describe the development of secondary deviant behavior. They emphasize that deviance is partially a product of interaction between those who "drift" or "happen" into temporarily deviant behavior and are formally labeled by authorities, and the institutional arrangements for those who are so labeled. Thus, Howard S. Becker writes:

> *Deviance is not a quality of the act the person commits, but rather a consequence of the application by others of rules and sanctions to an "offender." The deviant is one to whom that label has successfully been applied: deviant behavior is behavior that people so label.*[17]

To Becker, Goffman, and others who have commented on secondary deviance, criminal categories in statutory law have been a major source of institutional control leading to greater degrees of deviance. A standard criticism of the criminal law from this school of thought has been that it increases crime instead of deterring it. Under certain circumstances, crime rates will rise in in proportion to the number of activities that are newly "labled" crimes.

This is especially true regarding criminal statutes designed to protect health and morals through prohibition of "immoral activity" in communities where such activities are considered legitimate. Legal sanctions on narcotics, homosexuality, gambling, and prostitution all fall within this group of "crimes without victims," to use Edwin Schur's phrase.[18] Thus, when drug use was proscribed by the Harrison Act of 1914, sanctions were mild.[19] Initially, the act envisioned controlling drug use by a licensing system and tax, to be administered not in the Justice Department, but in the Department of the Treasury.[20] Gradually, the

[15] Erving Goffman, *Asylums,* (New York: Doubleday, 1961), pp.127-169.

[16] Matza, *Delinquency and Drift.*

[17] Becker, *The Outsiders,* p. 9.

[18] Schur, *Crimes without Victims.*

[19] Lindesmith, *The Addict and the Law,* p. 35.

[20] As a result of a Presidential Reorganization Plan in April 1968, the Bureau of Narcotics in the Treasury Department merged with the former Bureau of Drug Abuse Control in HEW to form the Bureau of Narcotics and Dangerous Drugs under the U.S. Department of Justice. See Statement of

penal sanctions were increased to present levels where in federal cases prior to the penal revision of 1970, possession of marihuana alone was punishable by a mandatory 2-year prison sentence for first offenders, 5 years for the second, and 10 years for the third and subsequent offenses. At the same time, suspension of sentence and probation were prohibited for second offenders.[21]

Most states have similar penalty provisions. Recently, both the federal government and some of the states have been reducing penalties for marihuana and hard drug possession and use.

However, during this same period, the use of dangerous drugs has probably increased in the United States, especially the use of marihuana.[22] U.S. Government estimates in 1969 have placed the number of opiate addicts at over 64,000. However, John E. Ingersoll, Director of the Bureau of Narcotics and Dangerous Drugs (BNDD), in testimony before the House of Representatives Select Committee on Crime, state that "this recorded number is an absolute minimum—there are thousands more."[23] In 1971 the BNDD had 82,294 addicts in their national register. The BNDD list is compiled from voluntary data submitted by state and local law enforcement authorities and underestimates even when compared with state enforcement data.[24] No one knows the addict population in the United States, and estimates range from the BNDD data up to 315,000.[25] It is fair to say that nongovernmental authorities on narcotic addiction believe government figures to be extremely conservative.[26]

John E. Ingersoll, Director, Bureau of Narcotics and Dangerous Drugs, "The Improvement and Reform of Law Enforcement and Criminal Justice in the United States," *Hearings Before the Select Committee on Crime,* p. 331.

[21] In 1951, following the post-World War II upsurge in reported addiction, penalties for illegal possession and sale of narcotics, including marihuana, were sharply increased by the Boggs Act. The 1956 mandatory minimum sentences were raised to 5 years for the first offense and 10 years for the second and subsequent offense for unlawful sale or importation. *Internal Revenue Code of 1954,* § 7237.

[22] Richard H. Blum, assisted by Mary Lou Funkhouser-Balbaky, "Mind-Altering Drugs and Dangerous Behavior: Dangerous Drugs," Consultant's Paper, The President's Commission on Law Enforcement and Administration of Justice, *Task Force Report: Narcotics and Drug Abuse* (Washington, D.C.: U.S. Government Printing Office, 1967), p. 24.

[23] Ingersoll, *Hearings,* p. 331.

[24] William H. McGlothlin and Victor C. Tabbush, "Costs, Benefits and Potential for Alternative Approaches to Opiate Addiction Control," in *Drugs and the Criminal Justice System,* p. 80.

[25] J. A. Greenwood, "Estimating Number of Narcotics Addicts," SCID-TR-3, Bureau of Narcotics and Dangerous Drugs, 1971.

[26] Alfred R. Lindesmith has done extensive analysis of Federal Bureau of Narcotics statistics for the years 1914 to 1960. His conclusions point to much higher incidences of addiction than the Bureau indicates. Lindesmith contends that the Bureau's figures were designed to demonstrte the effectiveness of greater sanctions on narcotic possession to the Boggs Committee in 1960, since this committee was principally responsible for proposing an increase in penal sanctions for possession in 1951 and 1956. For a review of statistical material on narcotic addiction see O'Donnelly and Ball, *Narcotic Addiction,* pp. 6-10.

Jerome Skolnick has illustrated some of the difficulties that law enforcement officials experience in enforcing "crimes without victims." Since prostitution, gambling, and narcotic usage take place between consenting individuals within a supporting subculture, special problems present themselves. Unlike crimes against property or crimes of violence, aggrieved witnesses are not available to file complaints or testify as friendly witnesses for the prosecution. Police must rely on paid informers and subterfuge to obtain evidence. Such informers are often recruited from the ranks of prostitutes or junkies and give information in return for leniency or a dismissal by the police of complaints leveled against them or for tolerance for their illicit trades.[27] Obviously, this practice encourages disrespect for law as well as nonfeasance of duty on the part of the police, but its employment is widely tolerated by lower-level detectives and police supervisors, according to the Skolnick study. Skolnick also discovered that search-and-seizure guidelines, handed down by the U.S. Supreme Court in *Mapp* v *Ohio,* were also evaded to obtain evidence,[28] particularly in narcotic cases, and "entrapment," the enticing of a suspect by law enforcement officers to commit a crime, was freely used to make arrests on prostitutes.[29] All of the above practices are justified, in the policeman's mind, on grounds of the difficulties of enforcing such laws and the necessity to cut corners to meet public demands that they be enforced.

Much has been written on civil liberty problems raised by antivice legislation. The core of problems raised by antivice legislation seems to be the social pattern of sanctions. Punishment is meted out for behavior disapproved by a large number of people, but accepted in minority communities.[30]

It is beyond the scope of this volume to develop this theme. However, research seems to imply that some of our rising crime rate and the subsequent development of administrative processes inconsistent with traditional due process is more a product of American Victorianism, persistent pluralism, and the attitude "there ought to be a law!" than either appellate court soft-heartedness or police heavy-handedness. As long as police are given heavy responsibility to prevent social "ills" of homosexuality, public drunkenness, prostitution, gambling and, especially, narcotics, they can hardly follow the formal rules of law and still deal with crimes of property and violence. Our system of procedural safeguards for the

[27] Skolnick, *Justice without Trial,* pp. 112-136.

[28] Ibid., p. 211.

[29] Ibid., pp. 102-103.

[30] Arnold, *The Symbols of Government,* p. 48. Arnold writes: "Before . . . prohibition . . . the problem of search and seizure was a minor one. Thereafter, searches and seizures became the weapon of attack which could be used against prohibition enforcement. For every dry speech on the dangers of disobedience, there was a wet oration on the dangers of invading the privacy of the home. Reflected in the courts the figures are startling. In 6 states selected for the purpose of study we find 19 search-and-seizure cases appealed in the 12 years preceding Prohibition and 34 in the 12 years following.

accused in an adversary process cannot operate with large numbers of criminal offenders and crowded dockets.

Earlier it was suggested that informal administrative devices have been developed to handle the defendant who, because of his juvenile status, emotional status, or drug addiction, is considered lacking in *mens rea* to some degree. Although it has recently been criticized, the informal, expert hearing has been substituted for criminal court proceedings in determining who will assume the status of exculpatory or irresponsible violators of the law or public order. Juvenile courts[31] and mental health commitment commissions[32] historically were designed to introduce a greater degree of individual justice in difficult areas by referring cases to behavior experts. Narcotic addiction is being dealt with in similar fashion.[33]

Informal hearings have the advantage of being efficient, which leads to the support of those concerned with the efficiency of court administration. Those puzzled concerning what to do with youthful offenders, the insane, and the persistent growth of drug addiction advocate giving greater decision-making responsibilities to the experts in these areas, yet without abandoning altogether the coercive character of the law. Informal hearings by experts also have the support of liberals who question on humanitarian grounds the justice of punishing the apparently irresponsible. Curiously, many liberal critics who vigorously defend the rights of individuals in these three categories against criminal prosecution paradoxically accept a civil administrative denial of liberty if it is medically oriented. References to health seem to have more appeal as justification for incarceration than criminal sanction.

Serious questions have been raised whether or not large numbers of juvenile offenders, mentally disturbed persons, or narcotic users are dealt with wisely, regardless of the professional competence and dedication of those who determine their fate.[34] Certainly the degree of discretion accorded those who apply categories of irresponsibility has grown both in the law and in the actual administration of justice through the weight of sheer numbers of individuals to be processed.

As crime policy is substituted for social policy and social institutions to promote personal morality and private and public health, we have the makings of tragedy. It is particularly important that value-laden terms such as hospitalization, individualized justice, and treatment be placed in the context of actual functions. The primary capability of the criminal justice system is not to practice

[31] Lemert, "Juvenile Justice," pp. 91-93.

[32] Wilfred Guttmacher and Paul Weilhofen, *Psychiatry and the Law* (New York: W. W. Norton, 1952).

[33] "New Narcotic Addiction Control Act," *Albany Law Review* (1967), 32:336; Dennis S. Aronowitz, "Civil Commitment of Narcotic Addicts and Sentencing for FOR Narcotic Drug Offenses," Consultant Paper, *Task Force Report: Narcotics and Drug Abuse,* Appendix D.

[34] The literature concerning these questions is enormous. For examples of such criticisms of juvenile

benevolent science. Indeed, there is little benevolent, from the perspective of the defendant, about the restraint of the criminal law, regardless of the manner in which that restraint is rationalized by terms such as treatment, hospitalization, and nonpunitive court procedures. Overemphasizing the criminal justice system as an instrument to reduce vice and drug use may result in serious infringement on civil liberties, no advance at all in protecting private health, and no reduction in victim suffering.

courts see Edwin Lemert, President's Commission on Law Enforcement and Administration of Justice, *Task Force Report: Juvenile Delinquency* (Washington, D.C.: U.S. Government Printing Office, 1967), pp. 94-95; for mental health commitments see *Hearings Before the Subcommittee on Constitutional Rights of the U.S. Senate,* 87th Congress, First Session, March 28, 1961, pp. 40-54.

13

DRUGS AND CRIME

We have regarded drugs as "public enemy number one," destroying the most precious resource we have—our young people—and breeding lawlessness, violence and death.
Richard Nixon
March 14, 1973

It will be recalled there were three potential tragedies associated with the criminalization of drug use. A criminalization policy may not protect public and private health and morality, while such a policy may seriously reduce personal liberty. However, civil liberty protection must, at times, be weighed against protection for victims of drug addicts. Some prohibitions of amenities, such as limiting the use of pleasurable drugs, and some abridgment of general liberties, such as legalized wiretapping and stop-and--frisk laws, may be worth the cost, if decriminalized drug programs can be demonstrated to be criminogenic. Examining the criminogenic nature of drug use, contrasted with moral and medical approaches is an additional perspective on the drug problem. It asks the question: To what extent is there a close relationship between drug usage and crime?

The answer does not come easily. Two sophisticated and, for the most part, opposite views on the question compete for attention. The first view proceeds from the position of Daniel Glaser[1] that "drugs and crime like other non-complaint generating behaviors are most related when the use of drugs is defined

[1]Daniel Glazer, "Interlocking Dualities in Drug Use, Drug Control and Crime," in *Drugs and the Criminal Justice System,* pp. 39-55.

by law as a crime."[2] Beyond the obvious point that possession and sale of drugs is a crime itself, other criminal behaviors are encouraged as an indirect result of drug criminalization. Drug use does not directly cause crime; excessive criminalization in a drug control policy may. There are several reasons why this is so.

First, many of the most widely abused drugs have physiological effects that impede criminal activity during the periods when the drug's effect is most pronounced. This is particularly true for opiates and barbiturates, but it is also true for marihuana, LSD, and other hallucinogens.[3] Instead of becoming crazed by these drugs, those intent on mugging, robbery, or rape would be impeded during this period.[4] The one violent crime that *does* seem to be committed by both users (30 percent) and nonusers (31.4 percent) of heroin is robbery.[5]

Second, drugs cannot cause "crime" by their chemical properties; complex social behavior requires a learning experience. For example, some people drink alcohol and become passive; others become assertive, even violent. How one behaves after consuming alcohol depends on other social considerations more than on biochemistry. Alcohol and other inhibitory drugs may indeed encourage assaultive tendencies or a willingness to steal, although Glaser minimizes this likelihood. But prohibition policies are even more responsible for serious crime related to illegal drug use. It is variously estimated that heavy-dosage heroin addicts spend between $20 and $100 or more per day to maintain their habit and, since they are usually poor, they must steal, commit prostitution, or engage in some other "hustle." Conversely, regulated drugs available through legitimate channels are not as expensive. The more effective law enforcement is in drying up sources of supply, the higher the price and, presumably, the greater the need to obtain money legally or illegally. Moreover, the margin of profit in narcotics and the difficulty of making arrests or making convictions stick provide a fertile environment for corruption in vice squads[6] and courtrooms. Making a highly desired substance illegal simply corners the market for those who are willing and organized or positioned to operate illegally.

The law enforcement approach to drug use, particularly heroin use, is not without its supporters. James Q. Wilson has argued that, if law enforcement is directed at the user and street dealer, taking users off the street in large numbers would retard the price of heroin over the long run for lack of a market.[7] Alterna-

[2]Ibid., p. 43.

[3]Ibid., p. 48.

[4]Blum, "Mind Altering Drugs and Dangerous Behavior: Narcotics," *Task Force Report: Narcotic and Drug Abuse,* Appendix A-2, pp. 40-63.

[5]William C. Eckerman et al., *Drug Usage and Arrest Charges* (Washington, D.C.: U.S. Department of Justice, BNDD—Office of Scientific Support, Drug Control Division, 1971).

[6]Glazer, "Interlocking Dualities," *Drugs and the Criminal Justice System,* p. 50; Rubinstein, *City Police,* pp. 375-401.

[7]Wilson, *Thinking about Crime,* pp. 151-152.

tively, sharp decreases in imported heroin resulting from restriction of supplies from Turkey, Mexico, or other countries, or interdiction of heroin moving across our borders could result in dealers "cutting" the heroin content of a "bag" from 10 percent to between 1 and 4 percent when it reaches the street. Wilson contends this may have occurred in the early 1970s after intensive interdiction efforts by the federal government when the heroin content of a bag run between 1 and 4 percent instead of the "purer" 10 percent.[8]

As law enforcement reduces the availability of heroin by intercepting the supply and arresting users, what heroin does remain on the streets will be cut below addicting levels, and individual use of opiates among middle-class Americans will drop sharply. Moreover, novice users are introduced to serious drugs by friends and peer pressures. For this reason distinctions between users and local "pushers" are meaningless, a point on which there is almost universal agreement. Although seriously addicted individuals drift off from early groups, early users are first attracted to the drug by friends and peers, not by shady outsiders in dirty trenchcoats loitering in school yards. The "high" and "rush" of heroin pleasure is often a group experience. Older addicts experience very little high, their bodies having developed a strong tolerance to the drug's physiological properties. Their use of drugs, usually in solitude, is primarily to prevent withdrawal symptoms.

If law enforcement is vigorous and actual sentences are imposed, Wilson argues, some of the contagiousness of peer pressure for narcotic use may be checked, since some peers will not be around and others may be deterred from experimenting. Wilson laments the fact, and it is a fact, that recently "only a few addicts are singled out for very severe punishment,"[9] most receiving probation or suspended sentences.

In our view, however, option for a law enforcement emphasis instead of a public health emphasis (they are never totally unrelated enterprises) rests on the question: Is drug usage related to crime? The literature on this topic is massive, often contradictory and inconclusive. Often relying on drug-user samples drawn from arrest records or treatment programs and probably not from the general addict population, it is very probable that a bias exists in most research associating crime with addiction. In addition, many studies fail to differentiate between arrests and convictions for narcotic violations and for nondrug crimes alike. But methodological qualifications aside, the bulk of several decades of research suggests the following. Prior to the 1950s narcotic addiction was not preceded by criminal records, although a majority of all addicts became involved in nondrug

[8] Ibid., p. 149; B. J. Prim and P. E. Bath, "Pseudoheroinism," *International Journal of the Addictions* (1973), 8:231-242; Mark Weisman et al., "Quality of Street Heroin," *New England Journal of Medicine* (1973), 289:698-699.

[9] Wilson, *Thinking about Crime,* p. 145.

criminal activity after addiction.[10] However, since 1952 and continuing into the 1960s and 1970s, the trend has been in the opposite direction.[11] The weight of evidence appears to support the hypothesis that addicts today are much more likely to be involved with crime prior to their using drugs than they were in the past. For example, Chein and Rosenfeld[12] found in the middle 1950s that almost all juveniles using drugs were strikingly similar to nonusing *delinquents* in terms of social attitudes. The conclusion that they drew is that juveniles in delinquent subcultures are drawn to drug use and become even more involved in criminal behavior, other than drugs, to support their habit. O'Donnell's study[13] of 212 southern, white, male addicts at the U.S. Public Health treatment center in Lexington, Kentucky also supports this trend into the 1960s and points to a crucial fact that may explain the greater preaddiction pattern of criminal behavior. In his earlier study O'Donnell found that 67 percent of addicts at Lexington were not arrested prior to addiction and only 15 percent had served a prison sentence. Superficially O'Donnell's results seem to support a tendency for addicts to become criminals and not the other way around, but further analysis reveals a different conclusion, since the year addiction occurred becomes a salient variable. *Ninety-five* percent of those addicted prior to 1920 had no arrest record prior to drug dependency and, prior to 1950, a majority of subjects were arrested only after addiction. But after 1950, 53 percent had been arrested prior to addiction. Furthermore, the younger the addict, the greater the proportion of arrests prior to addiction.

The preponderance of the literature on drug use in the 1960s and 1970s strongly supports O'Donnell's findings and suggests that today criminal behavior tends to precede addiction and that the use of heroin is characteristic of individuals who are members of social groupings that are crime-prone,[14] although re-

[10] A review of the literature on this question can be found in Alan S. Meyer, *Social and Psychological Factors in Opiate Addiction* (New York: Columbia University Bureau of Applied Research, 1952). Meyer concluded that criminal behavior was a direct result of addiction, not a reflection of subcultural norms of life-style.

[11] Carl D. Chambers, "Narcotic Addiction and Crime: An Empirical Review," in *Drugs and the Criminal Justice System,* p. 126. Also see Arnold Abrams et al., "Psychological Aspects of Addiction," *American Journal of Public Health* (1968), 58:2142-2155.

[12] Isador Chein and Eva Rosenfeld, "Juvenile Narcotic Use." *Journal of Law and Contemporary Problems* (1957), 22:52-68.

[13] John A. O'Donnell, "Narcotic Addiction and Crime," *Social Problems* (1966), 13:374-385; John A. O'Donnell, "Narcotic Addicts in Kentucky," Public Health Service Publication No. 1881 (Washington, D.C.: U.S. Government Printing Office, 1969).

[14] John C. Ball, "The Reliability and Validity of Interview Data Obtained from 59 Narcotic Drug Addicts," *American Journal of Sociology* (1967), 72:650-654. Ball found that 87 percent of 2213 addicts throughout the United States had been arrested some years prior to the mean age at which narcotic addiction begins. John C. Ball et al., "The Association of Marihuana Smoking with Opiate Addiction in the United States," *Journal of Criminal Law, Criminology and Police Science* (1968),

searchers differ over the causal factors for crime within the the social grouping. The same literature also suggests that once individuals are addicted, their criminal propensities grow.

Why the change from the less criminogenic 1920s' addict world to the more crime-prone world of the 1970s? The shift in the kind of addict *population* that O'Donnell noted is significant. Prior to the 1950s the typical addict was middle class, a musician, a bohemian, a nurse, or doctor. But, by the 1950s, the use of narcotics became stylish among the lower class, which had greater crime propensities. Why this shift took place is not entirely clear. Possibly it was because of increased affluence, even for "street" people, or possibly it reflected greater availability of narcotics. Additionally, after large numbers of people drifted into heroin use, we find merit in the agrument that rigorous law enforcement may have helped encourage illegal activities in a criminogenic class by driving up the price of a habit for those who were addicted, requiring a lucrative "hustle" to sustain it. On this point, my judgment differs with that of Wilson. It appears more likely that law enforcement, unaccompanied by the availability of alternative drug clinics of the methadone variety, produced "secondary deviance" of even more serious crime than would have existed with some alternatives.

Of course, not *all* addicts participate in illegal activities (excluding illegal use of drugs) to sustain their habit. Chambers found that 68 percent of black addicts supported themselves by illegal activities,[15] but support by criminal activity among white females[16] was only 32 percent. Moreover, 25 percent of black, male addicts and 23 percent of white, female addicts studied were legally employed as their means of support (Table 13.1).

Some crimes are more characteristic of addicts than nonaddicts. For females, illegal means of support range from prostitution and shoplifting to the sale of drugs, with the latter constituting 50 percent of all illicit fund-raising activity.[17] The sale of drugs was also a principal source of income for male addicts,[18] along with crimes against property. As mentioned earlier, crimes against property are more characteristic for addicts than crimes of violence. There is some evidence from limited samples that this may be changing and that addicts are more prone to personal crimes than in the past.[19] However, even these crimes tend to be motivated by high monetary return, not by a violence-prone personality. The

59:171-182. Also see Robert E. Jones, "The Characteristics of Addicts Opting for a Self-Care Program," *Drug Forum* (1972), 2:31-42; Barry S. Levy, "Five Years After: A Follow-up of 50 Narcotic Addicts," *American Journal of Psychiatry* (1972), 128:868-872; Harwin L. Voss and Richard C. Stephens, "Clinical History of Narcotic Addicts," *Drug Forum* (1973), 2:191-202.

[15] Chambers, "Narcotic Addiction and Crime," p. 130

[16] Ibid., p. 131.

[17] Ibid., Table 8 at p. 135 and text pp. 133-135.

[18] Ibid., pp. 132-133.

[19] Ibid., p. 131.

Table 13.1 Primary means of support during the six months prior to entering treatment

Primary Means of Support	N	%				
Illegal activities	66	67.3	39	68.4	105	67.8
Legal employment	30	30.6	9	15.8	39	25.2
Dependent on spouse	1	1.0	6	10.5	7	4.5
Dependent on parents	—	—	1	1.8	1	.6
Dependent on welfare	1	1.0	2	3.5	3	1.9
Total	98	100.0	57	100.0	155	100.0

Source. Carl D. Chambers, "Narcotic Addiction and Crime: An Empirical Review," in *Drugs and the Ciminal Justice System* (J. A. Inciar and C. D. Chambers, eds.) (Beverly Hills, Calif: Sage Publications, 1974), p. 130. Copyright © 1974. Reprinted by permission of the publisher, Sage Publications, Inc.

increase in personal crime among *all types* of drug users is robbery, not assault, rape, or homicide. In addition, several studies indicate that the probability for both arrest and incarceration is extremely low for criminal activities of addicts. In a study of heroin addicts in New York City, Inciardi and Chambers found that there were fewer than one arrest for every 120 crimes that were self-reported; less than half of those arrested were convicted, and less than half of those convicted were sent to jail or prison.[20]

CONTROLLING NARCOTIC-RELATED CRIME

While it is quite proper to caution against separating the regulation of public health—discouraging peddlers from selling dangerous drugs to youths, for example—from law enforcement efforts of reduce crimes with unwilling victims, using the apparatus of criminal justice to reduce the importation and sale of drugs as

[20]James A. Inciardi and Carl D. Chambers, "Unreported Criminal Involvement of Narcotic Addicts," *Journal of Drug Issues* (1972), 2:59.

an end in itself contradicts a victim-oriented crime control policy. This is particularly true if the control effort is, as we believe it is, counterproductive, even criminogenic. A victim-oriented policy will not have as its mission the elevation of character or the supervision of pleasures or the shielding of the young from moral corruption. Not because such missions are unworthy. They are very desirable social goals. And not because they are irrelevant to public policy concerns. Dozens of programs, federal and state, have these missions. Indeed, I would speculate that an income distribution program along the lines proposed by Daniel Moynihan to encourage and assist the working *poor* and strengthen the American Family as an institution may do more than all the LEAA programs combined for reducing crime and making the pursuit of happiness somewhat less than an overwhelming struggle for lower-income people.

But a crime policy with character-saving missions for *criminal justice* agencies is overly ambitious and remarkably unsuccessful. A criminal justice system that becomes the principal instrument of society to deal with character and individual failings *detracts* from the fulfillment of more vital missions. Vice and narcotics squads almost invariably produce police corruption, and their successful operation demand wholesale violations of civil liberties. Extensive search and seizures of persons and residences associated with drug enforcement go a long way to dismantle carefully constructed police-community relations, particularly for minority groups. Of course, street frisks, warranted searches, and even wiretaps are worth the temporary embarrassment they cause to the public and the expensive drain on criminal justice resources if the objective or reducing victim suffering is feasible and desirable. For example, federally warranted wiretaps for the control of organized crime are quite necessary. Moreover, a police department is not a public relations firm. But the enforcement of narcotics appears to be more successful at increasing complaint-oriented crime as a result of addicts hustling to maintain their habit than it is in reducing the use of addicting drugs.

Of course, my tentative conclusion could be quite wrong. The test of successful crime policy, as I have suggested, is its impact on victim suffering at the hands of others. Stated in this fashion, the cost-benefit framework of the economist provides a reasonable avenue by which alternative drug policies may be tested empirically in terms of their impact on victimization and other desirable social goals.

McGlothlin and Tabbush[21] have designed a model to estimate the costs, benefits, and potential of seven approaches or "modules" for narcotics addiction control. Figure 13.1 illustrated the model.

The horizontal axis (*A* to *C*) represents the addict or partient years of treatment

[21] William H. McGlothlin and Victor C. Tabbush, "Costs, Benefits, and Potential for Alternative Approaches to Opiate Addiction Control," in *Drugs and the Criminal Justice System,* pp. 77-124.

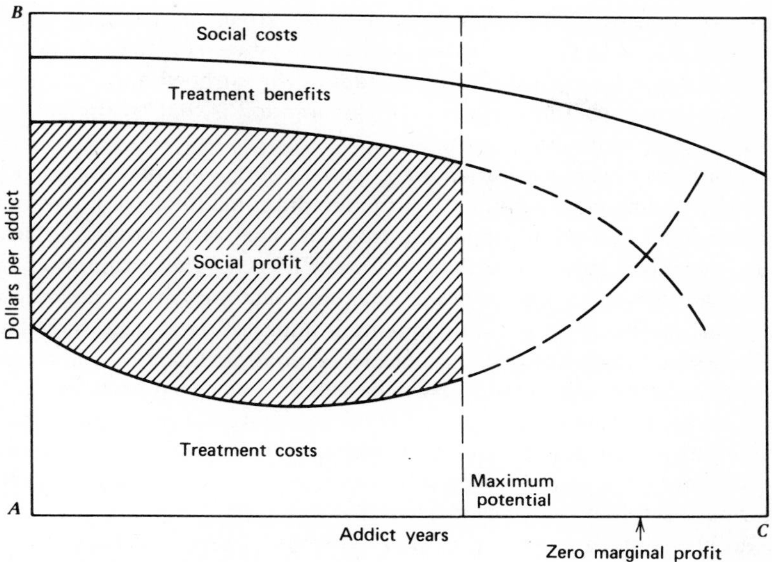

Figure 13.1 Costs, benefits, and potential for alternative approaches to opiate addiction control. [Source. *Figure 1 from "Costs, Benefits, and Potential for Alternative Approaches to Opiate Addiction Control," by W. H. McGlothlin and V. C. Tabbush is reprinted from* Drugs and the Criminal Justice System *(J. A. Inciardi and C. D. Chambers, Editors). Copyright © 1974 by permission of the publisher, Sage Publications, Inc.]*

for any of the alternative modalities. The vertical axis (*A* to *B*) plots the costs of treatment per patient year; the treatment benefits per patient year; and the social costs of an untreated addict resulting from theft, foregone production (unemployment) and criminal justice expenditures to counter addict-related crime. Although the data are hypothetical, they are based on several empirical propostions. The cost curve of a treatment program will initially be high, then drop down and rise again, reflecting initial fixed costs and lower unit costs as more voluntary patients enter the program and progressively higher costs in increased expenditures are made to attract and hold marginal patients to the program. It is assumed that the proportion of volunteer addicts who initially enter the program will be "burned out" and motivated to leave heroin and the streets for longer periords of time. The marginal patients are more likely younger, less interested in abandoning heroin, and likely to enter the program only under coercive direction from the courts. Still, dropping out is not restricted to young addicts. Some addicts prefer heroin to methadone. Some addicts would not enter a program unless they were forced to do so by the courts, because their street sources for heroin have dried up or are too costly, or all three. The treatment benefit curve drops precipitously after a given proportion of older addicts are enrolled and volunteer and marginal addicts enter the program. The assumption is that treatment will not be as effective for this latter group.

The treatment benefit, operationalized as the average number of addict years, is reduced by being enrolled in a "legitimate" drug maintenance program or by kicking the habit as a result of such a program. The social cost curve drops as additional average addict treatment years are logged. The assumption is that addiction does result in higher crime rates and that treatment can reduce the criminogenic nature of drug use by making it unnecessary to steal or sell drugs. As we have seen, this assumption is subject to serious qualification and the degree of the social cost slope is particularly debatable.[22] The social profit results from bringing each addict into treatment. The "zero" marginal profit point indicates the maximum theoretical potential for reducing the social costs of addiction. After this point, additional resource allocations would have negative returns, considering the treatment investment.

McGlothlin and Tabbush[23] provide a typology of seven alternative modules to control heroin use that is useful for purposes of comparison. (1) *Methadone maintenance I.* Methadone maintenance I dispenses methadone to registered volunteer patients and court referrals and includes: strict protections on methadone "leakage" from patients obtaining more than they need; prohibition of *other* drug usage during treatment by monitoring urine; termination of patients who run afoul of the law, participate irregularly (a sign of other drug use) or use illicit drugs repeatedly. Counseling and other social services are provided as well. (2) *Methadone maintenance II.* Methadone maintenance II permits administering oral methadone to registered addicts without imposing prohibitions against other drug use. Ancillary services are also provided addict patients, but these services are not conditonal on "clean" behavior. (3) A third approach, *heroin maintenance,* is permitted only in the United Kingdom. Prior to 1968, registered addicts were provided drug maintenance by private physicians. At present, only clinics can dispense heroin (50 percent) and they also dispense methadone (injected 40 percent, oral 10 percent). The estimated addict population of Britain in 1971 was around 2530 to 3000 and about 70 percent of these are registered in a clinic during any 12-month period.[24]

Three other approaches that differ somewhat from the above are Synanon-type

[22] See Leroy C. Gould, "Crime and the Addict: Beyond Common Sense," in *Drugs and the Criminal Justice System,* pp. 57-63; McGlothlin and Tabbush, "Alternative Approaches," pp. 83-85.
[23] McGlothlin and Tabbush, "Alternative Approaches," p. 79.
[24] Ibid., p. 99.

therapeutic communities, detoxification centers, and civil commitment hospitals. Therapeutic communities appear to have considerable success but can reach only an insignificant number of addicts. Detoxification provides little evidence of its effectiveness in discouraging addiction, and civil commitment is indistinguishable from incarceration, probation, or parole, without due process of law. Most of the issues in each of these methods can be explored by looking closely at MMI and MMII and at heroin maintenance programs and how they relate to a victim-oriented policy.

I am not in a positon to recommend categorically a given alternative, since empirical assumptions behind each alternative await further research for verification. For example, estimates of volunteer rates for MM programs run from 20 to 85 percent of the addict population. Some addicts apparently prefer detoxification to methadone maintenance, either because they prefer to return to heroin after a brief drying-out period (and most addicts, for one reason or another, desire several heroin-free periods per year) or because they wish to shake all drug habits, and methadone remains an addictive drug. But we do not know how many or what type of individual under what circumstance prefers detoxification. Nor do we know how long addicts will remain in treatment under various treatment alternatives or for how long they will remain in treatment. Finally, treatment costs vary tremendously, from $500 per patient for maintenance only to over $10,000 per prisoner in detention facilities. All of the above variables affect costs and affect the number of addict years in treatment, making it very difficult to perform cost-benefit analysis. For these reasons it would be prudent to continue funding each alternative on a pilot basis.

However, suppose we assume that increases in larceny, burglary, and robbery are partially correlated with heroin addiction. Suppose we also assume that the criminalization of use of all addictive drugs under all circumstances (excepting detoxification) generates insulated drug cultures in which the addict is more and more cut off from normal employment and nondrug-using friends and relatives. Given these assumptions, methadone maintenance in general and an MM program that is designed to reach as many heroin addicts who are engaged in crime as possible seem to offer the most promise.

Why methandone? After all, methadone is a synthetic narcotic and MM merely means addicting individuals to methadone instead of heroin. The reasons are found in the particular pharmaceutical properties of methadone. Unlike heroin, it does no produce a high, the rush that addicts find intensely pleasurable. In fact, properly administered, methadone can block the rush in a partient who experiments with heroin, as many patients do, while registered with an MM clinic. Additionally, the effects of methadone continue for 24 hours, as opposed to the 8 hours or so for heroin. The lack of both the high and the stupor that follows, added to long-term effects of methadone, permit those under its effects to hold a job, drive an automobile, maintain a normal sex drive, and engage in normal social relationships.[25] In fact, in the British system, methadone has surpassed the traditional drug heroin as the drug of choice for patients. For these reasons, methadone is far superior to heroin as a treatment drug, although some have argued that it may merely increase the efficacy of the professional addict-thief.

MMI programs may have the advantave of providing a disciplined structure for treating and rehabilitating addicts, although we do not know this for a fact. But the alternative has several drawbacks for a victim-oriented crime policy. The major problem is its limited appeal for voluntary addicts. Those who prefer heroin will not stay within the disciplined structure of the MMI program, but a large majority of this group would probably enter the MMII program. Here again we encounter the philosophical issue crystallized by John Stuart Mill. The MMI program may do a better job at rehabilitating. But the MMII program probably would reduce the criminogenic characteristic of criminalizing narcotics more effectively by (1) giving young addicts an alternative to high-priced street heroin, and (2) providing a narcotic substitute that will not be a barrier to "straight" employment and normal social relations for the addict who, for whatever length of duration, is coming off the streets. Moreover, official criminal justice agencies, including clinics, detoxification centers, and hospitals, have very poor records at drug rehabilitation, at any rate.

Indeed, an MMII program need not deter the police and courts from apprehending and sentencing addicts for crimes committed, including the sale of drugs, or coercing them into any "treatment" program the judge deems advisable. Nor is there anything inconsistent between an MMII program designed to minimize crime and strict record keeping of methadone patients. Clinics should not be sources of extra drugs for street peddling. The principle objective of a crime policy should not be health and personal character, but the reduction of corruption in the criminal justice system, the preservation of civil liberty and, preeminently, the reduction of criminal victimization. If MMI or MMII lead to a net increase in victim-oriented crime, obviously they should be scrapped. If the programs have no impact on crime, then their public health and social impacts have to be assessed for social policy. The point is not to express enthusiasm for methadone programs, but to emphasize the utility of victimization rather than health and morals as an indicator to evaluate crime policy.

POLITICAL CONSIDERATIONS

"By words are men governed," said Disraeli, a pithy note the drug *reformer* must remember. "Narcotic drug" is a phrase frightening in its connotations to the public ear and couched in myth. For any antidrug program to be successful, it

[25] Herman Joseph and Vincent P. Dole, "Mthadone Patients on Probation and Parole," *Federal Probation* (1970), 34:42-43.

must appear not to minimize the evils of drug use, and normally that means the program must contain stiff sentences. Former Governor Rockerfeller's draconian drug control measures for New York State in 1973[26] called for mandatory life imprisonment without chance for parole for all dealers in hard drugs and was met with widespread support across the nation. In interviews conducted with 1549 adults, 18 and older, in 300 samples throughout the contry shortly after the Governor's proposals, the Gallup poll asked the following question: "The governor of a state has proposed that all sellers of hard drugs such as heroin be given life imprisonment without the possibility of parole. Do you approve or disapprove of this proposal?" Fully 67 percent approved of the Governor's approach, with agreement generally cutting across categories of age, race, sex, and education.[27]

Drug maintenance programs have also been attacked by the NAACP on grounds that they were racially inspired to keep black people in subjugation and by moralists concerned, as well as are, with the destructive nature of drugs on character and by law enforcement officials who object to the sloppy administration of some clinics that permit leakage. [28] But there is a point at which concern for leakage produces overtly officious administration and discourages large numbers of addicts from entering programs. Excessive concern by law enforcement for saving character from narcotic despoilation may simply raise the price of street heroin, increase larceny, robbery, and burglary to feed heroin habits, and provide a profitable, illicit, market for unscrupulous entrepreneurs. On balance, we may be better off administering methadone through carefully regulated methadone clinics whose purpose is not to "detoxify" unwilling addicts (although these services and others should be available to volunteers) but to provide medication as an alternative to street crime and heroin use.

This, of course, does not in any way suggest not prosecuting addicts who engage in either crime or illicit heroin use or sale. Nor does it suggest that group homes, religious and community groups, or schools and families slacken in their

[26] Governor Rockefellor's State of the State Message, January 1, 1973. The New York State legislature gave the Governor most of what he wanted. It replaced the mandatory life prison term with a madatory life sentence, permitting lifelong parole after an offender served a mandatory minimum prison term. In the summer of 1975 the legislature removed the plea bargaining restriction for small drug pushers permitting a plea of guilty to a class C felony, carrying with it a term of 5 years of jail or less. The charge was made at the behest of prosecutors who argued that without plea bargaining they could not obtain testimony against larger dealers. *The New York Times,* Sunday, July 20, 1973, Section 4, p. 16.

[27] Gallup Poll, 1973; George Gallup, " 67% Back Life Terms for Hard Drug Sellers," *The Washington Post,* February 11, 1973.

[28] All methadone distribution clinics, as of the spring of 1974, have been place under federal control to curb the diversion of methadone from legal channels. The bill required that those conducting narcotic treatment programs register with the Attorney General, and expanded the Justice Department's authority to revoke a program's license. *Congressional Quarterly Weekly Report* (March 23, 1974), 32:774.

efforts to alter destructive drug abuse. Criminal justice agencies should support these efforts. But criminal justice policy has limits on its capacity to produce behavioral change. Crime policy should concentrate on the criminogenic aspects of drugs and, if carefully managed methadone clinics can contribute to that end, they have merit.

14

HANDGUNS AND HOMICIDE

"Many people do not realize that Pennsylvania hunters took 273 deer by handgun last year."
Pennsylvania state representative opposing abolishing handguns in 1973
Pennsylvania homicide rate, 1973 —745 persons, approximately 395 by handgun.
FBI Uniform Crime Report

With drug control and juvenile policies we have seen the potential danger of doing too much and expecting too much from the criminal justice system alone. But state and federal policies regarding control of firearms, particularly the cheap handgun, represent a rare occasion of doing far too little when the returns may be significant. On numerous occasions legislation, which would restrict or otherwise limit accessibility of firearms to unstable persons or to individuals in emotional trauma, has died from overwhelming opposition in Congress. For example, in 1972 the U.S. Senate rejected legislation that would have prohibited handgun ownership by a vote of 83 to 7.[1] Not a little opposition has been generated from the executive branch as well. President Ford has announced his opposition to regulating guns, a rhetorical generality that does not appear to cover handguns since, as of this writing, the White House has recommended legislation that would bar the manufacture and sale of "Saturday night specials" and restrict, by licensing, commercial outlets from selling federally unregistered firearms. The necessity

[1]Robert Sherrill, *The Saturday Night Special* (New York: Penguin Books, 1973), p. 14.

of reverent rhetoric from Congress and the White House regarding the right to keep and bear arms reflects the depth of emotion that the gun lobby can evoke. Firearms have historically played an important role in American behavior from folk heroes to the "coming of age" rites of American males, particularly in towns and rural areas. Gun control policy debate predictably awakens a vocal, intensely concerned, and well-organized minority of sportsmen[2] who fear that their life-style, their last vestige of frontier autonomy, their masculinity, and their ability to protect their family or business personally from criminal intruders are all threatened by arbitrary government edict. The sportsmen are supported in their lobby efforts by organizations such as the Sporting Arms Ammunition Manufacturers Institute, the lobbyist for gun manufacturers. Both sportmen and gun manufacturers are guaranteed a wide audience for their views in the *American Rifleman,* the official publication of the National Rifle Association.

Normally, our consensus-oriented governmental politics, at state and federal levels, respects such a sizable, active minority, particularly when its views are countervailed only by a tepid, less intensely involved, unorganized majority. Certainly, government policy cannot adequately respond to opposition motivated by frontier spirit and machismo. But protection of life and property is the business of government and the evidence is accumulating that stricter regulation of firearms is unavoidable if violent crime and property are to be protected. On the issue of handguns and homicide particularly, it appears unavoidable that government intervene to a degree if violent crime is to be significantly reduced. In all probability intervention such as abolishing handgun ownership today remains politically unacceptable. An outright ban on handgun ownership does not have the support of the American public, except, significantly, from those who live in cities of 1 million or more, from those who live in the East, and from women. But the debate over handguns among legislators has been constrained by the fear that the National Rifle Association can and will defeat elected officials who reveal themselves by public comment to be antigun. Recently, however, the political omnipotence of the gun lobby has been minimized as political analysts see much more room for open, vigorous debate on the merits of gun control measures.[3]

It has been estimated that Americans are accumulating handguns at a rate of more than 1.8 million weapons a year and that the total number of privately owned handguns is from 24 to 30 million.[4] That figure looms ominously, since

[2]According to a Gallup poll in July 1974, 67 percent of all Americans polled favored the registration of firearms. Joseph D. Alviani and William R. Drake, *Handgun Control,* Handgun Control Project, U.S. Conference of Mayors, 1975, Illustration 10 on p. 15.

[3]Ibid., pp. 15-18.

[4]National Advisory Commission on Criminal Justice Standards and Goals, *A National Strategy to Reduce Crime,* p. 213. The Task Force on Firearms and Violence in American Life in 1970 estimated 90 million firearms in civilian hands in the United States, 24 million handguns, 35 million rifles, and 31 million shotguns. George D. Newton and Frank E. Zimring, *Firearms and Violence in American*

our murder rate was 9.7 victims per 100,000 in 1974, a total of 19,510 homicides, and the weapon used in 54 percent of the cases was a handgun, while in 68 percent of the cases the weapon used was a firearm of some type (see Figure 14.1). These percentages have remained relatively constant over the years, as have our homicide rates, which remain the highest in the industrial world, except for Latin America.

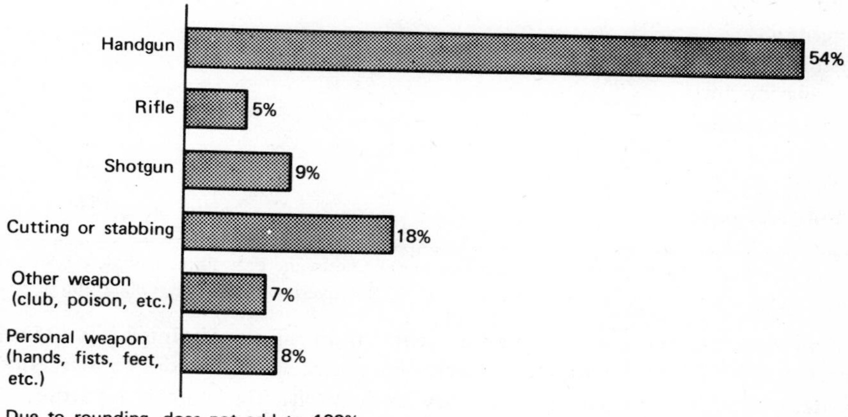

Figure 14.1 Murder, by type of weapon used, 1974. (Source. *FBI,* Uniform Crime Reports, *1974, p. 17.*)

As a crime of passion and contingency, except for the circumstances of gangland murders and the like, homicide has patterns of predictability at variance with other violent crimes. For example, the most likely perpetrators and victims of homicide are immediate family members, close friends, or intimate acquaintances (see Table 14.1). Felony or suspected felony homicides between 1969 and 1974 have made up only about 27 percent of all killings.[5]

The existence of a citizenry that is heavily armed, and this is an accurate characterization of American society compared with any other industrial society, has implications for other problems in criminal justice—police-community relations. It is curious that little recognition is given to the relationship between police-community relations and weapons. Yet, the presence of an armed citizenry

Life (Washington, D.C.: U.S. Government Printing Office, 1969), p. 4, Table 1-1.
[5]FBI *Uniform Crime Report,* 1973, Table on p. 10.

Table 14.1 Relationship between victim and attacker in homicide (Chicago, 1967)

Relationship	Percent
Friends or acquaintances	41
Spouse or lover	20
Other family	7
Neighbors	3
Business	3
No relationship	22
Undetermined	4
Total	100
Number of cases	554

Source. Staff Report to the National Commission on the Causes and Prevention of Violence, *Firearms and Violence in American Life* (Washington, D.C.: U.S. Government Printing Office, 1969), p. 42.

acutely increases the risk of injury or death to an officer. Skolnick has pointed out[6] that as the degree of danger is enhanced, police normally adopt a discretionary demeanor of personalistic authority to deal with the danger, regardless of formal procedures or the rule of law. Frisks are made more frequently and stop-and-search practices, certainly a point of resentment in minority communities, are supported by the general public, the police, and the courts.

The U. S. Supreme Court has frequently referred to the degree of danger that faces the patrolman as an omnipresent fact requiring the balancing of Fourth and Fifth Amendment privileges against the needs of the police. Typically, in *Terry* v *Ohio,* the court argued that it is necessary "for law enforcement officers to protect themselves and other prospective victims of violence in situations where they may lack probable cause for an arrest."[7] Judges are understandably reluctant to second-guess the experienced officer on the street who makes a frisk and an arrest because he suspects an individual to be armed and about to commit a crime. No area of constitutional law is more temporizing and confusing than that of searches incidental to arrest or searches resulting from suspicious circumstances where an officer believes a crime is imminent.

The ambivalence of the courts concerning Fourth and Fifth Amendment applications to police searches is understandable, particularly when one examines the relationship between handguns and the number of police killed in the line of

[6] Skolnick, *Justice without Trial,* Chapter 3.
[7] *Terry* v *Ohio* 392 U.S. 1 (1968).

duty. Between 1964 and 1974, 858 law enforcement officers were killed, over 71 percent by handguns, 12 percent by shotgun, 12 percent by rifle, and less than 4 percent by "other" means. Fourteen percent of these officers were murdered with their own weapons![8] Geographically, between 1969 and 1973, 218 police officers died in the American South compared to 89 in the Northeast, 144 in the North Central states, and 100 in the West. However, the number of officers killed in the line of duty outside of the South approximately doubled between 1946 and 1948 and 1969 and 1973.[9] The number of police officers who have been killed in the line of duty, while tragic, is not of epidemic proportions. But the presence of widespread ownership of firearms seriously affects the environment within which police work and, ultimately, affects police attitudes toward civilians.

Perhaps the profound influence that handguns have on police routines and attitudes can best be illustrated by the present controversy over the hollow-nosed, so-called "dum-dum" bullets that have been issued to some local police. The bullet is especially lethal or, at best, terribly damaging, due to a hollow tip that, upon contact, mushrooms back over its copper casing, thus widening the wound and shocking the victim. On the one side are aligned those who claim the bullet is necessary to protect the lives of police officers or others; they claim that it will only be used on those occasions. On the other are groups that charge that such extraordinary weaponry makes the police officer judge, jury, and executioner. Both groups have considerable merit to their argument, but the problem is broader in scope.

When compared to European police officers, American police are heavily armed. For example, some 5 percent of the Bobbies in the United Kingdom are armed, except in special areas where IRA partisans are particularly active. But very few British citizens, outside of Northern Ireland, possess weapons of any kind, whereas in the United States it is estimated that over 90 million weapons are in circulation.

The presence of weapons and citizens willing to use them against police creates an entirely different relationship between patrolmen and the citizens with whom they come into contact. Policemen look at the dum-dum bullet's killing power and its nonricocheting properties as advantages in situations where an adversary is armed. Police critics tend to conjure up a police victim who is youthful, unarmed, and possibly innocent. Both groups view the central issue to be how police should be armed instead of viewing the environment within which they work. Reducing the number of weapons in civil society would change the grounds of debate over this and other police-community issues considerably.

[8] FBI *Uniform Crime Report,* 1974, p. 19.

[9] Ibid., pp. 40-41.

AMERICAN VIOLENCE

Homicide in many cases is a consequence of violent behavior not necessarily intended to kill, since fatal attacks often grow out of rage or passion.[10] Consequently, homicide is a function of assaults in general. What is there in the American fabric that can explain such violent behavior? The National Commission on the Causes and Prevention of Violence spent several million dollars and several years on the issue, but their conclusions regarding criminal violence remain speculative and, at times, contradictory. They run from the anthropological conclusions that violence is a function of the realtive diversity of outside groups within a political jurisdiction[11] to lack of equality of opportunity and a stake in society.[12] There is, however, broad agreement that American violence is individual, not collective. We have had our periods of mass violence, even mass killings. The massacre at Wounded Knee and the anti-Negro riot in Chicago in 1903 and New York City in 1863 are shameful reminders of our capacity for collective brutality. And our technology gives us a frightening ability to destroy thousands of lives and millions of dollars worth of property in detached and systematic fashion during wartime. But our destructiveness in war results from our technology and industrial base more than from our character, and the history of our collective violence fortunately has been spasmodic when compared to that of most other nations.

Still, violence may be as "American as cherry pie." At least H. Rapp Brown did his best to prove his point. Social scientists have commented on the stimuli for violence that exist throughout our socialization process—T.V. programs watched by children, our historical myth, sporting events, newspapers, and even automobile advertisements. Annual traffic accidents alone for young people make even our high homicide rates appear small. Moreover, violence is closely associated with the American male's socialization. It is the male who fights, both legitimately in war and in athletics and semilegitimately in the school yard. It is the male who is expected to be a mortician, an assistant in the morgue, a doctor, an expert on guns and knives, and aggressive businessman, or a tough-minded thinker or lecturer. It is also a young man who commits the overwhelming number of murders that occur each year in the United States.

[10] Newton and Zimring, *Firearms and Violence in American Life,* p. 43. The authors quote the chief of the Homicide Section of the Chicago Police Department after Chicago's 600th homicide of 1968 had occurred: "There was a domestic fight. A gun was there, and then somebody was dead. If you have described one, you have described them all." Ibid., p. 43.

[11] Donald J. Mulvihill, Melvin M. Tianin, and Lynn A. Curtis, *Crimes of Violence,* A Staff Report to the National Commission on the Causes and Prevention of Violence (Washington, D.C.: U.S. Government Printing Office, 1969), pp. 467-842.

[12] Ibid., pp. 485-520.

At the same time the children of the middle class are also socialized *not* to be violent, at least in interpersonal relations. No one knows what impact violent stimuli have on macrolevel, middle-class behavior and on their support of repressive policy both foreign and domestic. My conjecture is that the impact is minimal and frequently overstated.

But violence at the interpersonal level and, therefore, at the level of street crime, is characteristic of particular subcultures where despair, poverty, and day-to-day outlooks prevail. Wolfgang has suggested a subculture of violence under these types of conditions that breeds its own impersonally violent life-style. In such a culture, little guilt is generated by illicit conduct and violence becomes a theme for solving problems, whether group or individual. Even the friendly companions of those who are members of the culture provide support for violent behavior and values.[13]

As young males are most receptive to the cultural transmissions of a violent life-style, the knife and the gun become both instrumental tools and sexual-psychological symbols in the young man's behavior and in his ability to manipulate and control others. Their possession becomes a vital part of what constitutes manhood.[14]

HOMICIDE

That the rate of homicide has been a very serious problem in American society throughout our history is beyond dispute. In 1974 we experienced 20,600 murders, 9.7 victims for every 100,000 population. Both sex and race were important variables; 75 percent of the arrests for murder were of males and 57 percent of all arrests for homicides were of black Americans. At the same time, 50 percent of all victims of homicide were black. Murder within the family and resulting from lovers' quarrels made up 29 percent of all killings, while suspected or actual felony murder constituted 28 percent, representing a general increase in felony murders over the past few years.[15] The remaining 43 percent of all murders arose from other arguments.

Curiously, a murder does more to bring praise or blame to the police and attention to the courts than any other event, yet police and courts, other than continuing to provide a specific deterrent, can probably not do very much more than they are already doing to reduce its occurrence. Moreover, from a victim-suffering perspective, murdered victims represent only a fraction of the annual violent death total that includes death by automobile, accident, and suicide. National legislation limiting speed limits on the highway has probably reduced

[13] Wolfgang, *The Subculture of Violence.*

[14] Wolfgang, ed., *Studies in Homicide,* pp. 4-12.

[15] FBI *Uniform Crime Report,* 1974, pp. 15-20.

violent death in the United States more than any crime policy that could be adopted.

But practical measures can be taken to reduce homicide if, as we believe, handguns are made less available to the general citizenry. As previously indicated, firearms, like football or Fourth of July picnics, are deeply embedded into American culture. There is no other way we know of to explain the appeal that popular shibboleths hold over millions of otherwise thoughtful American citizens. The slogan, "if they take away *our* guns only criminals will have guns," is an appeal, in fact, to frontier law and order. It suggests that civility and safety are the products of an armed citizenry, Davey Crockett style, instead of the function of the police and the law. Its companion rallying cry, "guns do not kill people; people do," presents a level of illogic that would also force us to conclude that reckless drivers, not fast, unsafe cars and winding, narrow roads cause accidents, or foolish people, not untreated water, cause typhoid. It is government policy, of course, to require inspections, straighten out dangerous curves, and treat public water sources to save lives.

There are more scholarly objections to prohibiting ownership of handguns and nationally registered rifles and shotguns. It has been argued that the Swiss have no restriction on private possession of firearms and yet they have a low homicide rate. The high rates of homicide in the United States, so the argument goes, may be a function of social conflicts, family instability, or subcultures of violence, not of the mere presence of handguns. For example, the high rate of murder in the southern states may not be the consequence of a lack of gun restrictions throughout most of the states, but a function of a violence-prone culture, particularly the subculture of poverty. It will be recalled that homicide is particularly common to violent subcultures. Given the existence of violent subcultures in the United States, it has been forcefully argued by some scholars that if firearms were not available, a substitute weapon would be used.

However, the presence of a handgun in a desk or bedroom dresser drawer "for protection" ironically makes homicide more likely for that reason. As a lethal instrument it is much more effective than a broken bottle, a knife, or a drape cord. Somehow it remains more difficult to kill another with a knife, in a fit of emotion, than a .22 caliber pistol. As Zimring and Newton pointed out, the substitution thesis assumes that the causes of deadly attacks and the resultant criminal homicides must be distinguished from the causes motivating the individual to use a firearm instead of a knife, bludgeon, or other tool to commit murder.[16] Many homicides, but not all, are probably the product of contingency, the availability of a handgun being one of them, not a single-minded intention to kill. If this were not so, if the substitution theory were correct, then we would expect no corelation between the *firearm* homicide rate and the *total* homicide rate. That is, the

[16] Newton and Zimring, *Firearms and Violence in American Life,* p. 43.

unavailability of firearms would not reduce homicides; it would merely reduce the number of homicides perpetrated by firearms. Seitz has demonstrated, however, that there *is* a correlation of .98 between the firearm homicide rate and the total homicide rate in each of the states for 1967.[17]

The reason for lower homicide rates in the absence of firearms appears to be that some weapons are less lethal than others. The Task Force on Firearms and Violence in American Life found the fatality rate of the knife, the second most frequently used weapon in homicide, to be one-fifth that of the fatality rate of a firearm.[18] The simple accessibility of firearms sharply increases the possibility of death resulting from both ambiguously motivated as well as intentionally deadly attacks. UCR reports of police fatalities tend to confirm this differential mortality rate. The rate of deaths per 100 police-reported attacks on their person is many times greater when an assailant used firearms, compared to occasions when the assault was with a knife.[19] In 1973 a startling statistic dramatized this differential. Out of 2656 police officers who were assaulted by firearms, 123 officers died of their wounds. Of 1017 police officers assaulted by knife, only 2 died of their wounds. Clearly, an accessibility to firearms and particularly to handguns sharply increases the probability of death resulting from ambiguously motivated as well as intentionally deadly attacks.

HANDGUNS AS SELF-DEFENSE

The musket hung high above the hearth is a universal American symbol of self-reliance, home defense, and masculine virtue. Many Americans continue to keep loaded firearms in homes and commercial establishments and on their persons for purposes of protection. In a poll conducted by the National Opinion Research Center, 66 percent of householders listed "protection" as one reason for having firearms,[20] a fact supported by other polls as well. Careful inspection of the available evidence strongly disputes the value of possessing firearms for purposes of self-defense, particularly when whatever advantages they do provide are weighed against the increased likelihood of interfamily assault and homicide or accident.

The three most likely household crimes are burglary, robbery, and sexual attack. Burglary represents the most frequent intrusion in the home, but it is not commonly prevented by a firearm. A successful burglary depends on eluding

[17] Steven Thomas Seitz, "Firearms, Homicides, and Gun Control Effectiveness," *Law and Society Review* (1972), 6:597.

[18] Newton and Zimring, *Firearms and Violence in American Life*, pp. 48-50.

[19] FBI *Uniform Crime Report*, 1973, p. 39, Table 61 on p. 170.

[20] Newton and Zimring, *Firearms and Violence in American Life*, p. 61. The analysis of handgun efficacy for purposes of self-defense draws heavily on Chapter 10.

discovery, usually by entering an unoccupied home during a vacation; by breaking into a summer camp during the off season; or, more rarely, by entering a home or apartment late at night when the residents are known to be out for the evening. Newton and Zimring found in a Detroit study that no more than 2 burglars in 1000 over a 4-year period were interdicted by being shot. Similar studies in New York City confirm this very low figure, although the studies do not include burglars who were frightened off with firearms. Indeed, the typical burglar would be more likely to steal the home-defense firearm than to be driven off by it. Professional burglaries (those involving total property loss of over $500) invariably involve furs, silverware, color T.V.s, cash—and firearms, if they are available.

Home robbery is considerably less frequent but far more dangerous than burglary. Although home-robbery killings probably make up only 2 to 3 percent of all homicides, it is a crime where the offender personally confronts victims in the sanctity of their homes under frightening and volatile conditions. But firearms are of limited utility under these circumstances, too. The offender is usually able to surprise and overwhelm the victim by gaining entrance through an unlocked door or being admitted by the homedweller. Given this advantage, it is a rare situation, about 2 percent of all home-robbery cases, where a robber is shot by the homeowner.

Although there is little empirical data, similar deductive arguments could be made regarding sexual assaults. Rape tends not to take place between strangers, anyway, particularly in the home.

In some commercial establishments in high crime areas a more plausible argument may be made for possession of a firearm.—plausible but not conclusive, since we do not have the necessary data to reach a conclusion one way or another. The Small Business Administration found that 3 percent of retail businesses with and without firearms reported being victims of a robbery, but it is quite likely that businesses with firearms are also in high crime areas. Thus, possession of firearms by businessmen might be reducing robberies in high crime areas. It is certainly correct that burglary and robbery are greater threats to businesses, both in terms of life and property, than to private homes, and it is also true that the possession of firearms by businessmen entails less risk of accident, homicide, and suicide than firearms in the home.

GUN CONTROL AND CRIME POLICY

Of course, the question must be raised, How will gun control statutes limit ownership? Is it realistic to confiscate 30 million handguns at a cost of several billion dollars? What distinctions should be drawn between regulation of handguns as compared to the regulation of shotguns or rifles? Finally, what of the argument that firearm-related crimes could be reduced if judges would follow the stiff sentences that are presently in the statutes for firearm-related crime? I would not dismiss this latter objection with regard to calculated robbery or gangland murder, and there is limited evidence that it is a correct position for selected crime types. But most assaults, as I have argued, are spontaneous, not premeditated, and utilitarian considerations of punishment on the part of the violator are not likely to enter whatever calculations he makes. Firearm-related crime is largely, although not exclusively, a problem of weapon accessibility for impassioned human behavior of violent, but ambiguous, intention.

However, prohibiting all firearms is both politically impossible and unnecessary. The major problem is the handgun, because it can be easily concealed and carried and is, unfortunately, readily accessible. Although handguns represent only about a third of all guns in the country in crimes involving firearms, they constituted 76 percent of all homicides, 86 percent of all aggravated assaults, and 96 percent of all robberies. As previously noted, handguns were used in the United States in 63 percent of all homicides, 37 percent of all robberies, and 21 percent of aggravated assaults. However, the volume of handgun involvement in serious crime has been significantly increasing.[21] Handguns alone each year account for more than half of all homicides. If the handgun were abolished, or at least if newly manufactured handguns were prohibited for all citizens except police and security guards, and larger rifles appropriate for legitimate hunting were registered and issued only by permit, the evidence indicates that rates for both homicide and violent crime would fall.

The major rationale behind registration of firearms is to provide a cooling-off period between an emotional interaction and the accessibility of a firearm. Additionally, law enforcement is, of course, substantially assisted if it can trace the ownership of weapons used in the commission of a crime. But, given the irrational, nonpremeditated nature of assaults, denying accessibility is a realistic, if politically painful, crime control policy directed toward reducing victim suffering.

As an example, Newton and Zimring point out that if the level of gun attacks in Houston in 1968 (a city in a state with little gun control) were reduced from 42 percent to New York City's low level of 24 percent (i.e., if gun attack would have been knife attacks), there would have been a reduction of 20 deaths per 100 attacks to 4 deaths per 100 attacks.[22] Legislation was proposed again in the summer of 1975 to ban the manufacture and sale of "Saturday night specials," the small handgun with an effective range of no more than 10 feet. The legislation will do very little to reduce homicide and crimes of violence, since it does not cover larger handguns, which can also be concealed and easily obtained. Even in this tepid form, however, the legislation is vigorously opposed by the gun lobby. Once again the politics of crime pits the values of a dubious portion of our American heritage and the economic interests of the firearms manufacturers in

[21] Ibid., pp. 46, 49.
[22] Ibid., p. 45.

the United States against the realities of modern, urban life in the formation of a crime policy.

15

CONCLUDING THOUGHTS

Much of our crime problem is rooted in the structure of American society and culture. However, knowing this does not provide much help in formulating a realistic crime policy. A democratic crime policy, relying as it does on the lawful use of force modified by discretion, can neither alter the social structure nor reform criminals. Most of what it *can* do well is very traditional and unexciting. It can defend social tranquility and protect citizens by deterring crime, preventing crime, and apprehending offenders. It can restrain for some time offenders who are likely to repeat their transgressions. No doubt, when these functions are not performed well, our crime problem is much worse. But criminal activity is likely to remain relatively high in the United States in the foreseeable future, regardless of the wisdom of crime policy.

The politics surrounding crime policy are characterized by competing perceptions of individuals both in and out of the criminal justice system. Policy analysis is arid, indeed, if it does not recognize the political context and the limits created by competing perceptions about what policy instruments should be used and what objectives should be pursued. For the problems that I have examined that *are* susceptible to solution—bail bond reform, alacrity in the courts, an effective deterrent policy toward the serious offender, victim-oriented drug control, and handgun control—a lack of consensus among political elites over the nature of the problem continues to block effective action. Here, political conflicts of interest and parochial perceptions of the ends of criminal justice provide barriers as difficult as the limits of our current technology and knowledge.

Paradoxically, the comprehensive end of the criminal justice system that has the most potential for a broad consensus on crime policy is the reduction of victim suffering. Yet the victim is undoubtedly the most ignored element in the criminal justice system. The system is much more interested in the question of public order, legal guilt and innocence, punishment, and rehabilitation—all of which are concerns remote from the citizen's interest in safety and protection of his property. The administration of justice generates copious data to measure the seriousness of crime in terms of police activities (time checks, complaint and investigation reports, and arrests), lawyers' activities (legal decisions), correctional officials (recidivist rates), and journalistic drama (public relations). Moreover, although the public is capable of identifying with those who suffer at the hands of the offender, that concern does not really lend itself to public support for crime policy with any specificity. The reduction of victim suffering may be a social good in the abstract, but it suffers from lack of an active political constituency where the victim's interest must compete with other organized interests.

Although concern for victim suffering is an advantageous perspective for determining the success or failure of the criminal justice system as a whole, as an indicator of success or failure for various subgoals in criminal justice it has obvious limitations. For example, we cannot measure the capacity of the police to keep the peace by victimization indicators. Nor can we assess the quality of due process. It hardly needs argument that the goals of criminal justice are multiple and that each subgoal requires its own indicators consonant with what it attempts to do. Obviously, nonvictim issues also are of interest to the policy analyst: prosecutor and defense counsel effectiveness, police ability to handle crowds, due process protection, and judicial competence.

But when state and national policy regarding firearm ownership is discussed, we are speaking of victims, police officers, and civilians, murdered or injured. We can compare the amount of suffering with the number of handguns in circulation and with their availability for acts of violence. Here the question is not tranquility or disturbance, guilt or innocence. Here the question is whether policy choices by the legislature regarding gun control, executed by the police, can reduce victim suffering.

To the extent we can identify, apprehend, and convict serious offenders who commit violent and serious property crime, we can prevent victim suffering. A deterrent policy is clearly related to victim suffering. The empirical evidence is that the certainty of punishment, and perhaps the alacrity of its application, and its severity in some cases, will deter crime. Moreover, we have provided some argumentation that incapacitation during crime-prone years for serious repeating offenders may have an effect, perhaps not very great, but an effect on serious crime. The evidence is mixed, however, and conclusions regarding what kinds of deterrents for what types of crimes are still tentative. Perhaps more important, an effective deterrent will depend more on a high rate of apprehension and conviction than on longer prison terms.

Criminology has too long neglected crime prevention research, a neglect stemming, in my view, from ideological bias. No one likes to calculate the deterrent effect of locking up a youngster who, out of his poverty and despair, lifts a T.V.

from some affluent businessman. But the image is misplaced in most circumstances. The victim is more likely to be an elderly woman whose savings have been expropriated by someone younger and stronger than she. We depend on the courts in their discretion to pass judgment on the malevolence of criminal behavior in individual cases. But to the extent that effective police work and prosecution can deter serious crime, victim suffering, often borne by the poor and helpless, can and should be reduced.

Research in deterrence is just beginning. More research is needed to explore the relationship between deterrence for different typologies of crime, between the speed of disposition and crime, and between incapacitation and crime prevention. But the research is crucial to crime policy; deterrence is a function that *can* be implemented by the criminal justice system.

Until such time that we can develop effective rehabilitative programs, crime prevention through a deterrent policy lamentably seems to hold the most promise for reducing serious, violent crime. This does not mean that we have to abandon diversionary projects whereby less serious offenders receive sanctions short of prison. Nor does it mean giving up on rehabilitative efforts or giving up on research to discover effective rehabilitative measures. Most especially, there is no reason why we should not vigorously move to put an end to brutal prison conditions, regardless of whether or not decent, humane conditions are related to rehabilitation.

Victimless crime has raised a special problem in this volume. My approach has been to examine the criminogenic quality of victimless crime, particularly for heroin use. The key question was: Has drug use resulted in increasing serious crime or has the criminalization of the use of heroin been responsible for the strong linkage between heroin and criminal behavior. My tentative conclusions are that methadone maintenance programs may be an effective means of reducing serious crime while providing a framework for assisting users of hard drugs to have a productive life. Again, I could be wrong. The evidence regarding the effectiveness of methadone maintenance programs is mixed. With the proliferation of methadone maintenance centers throughout the country, as well as the development of other alternative treatment programs, assuming there is competent evaluation, we should soon know more about the potential for alternate treatment of addictive drug users in reducing serious crime. My primary concern in this volume was to suggest an approach to crime policy and describe some of the techniques that can be brought to bear on the problem.

Finally, my analysis of crime policy has been constrained by the political realities that determine its boundaries and by the alternatives that the criminal justice agencies can realistically pursue, given legislative and financial support. That has necessitated not more than a superficial treatment of a number of fascinating and important issues. White-collar crime has received very little attention, and organized crime has been mentioned only in passing. A book must draw the line somewhere on substance, and I was primarily interested in traditional street crime. Of course, organized crime is intimately related with street crime at many junctures. But both organized crime and the very broad dimensions of white-collar crime are topics for separate volumes; the questions they raise for crime policy involve much more than the activities of police, courts, and corrections.

In addition, I have argued that for the most part crime causation is not central to crime policy. It might be in the future but, given the state of knowledge regarding the causes of crime, it is not today. It is one thing to know the causes of crime; it is quite another to know how criminal justice agencies can act on those causes. Criminologists do not agree for the most part on crime causation, at least to the point where causal analysis can inform criminal justice decision making. Where they do agree on the social factors correlated with criminal behavior, family instability, lower-class behavior, violent subcultural phenomena, differential association, or whatever, their conclusions lend themselves to suggesting alterations of the social structure far beyond the capacity of the criminal justice system. I do not discount the possibility of such alterations or their desirability. But people are being victimized *now,* and practical policy questions cannot wait for a wholesale alteration of the social structure to resolve the problems of crime.

An enormous number of issues, many of them volatile and highly charged, have been covered by this volume. No doubt, my treatment of many of those issues has been deplorably brief. Each topic—drug control, bail bond, court delay, deterrence, the measurement of crime, the politics of crime, correctional reform, and planning and policy analysis—deserves and often receives treatment in a separate volume. However, there is an advantage in surveying a broad number of issues, since they are interrelated. A comprehensive treatment allows the student to appreciate both the complexity of criminal justice problems and their interrelationships.

Finally, I return to my initial theme—the intransigence of so much of our crime problem. Our inability to resolve the problems of crime is partly due to the lack of an active political constituency for victims and partly due to conflicts of interests in American society at large. Intellectuals (even between the disciplines of political science, sociology, law, economics, and psychology) have separate, competing paradigms over the issue. In addition, attorneys on and off the bench, police officers, probation and parole personnel, planners, and the bureaucracies accompanying these occupations have contending perspectives, not to mention the special-issue lobbyists for and against blue laws and victimless crimes, and the legislators themselves. I agree neither on the problems of crime nor, not surprisingly, on the solutions.

Perhaps I am wrong. Perhaps victim suffering will become the standard measure of public policy in reducing crime in the future. If so, my analysis may prove useful in examining anew some of the traditional problems of crime. But even if this is the case, the impact of an effective crime policy will still be limited. Violence, theft, greed, and exploitation will not go away with government action. But it might be reduced from the extraordinary levels it has reached in recent years. At any rate, hopefully, we can avoid the simplistic crusading zeal of either the left (eliminate poverty or racism or capitalism and crime will disappear) or the right (make everything illegal that is immoral, lock everyone up for long periods of time, eliminate permissiveness, and crime will stop). Crusades produce either pyrrhic victories or dangerous frustration. To the extent our crime problems are successfuly addressed, they will be addressed incrementally, with full recognition of the political realities and human limitations that exist.

Author Index

Subject Index